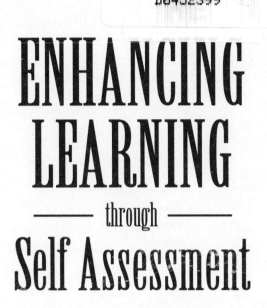

D0452399

# ENHANCING LEARNING

—— through ——

# Self Assessment

# ENHANCING LEARNING

## LEARNING
—— through ——
## Self Assessment

DAVID BOUD

KOGAN
PAGE

London • Philadelphia

First published in 1995
Reprinted 1997

Apart from any fair dealing for the purposes of research or private study, or criticism or review, as permitted under the Copyright, Designs and Patents Act, 1988, this publication may only be reproduced, stored or transmitted, in any form or by any means, with the prior permission in writing of the publishers, or in the case of reprographic reproduction in accordance with the terms of the licences issued by the Copyright Licensing Agency. Enquiries concerning reproduction outside those terms should be sent to the publishers at the undermentioned address:

Kogan Page Limited
120 Pentonville Road
London N1 9JN

© David Boud and contributors 1995

**British Library Cataloguing in Publication Data**

A CIP record for this book is available from the British Library.

ISBN 0 7494 1368 9

Typeset by Books Unlimited (Nottm), Mansfield, NG19 7QZ
Printed and bound in Great Britain by Biddles Ltd, Guildford and King's Lynn

# Contents

## Part IV  DESIGN, IMPLEMENTATION AND EVALUATION

## Part V  CONCLUSION

# Acknowledgements

I wish to particularly thank my co-worker in this book, Angela Brew. Not only has she written two chapters of her own, but she has given support and encouragement throughout. Her contribution has been invaluable. Three of my colleagues made helpful comments on earlier versions of some of the chapters: Ruth Cohen, Susan Knights and Rod McDonald. I also owe a lot to my collaborators over the years in exploring self assessment. In particular, I wish to acknowledge Alex Churches, Nancy Falchikov, Harvey Holmes, James Kilty, Jackie Lublin, Finn Thorvaldsson and Alan Tyree.

Some chapters draw on previously published papers. Where the original papers were written with others, this is indicated in the contents list. The chapters which include content from previous publications which is not otherwise indicated are: Chapter 4: Boud, D (1995) 'Assessment and learning: contradictory or complementary?' In Knight, P (ed) *Assessment for Learning in Higher Education,* London: Kogan Page, 35–48; Chapter 6: Boud, D and Holmes, W H (1981) 'Self and peer marking in an undergraduate engineering course', *IEEE Transactions on Education E-24,* 4, 267–74; Chapter 7: Boud, D, Churches, A E and Smith, E M (1986) 'Student self assessment in an engineering design course: an evaluation', *International Journal of Applied Engineering Education,* 2, 2, 83–90, with permission of the Editor, *International Journal of Engineering Education*; Chapter 8: Boud, D and Tyree, A L (1980) 'Self and peer assessment in professional education: a preliminary study in law', *Journal of the Society of Public Teachers of Law.* 15, 1, 65–74, with permission of Carfax Publishing Company, Abingdon, Oxfordshire; Chapter 9: Boud, D (1992) 'The use of self-assessment schedules in negotiated learning', *Studies in Higher Education,* 17, 2, 185–200; Chapter 10: Boud, D and Kilty, J M (1981) 'Self-appraisal for university teachers: a guide for workshop leaders', *Tertiary Education Research Centre Occasional Publication No. 19,* Kensington: University of New South Wales, and Boud, D and Kilty, J M (1984) 'Self-appraisal: an approach to academic staff development', in Cryer, P (ed) *Training Activities for Teachers in Higher Education, Volume Two,* Guildford: SRHE and

NFER-Nelson, 33–44; Chapter 12: Boud, D and Falchikov, N (1989) 'Quantitative studies of student self-assessment in higher education: a critical analysis of findings', *Higher Education*. 18, 5, 529–49, with permission of Kluwer Academic Publishers; and Chapter 13: Boud, D (1989) 'The role of self assessment in student grading', *Assessment and Evaluation in Higher Education,* 14, 1, 20–30, with permission of Carfax Publishing Company, Abingdon, Oxfordshire. In addition, some of the specific ideas spread throughout the book were first introduced in my HERDSA Green Guide: Boud, D (1991) *Implementing Student Self-Assessment*. 2nd ed, Sydney: Higher Education Research and Development Society of Australasia, included with permission of the Series Editor, HERDSA Guides.

The following made useful contributions to the work reported in these chapters: Lee Andresen, Kate Day, Dick Frost, Paul Hager, Jan McLean, Doug Magin, Alex Main, Haydn Mathias, Peggy Nightingale, John Powell, Mike Prosser, Peter Reason, Wendy Richards, John Rowan and Helen Simpson. We acknowledge the assistance provided by all those who responded to our survey and especially to those colleagues who have permitted us to use extracts from their work in Chapter 11. Most importantly, this book would not have been possible without the support and encouragement of all those students who have participated in the self-assessment activities reported here and who in their own ways have contributed to the development of the ideas.

# Chapter 1

# Introduction

Whenever we learn we question ourselves. 'How am I doing?', 'Is this enough?', 'Is this right?', 'How can I tell?', 'Should I go further?' In the act of questioning is the act of judging ourselves and making decisions about the next step. This is self assessment.

In starting this book, I began to pose myself some questions. I wanted to bring together previous work on self assessment, work on student learning and ideas which have followed the renewed interest in self assessment in higher education in the 1990s. As I progressed, I began to ponder on what self assessment meant to me now. Did it rest in my earlier conception of it as a vital skill and attribute of lifelong learning? Was it the one which has unfortunately become fashionable in some places: a warm up to assessment by others that often had severe consequences in terms of status and financial support? Or was it something altogether more personally challenging?

As I began to write, I realised that my motives for focusing on this topic were much more related to my own history and experiences than I had expected. Self assessment, while commonly portrayed as a technique to enhance learning, is more transformative, elusive and confronting to conventional teaching than it is normally expedient to recognise. As I thought back to my own images of self assessment and those of students I knew, I thought of it first as a task with defined outcomes, but then reflected that, when it is conducted in a context of openness and critical reflection, it allows for the possibility of seeing oneself and the options which lay before one in a radically different way. In other words, beyond discussion of technique and strategy, in self assessment lies something worth striving for that is more than simply an addition to the teaching and learning repertoire. To reach this further point involves getting to grips with a range of issues to do with power and the influence of others. It involves confronting the controlling role of assessment in educational institutions. And it involves noting that self assessment is much more than personal introspection. As we shall see later, it can take on many guises and be used to many different ends.

The book is grounded in my experience of using self assessment in a range of higher educational and professional settings. It is also grounded in experiences of being assessed and the feelings which accompany this. Above all I wanted a pragmatic book which would be helpful to teachers and students considering using self assessment. To start with the transformative and challenging aspects is not a good way to commence a practically oriented book. Faced with the practicalities of how to approach the task, I had to acknowledge that the starting point for the book was very much my own.

Although my experience is necessarily unique, the issues with which I deal in this volume are very common. The many people who have explored the relationship between assessment and learning will recognise features of the story. The book presents an account of a number of self assessment projects undertaken in higher education in a wide range of disciplines and professional fields of interest, interspersed with my own reflections. At various points, there are summaries of useful ideas and warnings of pitfalls to enable the reader to avoid some of the many traps that will be met in using ideas of self assessment. The realities of working within a system that places many barriers on the educational innovator are to the fore. Practical approaches that work within normal constraints on teaching are emphasised. However, some chapters focus on more fundamental educational issues and discuss self assessment in relation to them.

The question that had been constantly with me was: what are the implications of writing a book about self assessment? I had assembled a large volume of useful material, but I had failed to reckon with the reflexive nature of the task. How could I write a book on self assessment without engaging in the very act that I was commending to others as worthwhile? There is a unique challenge and a curious irony in writing about self assessment: attention is inevitably drawn to the act of self assessment itself and that can be inhibiting.

Such thoughts are not helpful when it comes to writing any book, let alone a book on self assessment. Discussing this with my co-worker on this enterprise led me to ponder on whether there is a model for self assessment that says one can't continually be assessing oneself; to do so is to inhibit action. One has to act and then assess; but not both at the same time. So I had to think of a way of writing without my critical self assessment stopping me.

The solution to this problem was to accept the advice I give to others using self assessment (which appears in Chapter 14). This is, identify some criteria for judging success early in the process then set these aside to be returned to later. I therefore listed the following:

- inclusion of some autobiographical material to help make the ideas come alive
- clarity about what is and what is not covered
- rooted in actual practice with examples given
- underpinned by theory and research
- reasonably comprehensive in coverage of higher education
- of practical use to others in implementation
- linked to key ideas in teaching and learning.

Starting with the autobiographical is a way of indicating the very tangible roots of ideas that might otherwise appear to be a little arbitrary. It provides a context for my introduction to the sections that follow. Those readers who prefer not to focus on a personal introduction should skip the next few pages and proceed directly to the section headed 'Structure of the book'.

## My background in self assessment

Why have I been interested in self assessment? I hold the view that research interests are always prompted at some level by personal experience (Marshall and Reason, 1993; Reason and Marshall, 1987). So what is it that has made this an interest which spans more than 20 years? As I thought about it I realised that my interest in assessment goes back ever further, to experiences of being assessed, and subsequently to the problems of assessing my own work. I also suspected that the concern of others with self assessment is also related to their experiences of being assessed. This therefore seemed a fruitful place to start.

In reflecting on being assessed what comes to mind are not the successes. My interest in assessment was related to experiences of failure, feelings of unfairness when being assessed, increasing doubts about the validity of the judgements of others, and a slow dawning that it was not others whom I should be satisfying in my learning endeavours, but myself!

I have been reinforced in my view of the personal impact of assessment by the work of my former colleagues in the Professional Development Centre at the University of New South Wales. Sue Toohey teaches a subject on assessment in the postgraduate course for university teachers. At the beginning she asks them to write a short autobiography focusing on their experiences of being assessed. The results of this are devastating and students can't stop themselves from referring to it in other classes. They emerge from the exercise saying to themselves that they must not treat their students in the same ways in which they were treated. It is clear from their reports that even successful, able and committed students – those who become university teachers – have been hurt by their experiences of assessment, time and time again, through school and through higher education. This hurt did not encourage them to persist and overcome adversity: it caused them to lose confidence, it dented their self-esteem and led them never to have anything to do with some subjects ever again.

I found it strangely reassuring that some of my own problems with assessment were shared by others. However, the effects in each case are personal and have a very specific influence over one's life and work. Sometimes they lead us to avoid entire areas of activity. Sometimes they lead us to overcompensate and nag away at those areas in which we were found wanting. Some of the assessment incidents which I recalled having had an influence – both negative and positive – on me were: first, being told in primary school that I couldn't write and had nothing to say; a remark which for many years was self-fulfilling and probably led to me failing 'O' level English Language twice. Then, I was surprised about my success in school mathematics and later physics. This led to successful completion of a physics degree. I remember my experience of 'A' level chemistry as I discovered the fallibility of my teacher in covering the appropriate syllabus and realising that I had to make my own assessment of what was required and prepare myself for the examinations accordingly. Then as a postgraduate student I was given useful, detailed feedback by a friendly colleague on my first paper for an international journal. Uncomfortable though this was then, I realised that this was the first time that I had been given feedback of a type that I could use, in a context which was supportive and which respected my intentions – Sid O'Connell was a true teacher. The experience of this helped build confidence and began to demystify the process of writing.

These experiences laid the foundation for my later interests in self assessment. My discovery and use of the chemistry syllabus was my first conscious involvement with self assessment in a relatively structured way, and my positive experience of getting good quality feedback focused my mind on the role of peers in the process, the subject of a later chapter. Following these reflections on being assessed, I recalled meeting the formal notion of self assessment for the first time. This came in the early 1970s when I was involved with the Human Potential Research Project at the University of Surrey. There was a jolt of recognition along with a degree of suspicion generated by the challenge it presented to someone like me who had succeeded in a system in which the assessments of others were supreme. Through my interactions with John Heron on this project, I was conceptually convinced of the significance of self assessment and started to realise how it connected to my own biography.

The project I became involved in focused on ways of working with people in professional and non-professional contexts to help them develop themselves. Under the inspired leadership of John Heron, the project explored how the potential of human beings could be more effectively realised in practical ways. One of these was the design and development of in-service training courses for groups who previously had no access to any kind of training or development. Courses for such groups were developed around the actual needs of the participants, without constraint from an external syllabus, assessment boards or competency frameworks. Success was judged on the extent to which the expressed needs of the participants had been met. These groups were particularly challenging to work with because many participants worked in contexts which were brutalising and not respectful of them or their clients. I clearly recall visiting one of the institutions from which they came. I found a hospital for the mentally handicapped (as they were then called) that could have come direct from the pages of Dickens: in the Victorian gloom of the brown-painted corridors nurses acted as jailers carrying huge bunches of keys for the locked wards; patients were punished by being placed in padded isolation cells if they 'misbehaved'. Some of the staff who came to our courses had been in the same job for the past 40 years with no opportunity to step aside and reflect on their practice. Meeting the needs of these participants involved overcoming their suspicion and resentment about being 'sent' on a course and dealing with a degree of personal inflexibility that was not surprising in the circumstances.

In these courses, if learners were to take responsibility for their own learning then part of this process was, inevitably, their involvement in making assessments of their own learning goals, the activities in which they were to engage and the ways in which they would judge the outcomes. Doing this was easier said than done and much effort was directed towards establishing a climate in which participants could set aside their job role and respond as people whose own needs were important. As course leaders we would often spend time licking our wounds after emotionally-draining sessions which were part of the process of working with the needs presented. In that context the only form of assessment which was conceivable was self assessment by the course participants, informed from time-to-time by the comments of peers and staff members.

This experience was a great shock to me, as a science graduate of only a few years standing. It seemed to turn my previous experience of teaching and learning on its head. It posed the fundamental question: what are teaching, learning and assessment really about? Are they the relatively well-ordered and formalised process which I had experienced as a student or did they constitute the searching, challenging, agonising struggle for meaning and growth which I was now confronting? My conception now encompasses both, but my faith in existing structures of teaching and assessment had gone. At school and university I had had doubts about the strange processes I was expected to participate in as a student, for example, spending hours memorising information which I knew I would never use again. However, the arbitrary, socially-constructed nature of university courses and particularly the assessment element, became apparent in a way that meant that I could never return naively to the cosy assumptions of the examination, the assignment and the rest of the teacher-determined paraphernalia of the educational institution.

Although this experience had challenged my conceptions of assessment, it occurred in a university context that was quite unusual. The next step therefore was to consider the consequences for more conventional settings. The Human Potential Project was also committed to working with 'normal' university courses and a little later organised the first of a pair of intensive workshops on what were called experiential techniques in higher education. In these workshops a group of people explored the application of strategies and techniques which had previously been used in the personal and professional development context to see how they could be used within the mainstream of the university. Apart from the realisation that experiential exercises could be used as readily in academic subjects as in practical areas such as communication, the main impact on me was in the clarification and development of ideas about self and peer assessment (Boud *et al.*, 1972).

While I was becoming increasingly confident about the importance of self assessment in higher education, I did not have the opportunity to apply the ideas in my own teaching until I moved to Australia in 1976. I was given responsibility for the design and teaching of the two core units in a postgraduate course in science education at the Western Australian Institute of Technology (now Curtin University). As I was surrounded by colleagues in the Department of Applied Physics who did not regard this as their own field of expertise, I was left very much to my own devices. The course I developed included a major emphasis on students setting their own goals, curriculum negotiation and, of course, self and peer assessment. As I appeared to know what I was doing and I presented it in a way which suggested that such an approach was not unusual, my ideas were accepted and students took readily to making their own assessments, though not without some initial trepidation. In keeping with the spirit of staff-student collaboration which the course aimed to engender, one of the students worked with me to write an account of the process (Boud and Prosser, 1980).

We saw self assessment as a significant component in a mix of strategies which aimed to create collaboratively designed courses to meet the needs of students and the subject. I thought this design was simply an application of what I had learned from the in-service courses, to a mainstream, accredited course, but it was regarded by others as a rather more significant shift of approach and a version of our paper appeared in Malcolm Knowles' well-known collection *Andragogy in Action* (Boud and Prosser, 1984).

Self assessment appeared to be effective but I soon discovered an additional challenge. I was responsible for offering the same subjects in distance learning mode. Could I use the same emphasis on collaborative design with self assessment when I did not have direct contact with students? At first I was intimidated by the prospect. There was only a small group of students but they were spread over the state – which was of a similar area to Western Europe. They couldn't afford to travel to a single face-to-face meeting and telephone contact was prohibitively expensive. I had already designed the internal version of the course so there was no alternative to making the distance version equivalent, even though curriculum negotiation by post over many thousands of kilometres was a very slow, and singularly non-spontaneous, process. Peer feedback and self assessment were in fact not particularly difficult to incorporate although I felt that the students had much less opportunity to explore and contribute to alternatives approaches than they would have had if they were sitting together in the same room (Boud, 1981). Teaching through paper and tape provided a discipline which forced me to be much more explicit and unambiguous about what was involved than I had been previously. The crucial importance of such explicitness in all communications about self assessment became apparent much later.

My next move took me to the Tertiary Education Research Centre at the University of New South Wales (UNSW) and away from teaching students. My only access to students was through the colleagues I was assisting with their teaching and learning concerns. While it was frustrating not being able to work directly with students, I was presented with the challenge of communicating my ideas about self assessment to colleagues in many different disciplines and developing self assessment strategies which fitted their particular context. This led to many fruitful projects in architecture, engineering, law and social work. Many of these were written up and published in collaboration with the staff concerned. The examples in Chapters 6 to 8 of the book draw from these papers. What I discovered was, not surprisingly, that self assessment practices need to be created for the particular subject matter within a particular context. It is not possible to take an idea off the shelf and translate it easily into another situation. I also discovered that self assessment is an innovation which, if suitably designed, can fit any context. Some of the courses with which I was working were very conventional in format; nevertheless self assessment could be introduced into these as readily as into more innovative courses.

Although I was not teaching students, I was extensively involved in staff development. Ideas about self assessment surely could be used in the professional development context as well as the undergraduate. Prompted by some earlier work by John Heron (Heron, 1981), I developed with one of John's colleagues, James Kilty, an approach to staff development workshops which revolved around participants focusing on their own practice, making a self assessment of it informed by peers and subsequently implementing the outcomes. This approach proved quite robust and it has now been used with many different professional groups beyond the immediate teaching context (see Chapter 10).

Finally, after many years of working only through others, I taught classes of my own again. The first was a Masters subject on the evaluation of educational programmes – a suitable subject in which to explore self assessment both theoretically and experientially. I adopted a similar negotiated approach to the one I used in Western Australia. Over many cycles of modification in collaboration with different classes of students I developed an approach to self assessment which seemed especially suited for courses which emphasise student autonomy and collaborative learning and which had the advantage of students producing a document which summarised their learning at many different levels (see Chapter 9). After moving to my present institution, the University of Technology, Sydney, I have been able to use this approach without the constraint of having to generate marks which fitted a normal distribution.

This brings me almost up to date. Towards the end of my time at UNSW I had been increasingly undertaking empirical research on self assessment ranging from evaluations of the innovations which I have described, to analysis of quantitative research on self marking. The time had come to put this together in one place. Hence the present volume.

## Structure of the book

The book is about self assessment in higher education. It is concerned exclusively with self assessment of learning. The learner may or may not identify as a student and may not necessarily be enrolled in a formal course of study. Self assessment has as important a role in staff development, management development (eg, Boydell and Pedler, 1981) and informal learning as in award bearing courses.

Self assessment as a term is now used in many different ways, so it is important to distinguish different uses. Self assessment has been applied to individual learners and assessment of their learning as well as to institutions and departments. In the latter, self assessment is applied to an internal appraisal of aspects of institutional performance, often as a prelude to an external judgement, possibly associated with funding. In the higher education quality movement in the UK self assessment is used in this latter manner. In my view, this aspect is appropriately called self evaluation, as it relates more to the evaluation of departments and courses than to the assessment of individuals.

More widely, self assessment is being used for purposes which have nothing to do with education and training. It is worth mentioning them in passing as they may begin to influence learners' perceptions of self assessment. Australians, for example, are now very familiar with what is termed the 'self assessment' of personal income tax. Self assessment in this context is a substitute for the detailed checking of each tax return by a tax officer. The return is accepted on trust, but the number of random audits has dramatically increased. Self assessment thus has a sting in its tail. Such usage can influence the conception of taxpayers towards what might otherwise be a more friendly view of self assessment. As self assessment becomes associated with other social practices it will be increasingly necessary to consider its connotations to learners. The apparent essential 'self-ness' of self assessment may be an illusion, as in the tax case, or a sweetening of the pill of external assessment.

This book is not about a new strategy for assessment nor even an approach to course design. It is about an issue which is central to all education and training in whatever context it occurs. Self assessment is not something to be added to the repertoire of teaching activities. It is a matter which needs to be taken into account in all considerations of learning.

Although the book focuses on self assessment, it necessarily reflects my own conceptions of what is important in teaching and learning in higher education. It stresses the importance of learners constructing rather than receiving knowledge, of promoting the taking of responsibility for learning, of communicating and expressing what learners know and understand and of taking a critical stance to received wisdom.

Part I provides a framework for discussing self assessment. It starts in Chapter 2 by addressing the questions of what self assessment is and why we should be concerned with it now. This places the discussion which follows in context and emphasises the key features of self assessment and the varieties of ways in which it can be used.

Chapters 3 and 4 consider the broader context of self assessment and discuss ideas which are closely related to it. The first of these chapters looks at what is known about learning and how ideas about student learning, learning from experience and reflective practice can link with self assessment. Chapter 4 reviews current ideas about student assessment in higher education and extracts issues which must also be considered in the self assessment context.

Chapter 5 starts by presenting self assessment in a wider social context – how it relates to the aims of education and the concerns of society. It proceeds to explore different conceptions of knowledge and how these can influence the design of self assessment procedures. The chapter establishes a framework for categorising self assessment practices in terms of knowledge interests of teachers and points to the use of self assessment in different subject areas.

Part II presents a range of specific examples of self assessment in practice. Each chapter describes different strategies in the context of different disciplinary areas. Chapter 6 considers how self and peer marking can be used in a technical electronics subject; Chapter 7 looks at self assessment of engineering design exercises; Chapter 8 examines the use of self and peer assessment of class participation in law; Chapter 9 presents the use of an intensive self assessment process in a postgraduate subject in education; and Chapter 10 provides an example of the use of self appraisal informed by peers in staff development. The section concludes with Chapter 11 where samples of strategies which have been developed in other subject areas for different purposes are discussed in terms of the framework established earlier.

Part III, on self assessment and marking, starts with research on self assessment. The empirical literature comparing student self marking with marking by staff is considered in Chapter 12. Chapter 13 proceeds to address the question of whether self assessment can be used for formal assessment purposes and, if so, under what circumstances.

Part IV considers some of the practical issues which arise from the examples given and the research presented. Chapter 14 looks at implementation and evaluation issues; Chapter 15 provides guidance on the design of self assessment procedures and Chapter 16 considers how peers and other parties can be used to enhance self assessment. The book concludes with a summary of good practice and speculates on issues of importance which have yet to be explored. Chapter 17 proposes some ideas for future development and returns to the criteria outlined earlier.

In keeping with the different emphases of each section, the voice changes from autobiographical to descriptive, to analytical, to pragmatic and to speculative depending on the material being considered. Many people have contributed to the development of the ideas and practices described here and these are either indicated as chapter authors or mentioned in the acknowledgments section.

# PART I

# SELF ASSESSMENT, LEARNING AND ASSESSMENT

## Chapter 2

# What is Learner Self Assessment?

While traditionally self assessment has not been part of courses, it has had an important role in learning. Students are always self assessing. Before they hand in an essay or report, many have formed some notion of how good they think the piece of work is. Language students have routinely tested themselves on lists of vocabulary, medical students have traditionally closed their anatomy books and drawn diagrams to check their understanding, mathematics textbooks have provided examples for students to try out and given answers for students to check their calculations at the back of the book. In open learning materials, in-text questions have encouraged students to think about and check their learning. All of these are examples of ways in which students have traditionally tested their academic discipline knowledge and skills: what they know and what they can do. Although this kind of self assessment is ad hoc and appears peripheral to formal assessment procedures, it is a commonplace part of learning. There are good reasons, as we shall later see, for treating it more consciously and systematically.

All assessment – whether conducted by teachers or by learners – involves two key elements. The first is the development of knowledge and an appreciation of the appropriate standards and criteria for meeting those standards which may be applied to any given work. Unless it is known what counts as good work, it is impossible to tell whether the specific work being considered is adequate. The second is the capacity to make judgements about whether or not the work involved does or does not meet these standards. Unfortunately, emphasis is normally given, by both staff and students, to the latter of these two elements. Engagement with the standards and their criteria is down-played to the detriment of learning.

Of course, not all standards and criteria are such that they can be easily articulated or appreciated without prior learning and experience in a particular domain of knowledge. Even with such experience, they may not be able to be articulated in an accessible form. Similarly, the application of standards is a task which involves considerable critical thinking and the ability to manipulate criteria in ways which allow them to be applied to the work under consideration. Nevertheless, all acts of assessment, whether by teachers, subject matter experts, peers or the individual learner, involve these two stages: establishing criteria and judging work in the light of them. The outcomes of this process might vary depending on who is doing the judging, but the basic process remains common.

In an earlier publication, I proposed the following as the defining characteristic of self assessment:

> the involvement of students in identifying standards and/or criteria to apply to their work and making judgements about the extent to which they have met these criteria and standards. (Boud, 1991, p.5)

This focuses on the two key stages discussed previously. The latter stage, which we might call self grading or self testing is, on its own, a limited aspect of self assessment. It may be useful for the development of self assessment skills, but an overemphasis on this aspect can direct attention away from involving students in identifying and engaging with criteria, a stage which is both difficult and, in my view, neglected.

Self assessment means more than students grading their own work; it means involving them in the processes of determining what is good work in any given situation. It requires them to consider what are the characteristics of, say, a good essay or practical report and to apply this to their own work. Students can be credibly involved in determining or discussing criteria in all areas. However, there do exist some aspects of subjects of either a highly technical or conceptually sophisticated nature in which it may not be practicable at introductory levels to involve students in the specification of criteria. However, students can often recognise the applicability of criteria provided by others. To eliminate completely students' consideration of criteria is to remove them from participation in the core processes of learning in any field of knowledge.

The identification of standards and criteria by students can involve many activities. In some courses, particularly in professional fields, there are published statements of what constitutes good practice. An effective self assessment would need to take account of these, although part of the preparation for such an assessment may involve students developing their own views of good practice first. This preparation can demonstrate that good practice guidelines are based on common foundations of what practitioners believe to be desirable and that they are able to come up with many items which closely reflect those of existing professionals.

It is important to identify what the definition does and does not imply as there are many misconceptions about self assessment. Self assessment is used as both a verb and as a noun: a process, as well as an activity with a distinct identity. It is a goal to which to aspire as well as a practice in which to engage. Without reference to the context it is often hard in the literature on self assessment to discern which of these two uses is meant. It is important to make the distinction as self assessment is so obviously a goal of higher education. However, the use of specific self assessment activities to meet this end requires a justification in the context of a particular course. Self assessment as a goal can be pursued through course designs which do not involve self assessment exercises as such. However, as many courses in higher education have been designed in ways which inhibit the development of self assessment skills, a useful first step is the introduction of explicit self assessment activities.

The term 'self evaluation', is commonly used in the literature and is widespread in North America. Although some authors have tried to distinguish between self assessment and self evaluation (for example, MacGregor, 1993, uses self evaluation to mean self assessment without any component of grading), other usage does not suggest a systematic difference and the terms can usually be regarded as synonymous.

## On what assumptions is the use of self assessment based?

Self assessment is coming to be regarded as an accepted and significant part of courses because it relates to one of the central goals of a university education: enabling students to become effective and responsible learners who can continue their education without the intervention of teachers or courses. Specifically, my own assumptions are that:

- *It is a necessary skill for lifelong learning*
  It is important for all learners to develop the ability to be realistic judges of their own performance and to effectively monitor their own learning. Learning can only be effectively undertaken when the learner monitors what is known, what remains to be known and what is needed to bridge the gap between the two. In the protected environment of the

educational institution it may just be possible for the learner to get by without being able to plan and organise their own learning, but in the world of life and work, this is rarely the case. The ability to self assess is a key foundation to a career as a lifelong learner who can continue their education after formal education has ended (Candy *et al.*, 1994; Justice and Marienau, 1988). Graduates who develop the skills of self assessment are more likely to:
- wish to continue their learning,
- know how to do so,
- monitor their own performance without constant reference to fellow professionals, and
- expect to take full responsibility for their actions and judgements.

- *It needs to be developed in university courses*
  Students manifestly do not enter higher education with this skill fully developed, although it is of course desirable that it should be developed at earlier stages of education. It is likely that it is in part subject-specific, ie, not a universal skill, but one that needs to be developed in relation to particular fields and types of knowledge. So it is appropriate to develop a range of self assessment skills through different subjects. The specific requirements for monitoring performance will, though, differ from one course to another.

  Its development therefore represents an important process which needs to occur in undergraduate education. If students are to be able to continue learning effectively after graduation and make a significant contribution in their own professional work, they must begin to develop skills of appraising their own achievements during their student years.

- *It is necessary for effective learning*
  The third premise is one which forms a particularly important part of the thinking of those who are committed to such goals as student autonomy, independence in learning or self regulation. It is one which is shared across the spectrum, from researchers of a strongly humanistic to those of a strongly cognitive orientation (eg, from Rogers, 1983, and Heron, 1988, to Corno, 1986, and Zimmerman, 1986). For effective learning of any kind to take place, learners – whoever they may be – must develop the capability of monitoring what they do and modifying their learning strategies appropriately. Such self monitoring is what educational psychologists include as part of their term 'metacognition', which is now a central plank in cognitive theories of learning (see, for example, Biggs and Moore 1993).

  Effective learning also involves learners being able to influence their own learning rather than waiting for others to do so, that is, being proactive. Those who are dependent on the continued impetus of teachers or work-place supervisors to develop and assess their knowledge and skills are severely handicapped in their learning.

In summary, it is argued that it is important to develop self assessment skills because they are central to effective learning now and for future learning and an essential feature of professional practice or for anyone who undertakes a responsible role in society.

## Enhancing learning

Of all ideas associated with assessment, self assessment provides the fundamental link with learning. Self assessment is concerned with learners valuing their own learning and achievements on the basis of evidence from themselves and from others. The judgements they make may be about what they have done, what they should be doing or why they should be doing it. Self assessment occurs within a particular context, with respect to particular domains of knowledge and with particular goals in mind. The kinds of activities in which students might be involved are diverse. Some would be purely for their own informal use in learning, others might form part of discussions with peers or teachers and yet others might be used on their own or in conjunction with other data as part of the formal system of assessment within an institution.

Self assessment does not imply that students develop their ideas in isolation from the views and judgements of others. We live alongside others in community with them and share common cultures and understandings. Therefore, peers, 'experts' and teachers are vital; teachers especially so as their actions and expectations tend to have a significant influence on learners. In terms of learning, assessment by peers, assessment by teachers or assessment by others with expertise are all moderated by one's own assessment. These other assessments have a useful part to play, and may control learners' access to future learning opportunities, but unless they inform and help develop a learner's ability to self assess, they are of little educational value. Ultimately it is only the decisions which learners make about what they will or will not do which actually influence the outcomes of their learning.

Peer assessment and peer feedback are activities which are commonly linked with self assessment and in the right circumstances can considerably enhance self assessment. Unfortunately, there are many examples of peer assessment which have the opposite effect. One is the common practice of using peer marking in the assessment of class presentations. If done in a way which emphasises the generation of marks rather than giving feedback on how the presentation can be improved, this form of peer assessment can undermine group cooperation and distract students from the steps they need to take to develop their presentational skills.

If students simply mark each other on a set of fixed scales and these data are collected and presented to the student being assessed, little more is contributed to the development of self assessment abilities than the familiar assessment by teachers. When such marks are formally recorded and contribute to students' final grading, then the distancing of students from making their own judgements is complete. However, when peer assessment is used to provide rich and detailed comments from other students about their reactions to the presentation, then students may be more able to take this, along with their own perceptions and whatever other information is available, and form a judgement which will influence future learning, rather than having to defend themselves and assess the validity of judgements from others which may not be supported by information and which allow for no opportunity to respond.

Heron (1988) explores different permutations of staff and student decision-making with regard to educational processes and proposes a model of assessment in which staff make some decisions, staff with students decide some and students decide some. He regards this as an appropriately comprehensive approach to assessment in higher education. He considers that,

> Once varying mixtures of self, peer and collaborative assessment replace unilateral assessment by staff, a completely new educational climate can be created. Self-determination with respect to setting learning objectives and to program design is not likely to make much headway, in my view, without some measure of self assessment. (p.85)

The role of others in self assessment is discussed specifically in Chapter 16.

Collaboration in assessment can also avoid some of the negative effects of unilateral assessment. Broadfoot (1979), arguing from the context of schooling, suggests that one reason for the lack of motivation of so-called 'less-able' students is that they have been alienated by the assessment processes which they have experienced, and that the essentially interactive basis of all learning is not reflected in the almost entirely one-sided nature of assessment. She suggests that the involvement of students in the assessment process, particularly through self assessment, can help to counteract the alienating influences through:

- mutual evaluation which recognises the dual responsibility of both teacher and student in the learning process. An awareness by students that their opinions are being taken into account should enhance their morale, involvement and thus motivation

- encouraging a good self-concept. If they can be encouraged to think positively about their learning and to see their progress in terms of their own previous achievement rather than merely in relation to others, students may come to have a better self-concept since whatever progress they do make, however small, can be recognised by both student and teacher
- helping students see a value in what they are doing and consequentially take more responsibility for their own learning.

So self assessment may be combined with other teaching and assessment practices, but care needs to be taken that it is not linked with activities which undermine the engagement of students in determining assessment criteria and in making their own decisions about their work.

Other teaching approaches which relate closely to the development of self assessment include the use of reflective strategies, self-directed learning methods and critical thinking activities. These are a few of the terms used to describe elements of courses which encourage students to take responsibility for their learning rather than follow the prescriptions of others, to process and reflect on their learning and to critically appraise the ideas that they meet. An overemphasis on the presentation of information or the overstuffed curriculum which seem at present to be endemic to higher education are antithetical to the development of reflection, the taking of responsibility for learning, critical thinking or self assessment. These ideas are discussed further in Chapter 3.

In summary, self assessment is about students developing their learning skills. It is not just another assessment technique to be set alongside others. It is about engaging learners with criteria for good practice in any given area and making complex judgements. It is not primarily about individuals giving themselves marks or grades. And it is not about supplanting the role of teachers. They are needed more than ever although their role will need to shift towards fostering students' self assessments rather than making judgements which do not take this into account.

## How is self assessment used?

Self assessment is not simply a substitute for activities in which students would normally be assessed by someone else, although there are many examples of its use in such circumstances. There are many purposes for which it is used, roles it plays and contexts in which it operates. Many of these fall beyond the traditional domain of assessment activities into the realm of teaching and learning. The major uses are discussed in later chapters but it is useful to note here the range of areas in which self assessment might be considered.

### For individual self-monitoring and checking progress

This is the area in which informal self assessment has traditionally found a place. Students monitor their own learning to ensure either that they are pursuing the goals they have set for themselves, or those which will meet the assessment requirements of the course in which they are enrolled. Students may be introduced to ways of doing this, but essentially they are left to their own devices to gain ideas and strategies from books and peers.

### As a way to promote good learning practices and learning-how-to-learn skills

In some situations self assessment finds a place in study skills courses or in the components of, typically, first-year courses in which students are introduced to worthwhile approaches to study and learning-how-to-learn strategies. These often apply to all students in a group and are designed to pre-empt learning difficulties which might arise at a later stage.

### For diagnosis and remediation

Students whose informally acquired self assessment skills are lacking and who find difficulties with their courses may need to undertake special study counselling. Self assessment here is introduced as a tool for demystifying study requirements and helping students through systematic approaches which may involve them in deconstructing course requirements to determine what might be the most effective matters on which to focus.

### As a substitute for other forms of assessment

The role of self assessment in other assessment activities might be the most obvious use, but it is often not the most frequently encountered. Self assessments, moderated or combined with assessments by peers, teachers and others may contribute to the final formal assessment in a course or unit of a course. Self assessment for formal assessment purposes is one of the few occasions on which the generation of marks or grades as such is involved. Issues in this area are discussed in detail in Chapter 13.

**As a learning activity designed to improve professional or academic practice**

There are many skills which need to be developed through practice and it is rarely possible for enough staff time to be devoted to the systematic monitoring of progress which is necessary for proper skill development. Self assessment, often in conjunction with peer feedback, is used in many areas in which such close monitoring is required. Many clinical skills are of this nature, for example. But its use goes beyond the area of skills into monitoring many forms of professional practice in which reflective abilities need to be fostered. For example, in teacher education and nursing education, a central aim of many courses is the development of the reflective practitioner, a person who can think critically about their own practice, plan changes and observe the effectiveness of these modifications. It is difficult to imagine how such goals might be pursued without resort to strategies akin to self assessment.

**To consolidate learning over a wide range of contexts**

Study is becoming increasingly fragmented through modularisation of courses, through independent assessment mechanisms in different parts of the same subject and through the use of mixtures of teacher-led and student-negotiated courses. One use of self assessment is to assist students in bringing these fragments together. (The use of a self assessment schedule within a single subject to consolidate all student learning in that area is discussed in Chapter 9.) As part of modular or self-directed degree programmes in the United States (cf. Waluconis, 1993) it is becoming increasingly common for students to take 'capstone' seminars after other course requirements are complete to integrate their learning through extended self assessment essays which link together learning from different course units.

**To review achievements as a prelude to recognition of prior learning**

Increasing numbers of students are being admitted into courses and gaining advance standing through mechanisms which involve the accreditation of prior learning. They prepare a portfolio which documents their achievements which is then assessed and its equivalence to formal qualifications determined. Self assessment plays an important part in the process of portfolio development (eg, Mandell and Michelson, 1990), although it is not common to explicitly identify self assessment as such in the procedure.

## For self knowledge and self understanding

Some self assessment practices conceptually take students beyond the present context. By reflecting on their learning they gain a greater appreciation of the influences on it and on the nature of their particular experience. In these cases, self assessment is emancipatory. It contributes to the development of the person because, through it, students' self knowledge and self understanding increase.

Self assessment thus encompasses a larger territory than might at first be apparent. It is as much concerned with planning learning and the questioning of existing learner practices as it is with recording achievements or checking understanding.

## Why is there such current interest?

Given the range of contexts in which self assessment is now used, it is interesting to speculate on why there is such a high level of acceptance of it now when it was relatively unusual only ten years ago. There are different levels at which this question can be answered, and self assessment is only one of many developments which are apparent in higher education.

At the macro-level there are major trends and forces of which individual teachers and students are usually unaware. These factors are diverse and in many ways contradictory. However, when arguments from different ideological positions lead to similar kinds of practice there is normally a clear trend apparent. Some of the macro factors include:

- a shift to individualism and market forces in education
- changes towards some democratic elements in organisations
- flattening of organisational structures which gives those lower in the hierarchy much greater levels of responsibility and thus greater need for skills to handle this
- reductions in resources; strategies which require less staff time and effort are seen as desirable
- students being better prepared for taking responsibility, for example, changing practices in schools which emphasise project work, student-created records of achievement and student choice
- shifts from a traditional (authoritarian) curriculum structure in which expertise in the discipline is the pre-eminent criterion for judgement to a competency- or to a problem-based one in which solving the problem or meeting explicit criteria is the measure of success.

Although at the pragmatic level of day-to-day decision-making such influences are normally invisible, they do affect the overall climate in which certain kinds of innovation are possible. Interestingly, self assessment is not an approach over which those with a 'progressive' educational philosophy have a monopoly – it is supported by those who wish to allow students more flexibility in their learning as well as those who wish students to engage more rigorously with a given subject area – and as such it is more likely to find a continuing place in courses.

At the micro level, there have been other developments:

- with the increasing number and diversity of students entering higher education it is no longer possible to assume that students will have a common range of often context-specific skills required to be able to judge their own work
- linked with this is the trend that courses are less likely now to be covering well-trodden knowledge in the traditional disciplines – combined degrees, modular structures and increasing options mean that different paths are followed by different students
- larger class sizes have led to a decrease in the number of separate items of coursework which are marked and an overall reduction in feedback at the early stages of a course. There are now fewer opportunities for students to discuss their specific work in detail with a member of staff and a need to pick up the cues and clues which can prompt the development of their own judgements on their work.

Whether or not it is wishful thinking to assume that self assessment skills were acquired in informal ways in the past, what is apparent now is that the current pressures on staff mean it is unlikely there will be a significant increase in the one-to-one feedback particularly helpful in learning-how-to-learn.

But is it not possible to acquire self assessment skills from the normal process of being assessed? The answer is of course it is possible to some extent, but it is not likely to be very effective because of the forms of assessment which are commonly used and the poor quality of feedback on assessed tasks which is now customary in almost all areas. Too often assessment tasks are set in a context which is artificial and unfamiliar to students and the tasks are fragmented. They are marked by staff on measuring scales which have vague and poorly understood divisions. Marks are frequently reported to students with inadequate commentary to explain what they signify. It is difficult in these circumstances for students to draw meaning from the experience. How does the assessment task relate to something which might realistically be expected of the student in the future (other than more assessment tasks)? What does the mark mean? It may be interpreted as good or about average, but what does that mean in relation to doing the task better next time around? What specifically was good and not so good about the work? Where is the starting point for further development? There are no satisfactory answers to these questions. There are often no answers at all when the assessment is one which terminates the course or the subject. There is no feedback loop to complete and no information of use to students *for learning* transmitted back to them. If detailed comments are available, they are far too late.

There are, of course, moves to clarify and make explicit marking schemes, to set tasks before the last few weeks of term and to improve the quality and timeliness of feedback to students. These are necessary and important steps, but in themselves they are likely to have little impact on the development of self assessment skills. If we regard the ability to self assess as important, then it should be pursued explicitly and in the light of the features which have been identified as to how it might best be supported. While these ideas form the focus of later chapters, it is necessary first to consider something of what is involved in assessment and learning to see how self assessment might link with these.

## Is self assessment as new as it might seem?

In preparing this book, I became intrigued with earlier ideas of self assessment which predate the modern idea. Prompted by the appearance of a student in one of my classes from the People's Republic of China, I started to think about the tradition of self criticism which featured strongly in the system of governance of Chairman Mao. Is this similar to self assessment and if so how can self assessment avoid the zealotry and the denial of the individual which the use of public self criticism appeared to promote? It is ironic to think of self assessment in this context of collectivism, as some contemporary critics have identified it as an approach which fosters an individualistic approach to education!

The feature of public self criticism which appears most objectionable in the West is the confessing of failures within a framework imposed on the person by the dominant ideology as manifest by peer group pressure in a totalitarian context. Shaming in front of members of one's community appears also to be part of the picture. Self assessment in front of an audience is rarely currently used in higher education institutions, and where it does take place (see, for example, Chapter 10) great care is taken to create a highly supportive small group with ground rules and a climate of trust and mutuality of self-disclosure. Decision-making remains in the hands of the assessee. The spectre of the exposure and ritual humiliation which has featured in some versions of self criticism should act as a salutary warning to teachers who may be tempted to implement a degenerate form of self assessment without regard to other values.

While the public act of self-criticism is associated mainly with the excesses of post-revolutionary China, there is a long history of officials reporting their own failings to their superiors in earlier periods (cf. the Qianlong period of the late 18th century: Franklin, 1994). It has been argued (Guptara, 1994) that self criticism was the secularised form of the Judeo-Christian practice of confession and that it continues today in our humanistic society via Marxism through psychotherapy. There is Hebrew confession via God, Catholic confession via the priest, Marxist' correction' of one's behaviour in the light of current doctrine and secular confession to a therapist or educator. The modern use of self assessment may or may not be in a direct line from that tradition and we will have to wait for educational historians to disentangle the many threads. However, we can identify ways in which self assessment as discussed here is different from these earlier social and spiritual practices.

Self assessment as discussed here:

- refers to particular work or achievements and does not purport to represent an account of the person *qua* person or an overall state of being; the person is conceptually separated from the work.
- is not normally public or directed at a specific person or entity, although declaring one's self assessment can be a useful part of developing a commitment to it and receiving feedback on it
- has the self as agent and audience
- is not undertaken for the sake of catharsis, although it may be associated with completion and making whole
- is essentially formative and not absolute, though it can be used for summative purposes.

Unfortunately, the use of self assessment has grown at a more rapid rate than the dissemination of good practice. There are many examples of strategies which are rejected by students because of poor implementation, which subtly undermine the taking of the very responsibilities which the approach is seeking to enhance or which combine self assessment with activities such as peer assessment which, while they can easily be made compatible, are used in a heavy-handed manner to impose a regime as rigid as the one it is purporting to replace. Self assessment has great potential when it is seen from the point of view of contributing to student learning and when it is used to engage students more deeply in the subject areas being studied. These themes are explored further in the following chapter.

# Chapter 3

# How does Self Assessment Relate to Ideas about Learning?

Self assessment, as we have seen, is one of a number of ideas having an impact on teaching and learning. For a full understanding of self assessment it is necessary to locate it in the current debates which are transforming the ways in which teaching and learning are regarded. From one point of view, self assessment is a subset of discussions about teaching and learning. From another, it is an aspect of assessment, which is considered in the next chapter.

In this chapter the starting point is the major change which is occurring in teaching and learning in higher education – from the teachers' to the students' perspective – and how self assessment has a central role in encouraging learning. The themes which are introduced are: the importance of considering students' approaches to learning, increasing emphasis on student autonomy and self-direction in courses, learning from experience and the role of reflection and reflective practice.

## The shift to a learning perspective

The greatest conceptual shift which has occurred in recent times in higher education has been from a perspective which focused on the teacher and what he or she does, to a perspective in which student learning is central. While much current practice has yet to fully reflect this shift, it is one which is not likely to be reversed. It is being strongly reinforced by research on teaching and learning which has specifically been conducted in relation to higher education (Ramsden, 1988a). The essence of the learning perspective is that it considers all decisions about teaching and assessment in the light of the impact or potential impact on student learning. From this point of view, it does not matter what other desirable outcome an existing practice or change of approach in teaching might have. Unless it results in improvements in student learning it is not worthy of consideration. It must be replaced by something which does influence learning.

There are many threads to this argument and different positions have been taken about the key factors in student learning which must be considered. What they have in common is the assumption that learners bring a great deal of experience to any new situation and teaching must start with what the learner already knows. This is true even when students are studying subjects which are quite new to them. They bring with them assumptions about how to approach the task and accumulated knowledge of matters which they perceive to be associated with the new topic. What is significant is not that this knowledge may be false or misleading from the point of view of the teacher, but that the teacher must start by assuming that such prior knowledge exists and that it will influence what students regard as important and where they will focus their energies. When prior knowledge is based upon direct experience of the topic under consideration it is again important for teachers to find ways of taking this into account and adjusting what they expect students to do in the light of it. This position is captured in David Ausubel's famous aphorism – when asked to summarise what psychology tells us about teaching, he replied 'Ascertain what a student already knows and teach accordingly'.

Rather than review all the various positions about learning which are current, I wish simply to describe four sets of ideas and associated research which I have found influential in developing my views.

## Student approaches to learning

The first of these ideas focuses on students' conceptions of learning. This is the aspect of teaching and learning in higher education which has been most thoroughly researched in recent years, and while the ideas which underpin it are simple, they are also powerful in their application. One of the best known ideas, based on research originally carried out in Sweden, is that of looking at students' differing approaches to learning. Marton and others (*cf.* Marton *et al.*, 1984) found that when they explored, through detailed interviews, the ways in which students went about studying specific subject matter there were a limited number of approaches which emerged. While these studies were always context- and content-specific, they found that students' two dominant approaches to learning could be labelled as 'surface' and 'deep'. Students who adopted a surface approach focused on the words used by teachers and found in textbooks and tried to remember them. Those who adopted a deep approach focused on the meaning of the words and tried to make sense of what they studied, relating it to their own understanding. This idea has been extended by other researchers who have identified an achieving or strategic approach in which students adopt an expedient position and use either a deep or surface approach depending on pressures of time or assessment expectations (Biggs and Moore, 1993).

What the researchers found was that the approach to learning which was taken by students varied according to circumstances. One person might adopt quite different approaches to learning in different subjects in the same course. The approach adopted was not simply a function of the person, but of the interaction of the person with the context in which they were operating. So, for example, someone might normally adopt a deep approach to a given subject, but under pressure from an examination they might switch to a surface approach. What was important though were not the intrinsic features of the examination, but the individual student's perception of it – different students could have quite different approaches under what appeared to be similar conditions. This way of viewing learning became known as a relational perspective. The approach to learning adopted by a particular student was related to their own goals in studying and their perceptions of the circumstances in which they found themselves (Ramsden, 1987). The researchers came to the conclusion that students' approaches to learning could be influenced by teachers, but not always in simple ways. Staff could have an impact on promoting deep approaches by changing student work loads, assessment requirements, and allowing students greater control over their learning. None of these influences however were independent of the total context as experienced by students. Students do not experience separate subjects in isolation; it is the overall effect of various requirements, their own aspirations and the cumulative influence of the total programme which governs how they approach studying.

While there have yet to be studies of self assessment which use the same methodology as this perspective, it is highly likely that students will approach self assessment in ways similar to those they adopt for the rest of their study. Self assessment must therefore be introduced in ways which take account of the context of study and involve activities which meaningfully engage students with the subject matter. Boyd and Cowan (1985) argue, for example, from an engineering perspective that it is only through methods such as self assessment in which students take significant responsibility for their learning that deep approaches to learning can be effectively fostered.

Recent research has extended work on students' approaches to learning by applying the same techniques to teachers' approaches to teaching. There is starting to emerge evidence from these studies which suggests that some conceptions of teaching, particularly a teacher-centred view of teaching as transmission of knowledge or concept acquisition, are counterproductive to student learning (Sheppard and Gilbert, 1991; Trigwell *et al.*, 1994). While teachers' views of self assessment have not been considered so far, it is unlikely that teachers who are not committed to fostering deep approaches to learning will be very active in promoting self assessment!

## Autonomy and self-direction

The second theme which relates to self assessment thinking is that which focuses on students taking greater responsibility for their own learning. While it is generally considered that higher education institutions require students to operate more independently than schools, the diet of teaching and learning in most universities is rather more directive and circumscribed than a reading of the goals of higher education would lead one to believe. This is true at least for the formal curriculum and the ways in which it is defined through assessment requirements. It is argued in many places (see, for example, Boud, 1988a) that it is fundamental to higher education that students learn to become independent of their teachers and that they should be placed in circumstances in which they are expected to make decisions about what and how they learn more often than is commonly the case at present.

Rather than leave this to chance, many innovations have been introduced to promote student autonomy and self-direction. These often involve very substantial changes in the organisation of courses. They also vary greatly and are normally designed to address a wide range of deficiencies in addition to promoting student independence. Those innovations which have a strong element of promoting student autonomy in learning include the following:

* Problem-based learning (Barrows and Tamblyn, 1980; Boud and Feletti, 1991) and variations such as 'enquiry and action learning' (Burgess, 1992; Burgess and Jackson, 1990).

   These approaches organise study around key professional problems rather than traditional disciplinary knowledge. With staff support and access to appropriate study materials, students plan their own learning to address problems with which they are confronted.

* Self-directed learning (Hammond and Collins, 1991), learning contracts (Anderson *et al.*, 1994, forthcoming; Knowles and Associates, 1986; Stephenson and Laycock, 1993) and the negotiated curriculum (eg, Brew, 1993; Millar *et al.*, 1986).

   The emphasis in these approaches is on negotiation between staff and students about what is to be learned and how it is to be learned. Such negotiation takes place on either an individual or group basis.

- Experiential learning (Kolb, 1984; Weil and McGill, 1989), experience-based learning (Higgs, 1988) and action learning (Beaty and McGill, 1992; Pedler, 1991).

  These approaches place particular emphasis on the past and current experience of learners. They involve either the construction of appropriate learning events and the processing of the experience gained, or working with students' experience of events outside the immediate context of the course.

Some of these approaches have had a substantial impact. There are notable examples of problem-based learning in medicine and health-related areas, action learning is widespread in management education, the negotiated curriculum in teacher education, and learning contracts in adult education. While each of these approaches has unique characteristics, there are features which they share. Students are actively involved in making decisions about what and how they study, there is a high level of cooperation (as distinct from competition) between students in their learning, particular outcomes are often negotiated between staff and students rather than being imposed, and students are expected to engage in a greater variety of learning activities than in the traditional lecture, laboratory and tutorial regime.

A common feature in most of these ways of organising courses is the role of assessment within them. Assessment is seen as an integral part of the learning process with greater emphasis on formative assessment than in the courses they replaced. Along with a focus on students planning and managing their own learning and learning from each other there is a concomitant focus on self assessment. In some cases this is explicit, but in others it is implicit in the fine structure of the approach. For example, in the use of learning contracts students are required to determine criteria for assessment at the negotiation phase and decide when their work is ready to be presented for formal assessment and able to meet these criteria. Often no mention of self assessment as such is made in this process, but it is one that strongly encourages the development of the skills which are discussed in this book. Another example of self assessment embedded in the teaching and learning approach occurs in problem-based learning. Students are confronted with problematic situations in which they have to define their learning objectives, plan their own learning to address the problem and make assessments of the extent to which they have achieved their objectives. In some instances formal self and peer assessment activities are used, but often the problem-solving sequence is structured to emphasise self assessment without the term as such being used.

Another dimension to this work has been the development of initiatives for learning-how-to-learn (eg, Smith and Associates, 1990). While such approaches are most familiar through study skills counselling activities for students at risk, the learning-how-to-learn movement is more widespread and aims to influence all aspects of teaching and learning practice. The idea is that all courses, but particularly those at the introductory level, are constructed around the central goal of developing in students effective study practices. For many years it was expected that these activities would be the province of special programmes conducted by study skills units, but it is now accepted that the best way to develop such skills is through everyday work in mainstream courses fostered by regular teaching staff. This can only be done if teaching staff focus on learning skills, such as self assessment, as well as the ostensible subject matter of the course. The making explicit of academic requirements, which is a feature of learning-how-to-learn initiatives, directly parallels the explication of criteria, which is a key element of self assessment. The careful raising of consciousness about and monitoring of performance of academic skills in introductory courses can clearly be a form of self assessment.

Candy (1988) has drawn attention to the importance of the development of subject-matter autonomy in students. He distinguishes subject-matter (or epistemological) autonomy from the notion of autonomous individuals who exhibit qualities of moral, emotional and intellectual independence – the common goal of higher education – from the notion of learners taking responsibility for their own learning through setting objectives, finding resources and evaluating their achievements – which is the sense in which autonomy is used in many of the innovations listed above. He argues that if the aim of higher education is to produce students who will continue their studies in a particular domain of knowledge they will need to have developed a degree of expertise which will enable them to distinguish plausible from implausible knowledge claims and convincing from unconvincing evidence. A person can operate as an autonomous learner in many respects without having the kinds of expertise which discern quality in a given field of endeavour. Subject-matter competence is often highly context-specific and does not necessarily transfer from one area to another.

Acknowledgement of the varying demands of different subject-matter domains has considerable implications for assessment in general and self assessment in particular. It means that it is not sufficient for students to develop general purpose self assessment capabilities as these will not equip them for the full range of learning tasks with which they will be confronted in the future. Self assessment does not just apply to learning processes, or communication skills (where it is commonly used at present) but to substantive problems in the discipline or profession. To ignore this aspect is to consign self assessment to the margins. The implications of this in the application of self assessment in different domains of knowledge are discussed in Chapter 5.

## Learning from experience

The third set of ideas about learning which is of significance for self assessment relate to the role of experience. While experiential learning was mentioned briefly in the section on autonomy and self-direction, ideas deriving from recent work on learning from experience are having a much wider influence than in the specific innovations described. As was fore-shadowed earlier, the importance of taking account of the prior experience of students to actively build upon and use it in learning, is becoming increasingly recognised. Some consideration of experience always needs to be made. The role of experience in learning has been summarised in the following propositions (Boud *et al.*, 1993). The implications of each for self assessment are discussed.

### Experience is the foundation of, and stimulus for, learning

Experience cannot be bypassed; it is the central consideration of all learning. Learning can only occur if the experience of the learner is engaged. Every experience is potentially an opportunity for learning, however. Experience does not necessarily lead to learning: there needs to be an active engagement with it.

Self assessment must in some way relate to the actual experience of students. It must engage them in tasks which are meaningful to them and it must be framed in such a way that it is connected with the act of learning. Tasks must not assume that all students bring a common set of knowledge to them. Self assessment exercises must have sufficient degrees of flexibility to enable students of different backgrounds to benefit from them in accord with their prior experience. The act of self assessment plays an important role in drawing meaning from experience.

### Learners actively construct their own experience

Each experience is influenced by the unique past of the learner. Individual meaning is attached to events even though others may attempt to impose their definitions of it. The meaning of an experience is not given, it is subject to interpretation. The major influence on how learners construct their experience is the cumulative effects of their personal and cultural history: the influences of the events in their lives which have helped form who they are now and their response to the world.

Self assessment activities need to acknowledge that different students will legitimately interpret the same events in different ways. The meaning of an experience is created in the interaction between the learner and the milieu in which he or she operates – it is relational. Self assessment has to take account of this. Standardised self assessment tasks which make assumptions about the responses of learners and which do not involve communication between the learner and others should therefore be used cautiously, if at all.

## Learning is an holistic process

Learning is normally experienced as a seamless whole; there is continuity between experiences even though they may be labelled as different. It is impossible to dissociate a learner from his or her context, from the processes in which they are involved or from their past experience. All of our experiences, past and present, are potentially relevant to any given learning task.

Ideally self assessment practices take account of the development of the learner as a whole person. Learners bring to the self assessment process the whole of their experience and are likely to be sensitive to practices which deny or negate some aspect of themselves which they consider to be important. Hence self assessment tasks which are realistic and complex and engage a number of facets of the learners' experience are likely to be preferable to those focusing reductionistically on a single dimension.

## Learning is socially and culturally constructed

While learners construct their own experience, they do so in the context of a particular social setting and range of cultural values. It is not possible to step beyond the influence of context and culture, although critical reflection on experience can expose some taken-for-granted assumptions. Indeed, the making problematic of the familiar is a useful strategy in moving beyond the norms which constrain us. The most powerful, and generally invisible, influence of the social and cultural context occurs through language.

Self assessment is not meaningful in a social vacuum. It includes and responds to opinions of others, experts and peers. The development and appropriate use of a vocabulary for learning in any subject area is a necessary part of self assessment. This can often only come about through interaction with others or with suitable learning materials. Self assessment, as we shall see in Chapter 11, can assist learners to go beyond their existing culturally defined conceptions. It can help learners to name their experience and therefore provides a means for exploring, appropriating and moving beyond it.

## Learning is influenced by the socio-emotional context in which it occurs

Emotions and feelings are key pointers to both possibilities for, and barriers to, learning: they are commonly neglected and devalued in educational institutions. Denial of feelings is denial of learning. Two key sources of influence are past experience and the role of others in the present (supportive or otherwise). Everyone carries with them their own socio-emotional context from the past – a set of expectations about what can and cannot be done – and the present context can reinforce or challenge this.

The ways in which experience is interpreted in the self assessment process are intimately connected with how learners view themselves. Developing confidence and building self esteem both flow from and are necessary for learning from experience through self assessment. A supportive micro-context therefore needs to be established if self assessment for critical reflection is to be accepted by learners. It is difficult enough for students to open themselves to judgements which may contradict their existing knowledge without having to defend themselves from the criticisms of others. The construction of a learning rather than an assessment context for self assessment, where learners feelings are honoured, is important.

## Reflection and reflective practice

Development of reflective skills is an important feature of thoughtful and meaningful self assessment. In parallel with the shift of discussion towards the learning of particular concepts and subject matter in higher education has been a shift towards consideration of the gap between what is learned in educational institutions and the world of professional practice. A key figure in this debate has been Donald Schön (1983, 1987). He introduced the idea of a reflective practitioner – someone who is learning in the act of reflecting on their own practice – and drew attention to the need to prepare students for professional practice. He argues that most courses emphasise technical knowledge which is well-ordered and systematic rather than the complex problem-solving world with which students will be confronted on graduation. He has used the vivid metaphor of the hard high ground of technical expertise, for which students are well-prepared, and the swamp of professional practice for which courses have left students singularly ill-equipped (Schön, 1987, p.3).

Schön distinguishes between reflection-in-action and reflection-on-action. Reflection-in-action occurs while practising. It influences the moment-by-moment decisions which are made by a practitioner, whereas reflection-on-action occurs after the event and contributes to the development of the skills which are needed in practice. Both are necessary parts of any course and need to be developed as part of a practice-orientated curriculum. Caution needs to be exercised though to avoid confusing the two.

The ideas of Schön and others working with the idea of reflection in learning have had particular impact on courses in professional areas and there is a rapidly expanding literature in teacher education (Grimmett and Erickson, 1988), medicine and nursing (Palmer *et al.*, 1994), law (Ziegler, 1992), social work (Gould and Taylor, in preparation) as well as significant interest in engineering and architecture.

Alongside work influenced by Schön on reflective practice there have been independent developments which have focused on the role of reflection in courses. The main concern of this work has been to acknowledge the importance of reflection in learning and to find ways of incorporating reflective activities into educational settings (both reflection-in-action and reflection-on-action). One of the models which has been developed from this is that of Boud *et al.*, (1983) and subsequently Boud and Walker (1990). This model has conceptualised the process of learning from experience – the experience can be one which is specially prompted or one which occurs in the course of other activities. It shows how learning from experience can be enhanced by carrying out clearly defined reflective activities before, during and after a learning activity.

Consideration of self assessment can take place at any stage. Prior to the event, learners will be concerned with what they know, what they don't know and what they want to know and how their engagement with the learning tasks will relate to their goals. During the event, learners will be involved in making assessments about whether their goals are being met and how they can intervene to ensure that their learning proceeds in the direction desired. And following the event, learners will be making assessments of which aspects to focus on to pursue their intents and how the knowledge they are gaining relates to what they want to know and challenges what they thought they knew. Again, the concept of self assessment was not used, but many of the processes can contribute to the development of self assessment skills if conducted with a consciousness of this dimension.

The Boud and Walker model points to some features which self assessment activities might include to move away from the narrowly instrumental approach which characterises many examples. The learning process they describe is not a linear one: it involves iteration through many cycles of reflection. Criteria are not specified in advance. They may emerge from giving detailed attention to experience and the emotions which are part of it. Divergent rather than convergent approaches to the making of meaning are used. And the final 'assessment' is tested against further experience.

Some of the features of any learning activity which are likely to promote students' reflection can be drawn from the model. They are:

- Learners are actively engaged with a task which they accept is for learning (they are not simply following a prescription or set of rules, but are contributing their own thinking to the task).
- The task is constructed to allow significant elements of choice by the learners so that they can begin to own it and make it meaningful and worthwhile for them – it is a task which is not undertaken simply to satisfy the needs of the teacher.
- The learning event is not totally predictable to the participants and learners are prompted to notice what they did not expect.
- Learners' experience is challenged or confronted in some way which allows them to reassess their experience and the assumptions on which they are operating.
- Learners are obliged to intervene in some way in their own learning process; they have to make choices and follow the consequences of their choices.
- Learners are required to link what is new to them to their existing frameworks of understanding or confront the need to modify these frameworks. (From Boud and Knights, 1994)

It is easy to imagine that students would necessarily adopt a deep approach to learning in any activity which included features of this kind. Unfortunately this is not assured. It is not possible through design of any learning event to ensure that students participate in ways desired by teachers. However, if the total learning milieu of the student – formal and informal – is taken into account, the chances of students slipping into a surface mode can be diminished.

The list of features likely to promote reflection directly parallels features likely to promote self assessment. The similarities are such that it is not useful to consider reflection and self assessment as entirely separate ideas. Self assessment is a reflective activity and, when well designed, develops reflective skills. There are close links between self assessment and reflection. Indeed, the former can be regarded as a specific subset of the latter. When courses are designed with a consciousness of the role of reflection in learning, there may be no need for specifically labelled self assessment activities to be included. Consideration of self assessment in future courses might fruitfully proceed in conjunction with explorations of reflection.

## Implications for self assessment of taking a learning perspective

Considerations of learning such as those discussed in this chapter give support to the use of self assessment practices, and provide indications of good practice:

- Well-constructed self assessment activities act as prompts to deep approaches to learning. However, there are no guarantees that any strategy will reliably lead to a deep approach as it is students' conceptions which influence their actions. Concerns other than those related to the learning task will always be present.
- Self assessment encourages students to take responsibility, particularly when they are actively involved in considering criteria which are meaningful to them.
- Self assessment activities need to take account of students' goals and experience, whatever other goals teachers may have. To ignore the students' perspective is to give a message to them which says that their concerns are not important. This will have wider consequences in terms of the value students place on these activities. Students should be actively involved in decisions about self assessment activities.
- Self assessment needs to engage students with central problems and issues in the field of study to equip them with subject-matter skills as well as more generic ones. Self assessment is not context- or content-independent.
- Self assessment can encourage students to reflect on their learning to consolidate it and move beyond it.

In summary, well-designed self assessment activities need to take account of:

- learners and the experience which they bring to the task,
- the particular demands of the subject matter, and
- the context in which they take place.

They will also take account of the extent to which courses have reflective activities incorporated as a core feature. Practical issues in design are considered in Chapters 14 to 16. The next chapter looks at how self assessment relates to another vital element in the teaching and learning process, namely, assessment.

# Chapter 4

# How does Self Assessment Relate to Ideas about Assessment?

For many years, assessment has been taken for granted and considered unproblematic. Assessment followed teaching and indicated which students had achieved most from a course. Results were reported as percentages, grades or pass/fail. Assessment was usually undertaken after the end of a course or subject and, in higher education, assessment tasks were usually set by the person teaching the course, with some oversight by others. Students clearly had no role to play other than to complete the assessment requirements under the conditions set for them.

Much has changed. There is now less emphasis on final examinations and the unseen paper. Assessment methods have diversified and multiplied, and work completed prior to the end of the course more often than not is weighted as part of formal assessments. There have also been moves towards assessment based on defined criteria or competences and the use of detailed profiles of achievement rather than marks or grades. These are still regarded as innovative and while they have attracted great interest, have not yet found a place in the mainstream. The involvement of students in assessment decisions is still uncommon.

Such a context provides a frame through which self assessment can be viewed. If self assessment is (mistakenly) seen as simply an addition to the repertoire of assessment practices it is in danger of being judged in terms of these conservative traditions of assessment. Its merits in contributing to learning may therefore be neglected. If it is seen as a learning activity alone, the inevitable connections with assessment may be ignored and concurrent assessment practices may undermine its development. There is no simple solution to this. Self assessment is both an assessment practice and a teaching and learning activity. It inhabits an uneasy territory between the two. However, notions of assessment are slowly changing and the powerful influence of assessment on learning is being more clearly documented. It is desirable for self assessment to take its place in a broader conception of assessment without it being viewed in terms of the conventions of a previous generation.

## Tensions between assessment and learning

One of the fundamental constraints on any change in assessment practice is that assessment serves conflicting purposes. These purposes serve the interests of groups who have quite different agendas. There are two generally accepted purposes of student assessment. The first is to improve the quality of learning. Students are given feedback of various kinds on the work they produce with a view to them reaching a greater understanding of what they are doing and becoming more effective in their learning. This is formative assessment or assessment for learning.

The second concerns the accreditation of knowledge or performance: students are assessed to certify their achievements. This occurs primarily for the award of a degree or diploma, though various components of assessment are usually taken into account in making this judgement. This is summative assessment or assessment for the record. In both cases judgement is involved, but in the first it directly serves the needs of the learner and in the second it primarily serves the needs of the external world. The external world – employers, professional bodies, other educational institutions – needs it to certify competence and to simplify selection procedures. Assessment is also used for various internal administrative purposes such as the allocation of students to particular groups, but these can be thought of as subordinate to the two main purposes.

Students tend not to learn well if the former purpose is not effective and they cannot be recognised as competent if the latter is neglected. Unfortunately, resource pressures increasingly result in protection of assessment for the record at the expense of assessment for learning. In the self assessment literature there has been too little distinction made between self assessment for learning and self assessment as part of formal assessment requirements.

An additional tension is present for teachers, especially those working in higher education, between teaching and assessing. There is continuing potential for conflict between being a facilitator of learning on the one hand and being an assessor who has a key role in certification on the other. These two roles are not as easy to separate or make compatible as is commonly assumed.

Over the past 20 years or so, there has been building a challenging literature on the relationship between assessment and learning (See Boud,

1990). It is not the place here to review it in great detail, but generally research has shown that:

- students are assessed on those matters easy to assess and this leads to an over-emphasis on memory and lower-level skills (eg, Black, 1969)
- assessment encourages students to focus on those topics which are assessed at the expense of those which are not (eg, Elton and Laurillard, 1979)
- the nature of assessment tasks influences the approaches to learning which students adopt (eg, Ramsden, 1988b)
- students who perform well on university examinations can retain fundamental misconceptions about key concepts in the subjects they have passed (eg, Dahlgren, 1984)
- students give precedence to assessment which is graded (eg, Becker *et al., 1968)*
- successful students seek cues from teachers to enable them to identify what is important for formal assessment purposes (eg, Miller and Parlett, 1974).

Findings such as these have led to the conclusion that existing assessment approaches can have effects quite contrary to those desired.

Concerns about assessment have not been restricted to the domain of higher education. There is currently a great deal more activity on this front in schools where substantial reappraisal of the role of assessment has been occurring. One of the most perceptive US analysts has discussed the changes to assessment in a historical context (Eisner, 1993) and identified what he describes as features of the new assessment in education:

- The tasks used to assess what students know and can do need to reflect the tasks they will encounter in the world outside schools, not merely those limited to the schools themselves.
- The tasks used to assess students should reveal how students go about solving a problem, not only the solutions they formulate.
- Assessment tasks should reflect the values of the intellectual community from which the tasks are derived.
- Assessment tasks need not be limited to solo performance.
- New assessment tasks should make possible more than one acceptable solution to a problem and more than one acceptable answer to a question.
- Assessment tasks should have curricular relevance, but not be limited to the curriculum as taught.

- Assessment tasks should require students to display a sensitivity to configurations or wholes, not simply to discrete elements.
- Assessment tasks should permit the student to select a form of representation he or she chooses to use to display what has been learned.

These portray a considerable shift of emphasis from the older conceptions of testing towards an emphasis on realism, links with the world external to education, cooperation in learning, diversity in representation of achievements and an holistic view of the entire enterprise. Features such as these are also finding a place in assessment in higher education.

## Assessment prompts learning

Every act of assessment gives a message to students about what they should be learning and how they should go about it. Assessment messages are coded, not easily understood and are often read differently and with different emphases by staff and by students. The message is always interpreted in context, and the cues which the context provides offer as much or more clues to students than the intentions of staff, which are rarely explicit.

Good assessment is not just a matter of finding the 'appropriate' method and using it sensibly in conjunction with given subject matter. There are always unintended consequences. Students will learn to adopt surface approaches to study in some circumstances and will adopt deep or strategic approaches in others. In so doing they will be prompted partly by the forms and nature of assessment tasks. They will learn that, in order to maximise their marks, they should use rote learning in many situations, even when this would lead them away from the most important features of the course. This response – and other undesirable ones – will not only be a function of the assessment tasks set, but of all the experiences of assessment students have had in the past. Kohn (1993) discusses the negative long-term effects of instrumental approaches to assessment and appraisal. If, for example, students get the idea that memorisation works for multiple-choice tests, then they will persist in that strategy even when reassured that this won't be helpful. Students are not simply responding to the given subject – they carry with them the totality of their experiences of learning and being assessed and this extends beyond concurrent and immediately preceding subjects.

Assessment is the most significant prompt for learning. One of the most important outcomes of research on student learning is the recognition that learning must fundamentally be seen as relational (Ramsden, 1987). That is, learning is a function of both teaching and the context in which it occurs. It is not a matter of learners engaging with a body of knowledge to which they have been introduced, but how this is interpreted by them and what actions they take as a result of these interpretations. Assessment can encourage passive, reproductive forms of learning while simultaneously hiding the inadequate understanding to which such forms of learning inevitably lead (Entwistle and Ramsden, 1983; Ramsden, 1988a).

This means that, in terms of assessment, student approaches to learning are a function of:

- the intrinsic qualities of the form of assessment being used. Some assessment methods are better for exploring some kinds of achievement than are others;
- the ways in which the assessor translates the material to be assessed into the given format and selects assessment tasks appropriate for the subject and the specific learning goals. An assessment approach which has tasks which do not relate well with what is being studied or the goals of the subject does not contribute to worthwhile learning; and, most importantly,
- how the student *interprets* the task at hand and the context of the assessment. An assessment strategy is effective only in so far as it communicates appropriately with the student.

Students' interpretations are not just dependent on the form of the assessment process, but on how these tasks are embedded within the total context of the subject and within their total experience of the course and of university life. The perceptions and interactions of a student are more important to learning than what staff take for granted as the 'reality' of the assessment. These perceptions cannot be assumed: they are only available from the students themselves.

But more is needed. Students experience the interaction effects of one form of assessment on another. In any given month they may have to complete ten assessment tasks, in another month, only one. The ways in which they approach each of these will be influenced by the others. A task which is intrinsically interesting and which may be approached meaningfully at any other time may be given short shrift when it is located among a thicket of examinations. Very little attention has been given to the compounding effects of assessment even though it is evident that the total array of demands in a given period influences how each one is tackled.

The use of self assessment activities gives a message to students that such activities are considered an important aspect of learning and that it is worth spending valuable time on them. How powerful this message is depends greatly on how well designed are the self assessment tasks and how closely they fit the courses of which they are a part. If students interpret them as an add-on or an optional extra the importance of self assessment will not be communicated.

## Judging assessment by its consequences

An important concept that links assessment with learning is that of *consequential validity*. This refers to the effect of assessment on learning and other educational matters (Linn *et al.*, 1991: Messick, 1989). It prompts the question, 'What are the broader consequences of a given assessment activity beyond those which are immediately apparent?' Consequential validity is high when there is a positive backwash effect on learning and low when it encourages ways of learning which are counter to what are desired. It points to links between learning and assessment. Assessment procedures of high consequential validity should be developed. These should, for example, encourage students to adopt good study approaches, learning what it is most desirable for them to learn and relate to potential further learning beyond the current context.

There is growing interest in exploring the dimension of consequences. While they have not been directly using this conception, Graham Gibbs and his colleagues at the Oxford Centre for Staff Development have been promoting the use of action research with academics to develop students' deep approaches to learning (Gibbs, 1995). A vital part of this work is finding out what it is that students actually do. It is necessary to know what approaches to learning students are adopting, what students' expectations are of different assessment tasks and what they choose to do and not to do in response to different assessment regimes. There is no substitute for knowing students' learning practices well enough to be able to intervene in helpful ways. This is not just a principle of good assessment but is, of course, fundamental to fostering learning.

Encouraging deep approaches to learning is one aspect which can be explored in considering consequences. Another is the impact which assessment has on the capacities and skills students have in being able to assess themselves. This is of greater long-term significance than the effect of any specific subject-matter learning. As discussed in Chapter 2, it is important for students to leave higher education equipped to engage in self assessment throughout their professional lives. They need to be able to make reliable judgements about what they do and do not know and what they can and cannot do. Too often staff-driven assessment encourages students to be dependent on the teacher or examiner making decisions about what they know. They do not effectively learn to do this for themselves. Well-designed assessment practices should be oriented around the key concepts and ideas that students should be able to deal with. However, the disturbing phenomenographic research on concept acquisition in first-year classes (for example, Dahlgren, 1984) shows that courses tend neither to develop basic concepts well, nor use assessment tasks which allow staff *or students* to know whether concepts have been learned.

Self assessment tasks should be directed towards those aspects of the course which are central to the overall learning outcomes desired. If they are concerned with engaging students in those parts of the subject which have the greatest consequences for further learning, they can help orient learning towards key objectives.

## The limits of unilateral assessment

The problems with most existing forms of student assessment do not end with the gap between intentions and outcomes. Most research on assessment has taken place in the context in which staff decide on the aims and objectives, the assessment tasks, the criteria for judgement and the final outcomes of the process. This unilateral conception of assessment in which students have little or no role other than to present themselves to be assessed has other intrinsic consequences and limitations. In particular, it can obstruct the attainment of one of the common goals of higher education – that students should become autonomous learners who can take responsibility for their own learning, ie, they are self-determining. As Heron (1988, pp. 79–80) puts it:

> Unilateral control and assessment of students by staff mean that the process of education is at odds with the objective of that process. I believe the objective of the process is the emergence of an educated person: that is a person who is self-determining – who can set his (*sic*) own learning objectives, devise a rational programme to attain them, set criteria of excellence by which to assess the work he produces, and assess his own work in the light of these criteria – indeed all that we *attribute* to and *hope* for from the ideal academic himself. But the traditional educational process does not prepare the student to acquire any of these self-determining competencies. In each respect, the staff do it for or to the students. An educational process that is so determined by others cannot seriously intend to have as its outcome a person who is truly self-determining.

If students learn always to look to their teachers to identify the objectives of their study, appropriate tasks and criteria for judgement, they are learning to be dependent. They are not being encouraged to learn how to learn, monitor their own work, establish their own criteria and make judgements about the worth of their achievements, all of which are necessary elements of professional practice. Of course, very good students do manage to develop these skills quite independently of what teachers do, but many end up graduating with difficulties and distress about some aspects of their chosen field of study which will inhibit their continuing education and upgrading of skills.

Along with this dependency is a conformity which is quite counter to what higher education stands usually stands for:

> Authoritarian control and assessment of students breed intellectual and vocational conformity in students. Given a pre-determined syllabus, learning in a way dictated by others, taught by those who make the continuous and final assessment often according to hidden and undisclosed criteria, the average student has an understandable tendency to play safe, to conform his (*sic*) thinking and performance to what he divines to be the expectations of his intellectual masters, to get through his final exams by reproducing what he believes to be staff-approved knowledge and critical judgement. (Heron, 1988, p.80)

The appropriate use of self assessment can help shift the focus of courses towards self determination away from a passive dependence on goals and activities set by others. Not all self assessment activities fulfil this requirement, however. If self assessment is imposed by staff it may give the superficial appearance of change in this direction, but it is likely to be seen by students as a hollow gesture. It can, if not presented appropriately, contradict the very moves towards independence which staff may believe the change is promoting.

## Holistic conceptions of assessment

We are now seeing moves to an holistic conception of assessment: no longer can we think of assessment merely as the sum of its parts, all of which can be considered separately, or make a distinction between the work as a whole and particular aspects of it (eg, Hager *et al.*, 1994). We need to look at the impact of the total package of learning and assessment and not simply at fragments of assessment. This means that we must inevitably look at the profile of assessment *as students see it*, from the point of view of the course, the total experience of the whole. The move to modularised courses which operate as a smorgasbord makes this task more difficult, but it is a challenge which must be faced.

Most discussion of assessment has been posited on traditional power relationships between student and teacher/assessor, but in an holistic conception this assumption must also be challenged. The very act of a person or authority making unilateral and final judgements over another has major consequences for learning. If students are to become autonomous learners as argued in statements of aims of higher education, then the relationship between student and assessor must be critically examined and the limiting influences of such an exercise of power explored. The new agenda for assessment research needs to place this as a high priority if we are not to be sidetracked, as has so often occurred in the past, by statistical and technical details of assessment procedures and tradition.

Self assessment contributes to changing power relationships, but only if it is used with a shift of control as, for example, can come about when it is used as part of assessment which counts for formal grading purposes. Such a use has risks, but risks are inevitable in such circumstances. There are huge risks in traditional assessment, but we are oblivious to them through familiarity. The formal use of self assessment in an overall assessment regime can, however, have symbolic significance for students over and above the amount of control which is shared with them.

## The language of assessment

The final issue to be considered relates to all assessment and it is particularly important because it concerns an aspect of practice which is all-pervasive but invisible most of the time. Earlier, the importance of student perceptions of assessment and the interaction of students with learning and assessment were discussed, but there is an additional and more insidious aspect. It is a key factor in a lot of the damage that many people have felt in their careers as people being assessed. It is the effect of the language used in talking about and making assessments.

Not surprisingly, in an act which involves judgement, judgemental language is used. Ironically, it is this which creates many difficulties. Teachers often judge too much and too powerfully, not realising the extent to which students experience the power of their teachers over them. Learning is an act which necessarily leaves individuals vulnerable: they open themselves to changes in the way they see the world, not knowing where they will end up. They might find a secure spot or be exposed. Rarely are they confident about what they know during the early stages (which may include most of the time they are being taught) – the very stages at which they are mostly likely to receive comments from a teacher. They know how little they know and they fear the depths of their ignorance. To have someone come along and tell them that, for example, what they are doing is all wrong or that they will never do it well or that they haven't read the book when they thought they had, is a direct attack on a person when they are least able to cope with it. In treating students in such ways and, indeed, with some students by using far less direct forms, teachers can go beyond the realm of valid statements into the world of abuse. It abuses in the sense of taking undue advantage of students by virtue of a superior position. It may not seem abusive to staff, but to those on the receiving end, it can be profoundly so.

Too often the distinction between giving feedback on a specific product which has been produced by a person and judging them as a person is not made. Teachers write and say things which can readily be taken as comments about the person rather than their work and in doing so they link in to the doubts and uncertainties which learners have of themselves. These remarks are often magnified at great cost to the self-esteem of the persons concerned.

Great care has to be taken in using what Rorty terms 'final vocabulary'. This is the use of vocabulary which includes terms such as 'good', 'right', 'rigorous', 'professional standards' and the like (Rorty, 1989, p.73). Even though it is apparently positive, it is language which leaves no room for manoeuvre. It has the final say. It classifies without recourse to reconsideration or further data, and it does not allow for other possibilities. Not only are terms such as these (even more so in the negative or implied negative versions) damaging, but they communicate nothing of substance about the work being assessed. They are empty rhetoric, and have no place in any discourse about learning.

These words are used probably because they come easily to hand; they avoid having to engage with the substance of what is being commented upon and they give an impression of concern about quality and standards without engaging with those aspects of the work in which such issues are manifest. If words are chosen carefully with an eye on the consequences, then learners can be provided with valuable information which they can use to change what they do without being distracted by words which imply that they are deficient as persons. The simplistic response of cleaning up terminology while retaining the same universalist sentiments (eg, by merely rephrasing final vocabulary) needs to be avoided. So long as the intention of the assessor is to pass judgement, rather than to offer suggestions expressed in a manner which suggests they may be accepted or not, the problem remains. The judgemental form betrays the intention; it is the intention which must be changed.

One way to begin to address this problem is to stick with descriptive feedback which conveys in detail from an explicitly *subjective* point of view what is and is not manifest in particular work. A statement by some apparently absolute authority about what the *learner* can and cannot do is not helpful. Not only are the negative global and abstract words of judgement to be avoided, but the positive as well, for implied negatives are always close at hand and learners read comments on other people's work. Grades are themselves a form of 'final vocabulary' and if they cannot be avoided they must be directly linked with rich statements of competence which meaningfully elaborate on what the grade purports to summarise.

Another important way of avoiding final statements is to move away from the practice of assessment which occurs only at the end of a period of study or which does not allow for the possibility of response. If dialogue between staff and students is a normal part of assessment practices, there is often a human incentive to avoid the grosser forms of final vocabulary and other dismissive language and there is the opportunity for rich and detailed information to be exchanged that is helpful for both parties. The use of negotiated profiles of achievement (Assiter and Shaw, 1993) and portfolios (Courts and McInerney, 1993) also have potential value here. These are documents which are constructed by students and validated by teachers and which aim to portray the range of a student's achievements in ways which allow the reader to appreciate the kinds of work which the student can do. Where profiles provide specific, descriptive information they are worthwhile but when they read like a collection of unsolicited testimonials – the playground of final vocabulary – they will be of use to no one.

There are, of course, forms of oppression in teaching and assessment which inappropriately and offensively discriminate between individuals or groups in ways which are anathema to academic purposes and which directly act to inhibit the achievements of students. This is not just a reference to obviously offensive racist remarks, the apparent invisibility of certain group members or the issue of gender-inclusive language. Important aspects of discriminatory matters include illustrations and examples which favour members of dominant groups, materials used in culturally insensitive ways and assumptions made about learners on little more than their appearance or apparent background. It is a matter of great importance which needs to be explored further in the assessment context, but a useful starting point is to examine the differential use of the types of language which have just been discussed. These are matters which deserve far greater attention in all aspects of academic work as the evidence of the deleterious effect of such matters on learning is building rapidly (see, for example, Hayes and Colin, 1994; Luke and Gore, 1992; Pettman, 1991; Thomas, 1990).

## Implications for self assessment

The above discussion of assessment points to some matters which need to be taken into account in the self assessment context:

- Any discussion of assessment carries with it many assumptions about what is right and proper in an academic environment and what are legitimate areas of manoeuvre. When self assessment is part of this discourse, then it can be limited by these expectations. Associating self assessment with discourses on learning may be a more fruitful strategy for acceptance by colleagues and external bodies, although associating it with assessment might be more effective with some students!
- Student perceptions of the self assessment process can have a more potent influence on their learning than staff perceptions of the processes they have devised. Student expectations of self assessment need to be explored and taken into account when introducing the idea.
- Self assessment should be judged in terms of its consequences on learning and modified accordingly. No matter how potentially worthwhile a given strategy might be, it is only as good as its actual influence.
- The use of appropriate language is an important consideration in assessment generally, but it may be more so in the self assessment context. While it is bad enough for staff to oppress students by their unthinking use of language, inappropriate use of language by a student to describe his or her own performance may well have an even greater impact as it goes to the core of how people see themselves.
- Self assessment will interact with other assessment activities, and account must be taken of this. As the demands of formal assessment exert such a dominant effect on student learning, it is important that self assessment is not established in circumstances where the proximate effects of other assessment activities will swamp it. Self assessment can, under some circumstances, form part of assessed work. Examples of this are discussed in Chapters 7 and 9.
- It is necessary to be clear about the purpose of any given approach to self assessment: is it primarily for learning or primarily for grading? While these two may not be mutually exclusive they are driven by quite different concerns and some compromises between the two may be necessary. The potential of self assessment is easily reduced if the requirements of grading dominate. The use of self assessment for grading purposes is considered in greater detail in Chapter 13.

# Chapter 5

# What is the Scope of Self Assessment?

*Angela Brew*

What is being assessed? This chapter looks at the areas to which self assessment can be applied. The simple answer to the question of what is the scope of self assessment is, of course, everything. Everything a learner does or thinks is potentially capable of self assessment.

This chapter traces the impact of developments in higher education on what is being assessed and, in particular, on self assessment. It is concerned to make sense of the many developments in self assessment practices as a whole; how they relate to and reflect the changes in higher education which are coming both from inside and outside the academic community; and how they reflect different purposes and interests. The chapter then provides a framework through which the many examples in Part II can be viewed.

## How is the scope of self assessment affected by changes in higher education?

Traditionally, higher education was allowed, indeed expected, to get on with its work irrespective of the world in which it was situated. The image of the ivory tower was a familiar one: higher education was viewed as broadly separate from social, economic and political activity. It was left to academics to decide the nature of the educational experience of their students and to consider or otherwise, as they saw fit, the vocational needs of their students. Recent changes can perhaps be summed up in the image of higher education being thrust out into the world. It is no longer viewed as an activity separate from society. On the contrary, higher education is increasingly being incorporated into the mainstream (Barnett, 1994).

A significant shift in higher education in recent years is the recognition that a number of people and organisations have an interest in answering the question of how to establish a world class workforce in order to face the challenges of the future. Employers, when asked what they needed \ university graduates, emphasised not specific discipline knowledge but the need for people who have personal, transferable skills and qualities; people who are capable of taking decisions and who are self-aware and can communicate (Ball, 1990; Mayer, 1992).

Changes in the demand for what students know and can do have also been linked with a recognition that the working environment is also radically changing. It is unlikely that the students of today will do the same job for the whole of their working lives. They will need to train and retrain (Ball, 1990). They will need to be flexible and adaptable; to know how to learn so that when they no longer have teachers to help them they will go on learning. Education is no longer being thought of as something you have a dose of when you are young only to forget it later. The rhetoric of lifelong learning has turned into the expectation that education carries on throughout life.

These exhortations may have touched a raw nerve among the academic community. The criticism implied in them, followed by a number of state-backed initiatives which were set up to address the perceived deficiencies in student achievement, eg, National Vocational Qualifications (NVQs) and Enterprise in Higher Education (EHE), provide an impetus to change the higher education curriculum to address employers' demands. But many university teachers have feared that if higher education is to be geared to the need to provide a more highly trained workforce, the academic world will need to change its emphasis away from the provision of a broad liberal or theoretical education and succumb to a narrow vocationalism. Advocates of the above initiatives would however argue that the new vocationalism rests on a new understanding of what is required by industry and a protestation that the personal skills and qualities, transferable skills and the like are what should be developed in students anyway.

Weaving their way through these tensions, a number of developments with implications for the scope of self assessment have emerged. The new higher education agenda has focused attention away from what Ryle (1949) has termed 'knowing what' towards 'knowing how'. Many practices in recent years have been geared towards the assessment of the very skills and qualities which employers have identified: transferable skills, communication skills, study skills, personal capability and competency. Self assessment has been an important element in these developments. So a tension has emerged between assessing knowledge of the discipline and assessing students' transferable skills or attributes. In Chapter 11 a number of such examples are presented.

## How has self assessment developed?

While self assessment might appear to be a relatively new idea in higher education, it has a long tradition and examples of its use in its present forms go back at least 60 years. Some work on student self assessment was reported as early as the 1930s, much of it based in the US, but most research up until the late 1960s was concerned with comparisons between the grades generated by students and those generated by their instructors. In summary, this kind of research has tended to find that, with some exceptions, students are able to predict the grades they would be given with reasonable accuracy (see Chapter 12). Students in introductory courses and in earlier years of their programmes tended to slightly overrate themselves, whereas students in advanced courses and later years tended to slightly underrate themselves. Many of these studies were not rigorously designed, and it was common, for example, for it not to be reported clearly whether or not the grades generated were to form part of a formal assessment. The results should therefore be treated cautiously as the effects of the context of assessment always need to be taken into account in any interpretation.

Interest in other aspects of self assessment increased in the early 1970s, especially in professional schools in medicine and education, and a shift of emphasis occurred towards developing ways in which students and practitioners could appraise their own work. Concern with grading still existed, but other more fundamental educational issues began to be examined. Studies were less concerned with the predictability of students' ratings than with engaging students in activities which related to their future professional tasks.

At that time the involvement of students' peers in assessment began to feature more strongly than self assessment as such, perhaps in response to the peer review movement which had begun to be established in medicine and related areas. Studies comparing grades or marks have continued to appear until the present day. Unfortunately, there have been no major investigations which aim to systematically identify what contextual factors influence the grades students will give themselves. However, it is clear that the grading practices of teachers and the extent to which students are competing with each other for grades are important.

By the late 1970s there was a more general recognition of the educational value of self assessment, something which has been stressed by a great many authors over the last decade. There were related developments in self testing where students complete multiple-choice tests which they mark themselves. The latter area has been developed in medical education at the University of Dundee and there has been much research on self testing in this form at the Open University (eg, Gale, 1984).

Around this time in the UK considerable impetus was given by Heron's conceptual work and its subsequent development (Heron, 1988). Heron, as was noted in Chapter 1, was working in the context of professional development and experiential learning. He provided a clear rationale for self assessment based on the importance of learners accepting responsibility for their learning and on the need for the development of self assessment skills for professional life (Heron, 1981). He also stressed the fundamental importance of self assessment to learning and discussed the valuable role peers can play in self assessments.

More recent work has attempted to extend previous research and development to an increasing range of self assessment strategies. Much of that published describes particular forms of self assessment in specific courses and unfortunately there is relatively little cross-referencing by authors. What is appropriate practice will of course differ according to the discipline area, the circumstances; or the context of the assessment. There are some interesting questions to be pursued about the relationship between self assessment and different kinds of subject areas and different educational aims. There are many subject areas in higher education in which it has been used:

| | |
|---|---|
| architecture: | Peterson (1979) |
| biological sciences: | Fazey (1993), Sclabassi and Woelfel (1984), Stefani (1994) |
| business/management: | Orpen (1982), Williams (1992) |
| computer science: | Edwards (1989), Edwards and Sutton (1991) |
| counselling education: | Bishop (1971), Borman and Ramirez (1975), Fuqua *et al.* (1984) |
| dentistry: | Denehy and Fuller (1974), Forehand *et al.* (1982), Ries *et al.* (1971) |
| education: | Boud (1992), Hoffman and Geller (1981), Kagal'niak and Iashchishin (1992), O'Neill (1985), Wheeler and Knoop (1981) |
| engineering: | Boud and Holmes (1981), Boud *et al.* (1986), Boyd and Cowan (1985), Cowan (1988), Larson (1978), Woods (1990), (1994) |
| English: | Butler (1982) |
| health science education: | Cochran and Spears (1980), Rotem and Abbatt (1982) |
| language teaching: | Oskarsson (1980), Peirce *et al.* (1993) |
| law: | Boud and Tyree (1980), Stover (1976), Ziegler (1992) |

medicine:                    Arnold *et al.* (1985), Barrows and Tamblyn (1976), Fincher and Lewis (1994), Fincher *et al.* (1993), Gordon (1992), Henbest and Fehrsen (1985), Kennell *et al.* (1973), Morton and Macbeth (1977), Stuart *et al.* (1980), Woolliscroft *et al.* (1993)

music therapy:       Greenfield (1978)

physical sciences:   Daines (1978)

political science:     McGeever (1978)

psychology:         Moreland *et al.* (1981)

religious studies:    Kramp and Humphreys (1993)

science education:   Boud (1981), Boud and Prosser (1980, 1984)

sociology:           Denscombe and Robins (1980)

statistics:           Lan *et al.* (1993).

Although self assessment has been used in most disciplines in higher education, there are many more examples of its use in education for the professions. This may just be a function of the pressure of practice on such courses and the more obvious need for students to develop self assessment skills as part of their initial training.

The use of self assessment has independently been adopted in many other parts of education and training. This has ranged from primary schools (Blatchford, 1992; Crocker and Cheesman, 1988; Towler and Broadfoot, 1992) to the workplace (Benett, 1993; Heron, 1981; Marienau, 1994; Taylor and Marienau, 1993).

While it not surprisingly found an early place in innovative institutions (Justice and Marienau, 1988; Loacker and Jensen, 1988; MacGregor, 1993), the late 1980s saw self assessment starting to become a normal and regular part of university teaching. It is rare now to visit a department in which there is not some explicit use of self assessment practices with the term 'self assessment' attached to them. In the UK, the Enterprise in Higher Education (EHE) Initiative stimulated much innovation in this area (eg, Fazey, 1993; Somervell, 1993; Stefani, 1994) as well as in others which aimed to promote students taking responsibility for their own learning.

The issue with which the remainder of this chapter is concerned is not what strategy to choose; that comes later. We are concerned here with broader issues to do with the different kinds of knowledge interests which are being served. This follows Habermas' idea that knowledge is always shaped by the needs and desires of human beings and that different kinds of knowledge give expression to different 'knowledge constitutive interests' (Habermas, 1987). The examples of self assessment which are discussed in this volume can be seen to lie within one or other of the three knowledge constitutive interests of Habermas. These knowledge interests are present whether what is being assessed is students' knowledge and understanding, academic, personal or transferable skills or whether they are assessing their own competency or learning outcomes.

Habermas' project was to show that knowledge does not exist independently of us. Scientific knowledge is built up because humans have a desire to exercise control over their world. They attempt to exercise this control by seeing the world as separate objects which can be observed and measured and about which predictions can be made. Such knowledge has what Habermas terms, a technical knowledge interest, 'interest in technical control over objectified processes' (ibid, p.309). This interest is not confined, however, to the physical sciences. It can be seen to be served whenever objectified statements are present. As far as self assessment is concerned, we say that a technical knowledge interest is being served where students are engaged in checking their knowledge, skills, understanding or competence against a set of more or less objective statements. Such statements are, like scientific 'facts', presumed to exist more or less independently of each other and to represent discrete aspects of the world.

In some domains of knowledge, however, objectivity is problematic. In the social sciences, for example, knowledge is more a question of interpretive understanding. Habermas views this kind of knowledge as being constructed in a process of mutual negotiation and communication. Such knowledge has what Habermas terms a practical or communicative knowledge interest which he says aims at action-oriented mutual understanding (ibid, p.310). In considering the scope of self assessment, a practical knowledge interest is being served when the self assessment involves elements of communication and interpretation, perhaps a negotiation of criteria, or discussion of the relationship of one element of the assessment to another.

But people do not only either build up objective knowledge or engage in a process of interpretive understanding. They also reflect on the processes in which they are engaged. Knowledge therefore, Habermas suggests, includes a meta-level analysis. This analysis is given expression in the humanities where reflection is part of the process of building knowledge. This third domain of knowledge pursues what Habermas terms an emancipatory knowledge interest. It is concerned with the pursuit of reflection as such, ie, self reflection is part of the process. It is emancipatory in the sense that the meta-level analysis has the capacity to bring into consciousness the very ways in which that knowledge is constructed and therefore to go beyond it. Self assessment where students radically change perspective by reflecting critically on the determinants of their work exemplifies this third knowledge interest.

In Chapter 11 examples of self assessment are mapped against Habermas' knowledge interests. In the remainder of this chapter the implications of the framework for different domains are explored: knowledge and understanding, skills and capability, and competence and learning outcomes.

## Knowledge and understanding

Traditional assessment through examinations makes the assumption that there is a body of knowledge which students are to acquire. The assumption often is that students are incapable of assessing the extent to which knowledge has been transmitted to them because in order to do this they need to have this knowledge in the first place. Self assessment is therefore not viewed as a serious activity and is relegated to 'fringe' activities such as project presentations and non-essential group work.

The traditional model of a university degree with students achieving a thorough grounding in the subject in three years has now to take account of the enormous expansion of knowledge in the last 50 years. A UK report by a working party set up by the Institute of Physics (1988), the Standing Conference of Physics Professors and the Committee of Heads of Physics in Polytechnics, for example, advised that the content of physics degrees should be cut by one third. Courses are quite simply overloaded.

We are becoming used, in our daily lives, to new insights replacing old ones. What students learn in their first year may be either out of date or disproved by the time they graduate. What were once thought of as invariant facts, are now known to be true only within a limited domain. We used to believe that if you drop an apple it will always fall to the ground. But all students have now seen pictures of astronauts and they know that this is not always true at all times and in all places. Many courses still operate on the assumption that there are eternal truths which students must acquire, and to all intents and purposes it is possible for students to suspend their disbelief and go along with the course's assumptions. But they live in a world in which there is scepticism about all questions of fact or value.

Another set of trends has to do with the way in which knowledge has traditionally been divided into subject disciplines. The concept of inter-disciplinarity is, Barnett (1994, p.126) suggests 'fast fading from the higher education lexicon'. Yet courses which cross traditional subject boundaries are becoming commonplace: environmental studies, for example. Traditional discipline courses, eg, in specific sciences, are on the decline. Interdisciplinary and multi-disciplinary courses are on the increase through the growth of modularisation and more student choice. Another trend is the breaking down of the subject into ever smaller specialist components towards narrow specialisation: eg, applied toxicology. There is a move towards a different kind of knowledge including knowledge of processes and knowledge of skills and competences shown in the rise in subject disciplines such as marketing and strategic management and human resources management. All of these trends have contributed to a questioning about the knowledge which students are acquiring.

During the course of this century we have seen that there are many problems associated with the view that science holds up a mirror to reality. Habermas says that this idea gives expression to a human desire to have technical control over objectified processes. It expresses, for him, a technical knowledge interest. But not only do we now know that we have to maintain contradictory definitions of reality (light is both waves and particles), the very act of making a judgement about whether something is true can now be seen as taking part in a cultural act (Lyotard, 1984, p.19). In this context, developing students' skills of self assessment encourages them to develop the critical skills needed to make informed decisions within their culture about what should count as knowledge for them. Knowledge in this conception is viewed as a construction (Berger and Luckmann 1967; Schutz, 1972). Rather than mirroring reality, knowledge is seen as an interpretation of our experiences as we experience them. The way students perceive the ideas which are presented to them is crucial to their personal understanding.

Once the exclusive notion of detached, impersonal knowledge is lost in favour of the individual's construction of reality, there are implications for the way in which that knowledge is assessed. If there is not an independent body of knowledge to assess in terms of how much of it students have acquired, what is left is a dialogue between the definitions of reality held by students and teachers. Barnett (1990, pp.44–5) suggests that seeing knowledge in this way means it is a kind of conversation. It then becomes possible for students to ask questions about their own understanding and knowledge and for teachers to ask them to reflect.

However, it is not enough to simply say that knowledge is a construction. There clearly are coherent sets of culturally agreed interpretations of numerous phenomena which form a backcloth and focus for personal knowledge construction. In other words, knowledge is a personal construction *and* it is a social construction. What is important is the inter-relationship between the personal constructions of reality and the public ones. This is what Habermas viewed as having a communicative knowledge interest. Understanding occurs through interaction: through the process of communication (Vygotsky, 1978). We should not confuse the coherent, socially constructed theory which explains a set of observed phenomena with the

**55**

knowing which the individual student experiences in the process of learning about it. The theory as expressed in propositions reflects what is known but is not itself what is known (Brew, 1988, pp.187–9).

Once we take on board the notion of knowledge as a construction it becomes pertinent to ask who it is who is doing the constructing. For Maslow (1966, p.145) the quality of the knower is all important. The mature, self-actualised knower, he suggests, is more likely to treat scientific discovery with awe and love, rather than being tied to neat rules and pathological defences. There is a need expressed by Maslow for the knower to become self-aware. This view is important in relation to the practice of self assessment. It suggests that it is important to direct attention to the process of coming to know which becomes at least as, if not more, important than what we know.

If knowledge is a social and a personal construction, a further set of questions has to do with who decides what counts as knowledge. Much traditional assessment in higher education is premised on the assumption that teachers have the authority to decide and can exercise it absolutely. If we say that in higher education teachers have the right as well as the power to decide what counts as acceptable knowledge, we have to reconcile this with questions about the violation of the individual's right to decide for themselves. Scientific method with its mirror view of reality once determined what counted as knowledge. Viewing knowledge as a construction, on the other hand, poses a whole series of questions about why certain ideas count as knowledge; why, for example, a mirror view should be appropriate; why scientific ideas have been given such prominence and so on. There is now a recognition that social, historical and cultural variables determine what counts as 'learning' as 'knowledge' and as 'assessment' (Lave, 1988). We now live in a world where there are questions about who has the authority and the power to decide what counts as knowledge. This points to Habermas' notion of an emancipatory knowledge interest. On one level, in self assessment terms, this is manifest in students' critique of or setting up of the criteria which are used to demonstrate their own knowledge. On another level there is a process of personal change brought about by the meta-critique of the very constituents of constructed knowledge. Both levels are emancipatory in that students go beyond culturally defined perspectives into new areas of self-understanding.

We know from research on student learning that traditional assessment is not good at testing understanding. Entwistle (Entwistle and Entwistle, 1991; Entwistle and Marton, 1994) has more recently drawn our attention to how little is known about the nature of understanding. When students make an assessment of whether or not they have understood something, they engage in a process of self assessment. As Barnett says, an element of critique is an essential ingredient in understanding because understanding is always *an* understanding. It always carries with it an evaluation. There is always the possibility of a meta-understanding; that of evaluating one's understandings (Barnett, 1994 pp. 104–5). But another person's understanding is always in some sense hidden from view. Our understanding of our students' understanding of a phenomenon is filtered through our own understanding of that same phenomenon. We should therefore perhaps not be surprised by Dahlgren's (1984) finding that conventional examinations do not display students' intimate understanding of even basic phenomena in their courses. Only through their own reflection on and evaluation of their own understanding does the adequacy of a particular student's understanding come to light. This means that the capacity to stand outside their own understanding and to evaluate its adequacy is crucial. In this sense all self assessment aspires to be emancipatory.

## Skills and capability

There is a growing recognition in higher education that we need to prepare students not just to solve the problems we already know the answers to, but to solve problems we cannot at the moment even conceive. There is, most importantly, the necessity for them to develop critical judgement over what counts as valid knowledge in a given domain. In a world where there are question marks over everything, students must have the skills necessary to research new knowledge for themselves. Being able to access data and organise them, critically evaluate them and so on, becomes more important than being able to regurgitate a set of facts. Being flexible enough to leave behind ideas as they are replaced is also a useful ability.

Barnett (1994, pp. 61–2) provides a helpful way of looking at skills in the higher education context and suggests they can be understood in terms of whose interests each serves. He differentiates two trends: one is a tendency for the skills interests of the world of work to prevail against the skills interests of academia; the other trend is away from specific skills, for example in a subject discipline or a professional area, towards skills of a general nature: cross-discipline skills or so-called 'transferable skills'. The similarity in language in the different domains (academia and employment) means that it is possible to buy into an agenda which serves competing interests without realising that this is what is happening. Clearly the concept of skill is used in many different ways.

The Enterprise in Higher Education Initiative illustrates this dilemma.

Interpreted broadly, EHE has stood for any educational activity in higher education which increased the level of responsibility students were able to exercise over their study. The emphasis was on developing a greater level of creativity and initiative among students. All too often, however, EHE has been interpreted narrowly in terms of sets of 'transferable skills': study skills and personal qualities which it is desirable for students to acquire for the world of work.

Another related trend in the UK is the encouragement of what has been termed 'capability.' The Higher Education for Capability initiative was a scheme set up by the Royal Society of Arts, Manufactures and Commerce. This initiative attempted to break down the distinction between education and training by setting up projects to enhance students' opportunities to take responsibility, to take initiatives, to be creative and cooperate within their learning programmes. All of these are aims to which many teachers in higher education would aspire. The new initiative contained, like EHE, an implicit criticism of the achievements of traditional teaching.

A number of academic skills are, of course, at the core of any academic discipline: critical reasoning, analysis, problem-solving, written communication, as well as laboratory skills and so on. However, we should not overstate the extent to which some academic discipline-related skills have been explicitly developed – attempts to include study skills overtly in courses being one moot point.

One of the problems in talking of skills is determining what they mean independently of their context. Skills are, as Barnett (1994, p.59) points out, intimately related to specific situations. In applying a skill, one has also to use one's knowledge. So what is the relationship of the skills and the acquisition of knowledge? If students give presentations and hence demonstrate 'communication skills', there must be something (some knowledge, insights or information) that they are communicating. We cannot just communicate *in vacuo*. This tendency to distinguish the acquisition of knowledge and understanding from their application and skills (Atkins *et al.*, 1993, p.15) is manifested in self assessment practices which demonstrate a technical knowledge interest. Skills are viewed as objectified processes.

But what about 'transferability'? Atkins *et al.* (1993, pp.33–4) suggest that even if general skills are used, it is possible that the way they interact with specific subject knowledge will differ from domain to domain. The question is whether knowledge can be acquired without also acquiring the skills. And then how does the experience of studying different disciplines affect the development of core skills and personal competences? Or, the other way round, how can the core skills be developed without the disciplinary context?

In a different context, the skill becomes a different skill requiring different knowledge and responding to different interests. Barnett (1994, p.64) says:

> the literature, especially that of the philosophy of education, has generated a near-consensus in expressing doubt over whether transfer-able skills in the . . . labour-market form at least, exist.

As far as self assessment is concerned, when we move from viewing skills as more or less independent statements of what students can do towards the integration of skills and discipline knowledge, we move from skills which have a technical knowledge interest to skills which have a communicative knowledge interest. The delineation of knowledge and skills is less clear cut and becomes a matter of negotiation.

EHE has been influential in the UK in encouraging the development of self assessment practices in relation to transferable skills. The transferable skills are frequently those intended to improve economic competitiveness, such as communication and negotiation skills, decision making etc., not academic skills nor wider social skills such as friendship, altruism, generosity (Barnett, 1994, p.45). At one end of the spectrum, as we have seen, they are viewed in an objectified way. At the emancipatory end, the skill of critical reflection means that students step outside their experience to evaluate it as a whole. In the emancipatory conception, EHE is interpreted as encouraging a change in the whole learning experience of the student towards the exercise of personal autonomy in the learning environment, and teaching has to change either to facilitate or to respond to this.

## Competency and learning outcomes

It is hard to imagine that competency-based education, which is now so pervasive in many areas of the curriculum, is a relatively new phenomenon. The idea of emphasising outcomes of learning or performance and of clearly specifying behaviours to demonstrate them to enable judgements to be made is now very firmly established. Again, however, each of the three knowledge interests is served in different interpretations and uses of self assessment of competences.

First, expression is given to a technical knowledge interest in Jessup's (1991, p.140) definition of competence as 'the ability to perform to recognised standards'. He suggests that a person who is described as competent in an occupation or profession is considered to have a repertoire of skills, knowledge and understanding which he or she can apply in a range of contexts and organisations. Gonczi (1994, pp.28–9) distinguishes three different conceptions of the nature of competence. In the first, the task-based or behaviourist conception of competence is conceived in terms of the discrete behaviours associated with the completion of atomised tasks. In the second there is a focus on the general attributes of the practitioner that are crucial to effective performance irrespective of the context in which they are applied. In these two conceptions assessment (by self, peer or teacher) takes place by matching an individual's performance against a set of objectified competences which is what leads to saying they are expressing a technical knowledge interest. This conception ignores the distinction between having the skills or being competent and being willing to use them in particular circumstances, or of being able to judge when it is appropriate to use them.

Further, competency is about action so there is an issue here about how knowledge relates to performance or to action. What we notice here is a tendency to separate 'formal knowledge' from its application. There is also a separation between theory and practice. Competency is expressed in terms of objectified statements of learning outcomes.

So can competency ever overcome the problem that it is either focused on performance, on action, or dependent on the knowledge and understanding which makes that action possible? Or that it is focused on practice but dependent on theory? Gonczi (1994, pp.28–9) argues that his third, holistic, conception of competency does. This is the notion of competency which is most used in higher education and education for the professions. This conception relates the attributes (knowledge, attitudes, values and skills) to the context in which professionals find themselves and with which they have to deal. This is consistent with Otter (1992) who found that it was not helpful for academics to attempt to separate learning outcomes under headings like knowledge, skill and competence. All groups in her study began in this way but they found that it was:

> impractical to assess competence separately from knowledge since knowledge acted as a vehicle through which the competence was demonstrated. Similarly the assessment of knowledge invariably required the demonstration of some sort of competence in communication, however defined. (Otter, 1992, pp.29–30)

In higher education then, there is, among advocates of a competency-based approach, a desire that any assessment should reflect the nature of the actual work carried out within a given profession. This is all well and good for our purposes. Self assessment practices designed around a competency approach can and do, as we shall see, encourage learners to judge the extent to which their performance is of the required standard. Assessment in this conception of competency has a communicative knowledge interest.

But if competency-based assessment is the assessment of a person's competence against prescribed standards of performance or outcomes (Hager *et al.*, 1994; Wolf, 1995) we have again to ask who is doing the prescribing. We have argued that the question of who has the authority to decide what counts as valid knowledge is an open one and have viewed self assessment as a way of encouraging the development of students' critical judgement in relation to appropriate and valid knowledge. But as Barnett (1994) suggests, competency statements are always someone else's standards. Usually they are written by professionals in the field who are the people who decide on the standards. But what about the standards of clients, or of professionals in related fields or indeed teachers who prepare students to meet the standards?

Crucial to the practice of self assessment is the question of the relationship of the learner, or student, to the standards. Competency statements provide criteria for determining the adequacy of learning outcomes, but learners come to the learning process with their own ideas about what they want to learn. There is a need for a dialogue between what the student wants to achieve and the defined competency assessment. Students may, for example, wish to question the validity or relevance of a given set of competency criteria. The trouble with competency standards is that without fully integrated self assessment procedures they leave out of the reckoning critical reflection of the standards themselves. Without an adequate dialogue taking place, students may be asked simply to accept competency criteria. Yet it is the task of professionals to themselves be in a position to decide what counts as acceptable practice. If students are to be prepared for professional practice, critical questioning of competency standards and learning outcomes must take place. Self assessment procedures can provide an important arena for this to happen. If they do, they give expression to an emancipatory interest.

Barnett (1994, p.73) suggests that change presents an insurmountable challenge for notions of competency since 'today's competencies are not tomorrow's'. What is needed is for professionals not only to be competent but also to be able to carry on a conversation about competency; to be able to evaluate and reject those competences which are no longer applicable. We cannot just get round this with a competency statement which says that the ability to define competences is a mark of the competent professional. Competency statements are relatively stable and static representations of a critically reflective dynamic, creative process. What this suggests is that they must be part of an on-going dialogue. Without self assessment, a competency-based education is barren.

## Whose interests?

We have seen that all the domains which provide the scope of self assessment – knowledge, competency, transferable skills and so on – can be understood in a number of different ways. We have also seen that each is problematic and serves a number of different interests: of the state, the economy or academia. Value-freedom is not an option. In addition we have noted that the way in which self assessment is used depends upon the knowledge interests which are being served. The scope of self assessment is therefore a set of dynamic discourses involving participation and interaction.

In this chapter we have used Habermas' conceptions of knowledge interest to provide a way of mapping self assessment and to bring together the differing perspectives discussed. Design considerations are directly related to intent and the kinds of interests being dealt with. Our classification can look at different forms of self assessment at different stages of development both within a given subject area and more generally over time. The framework suggested here differentiates qualitatively different kinds of outcomes arising from the approach to self assessment which is adopted. It is only one way of categorising the scope of self assessment and is merely one device for looking at our examples. It helps to make sense of them, but at the emancipatory end it begins to break down as knowledge, skills and competency are assessed as a whole. Perhaps in this sense all self assessment should aspire to be emancipatory, at least in the sense of taking a learner beyond their existing conceptions of knowledge, skills and competency and perhaps the extent to which a given self assessment approach does this is one measure of its quality.

# PART II

# EXAMPLES OF PRACTICE

Ideas on self assessment, like many other aspects of teaching and assessment, need to be translated carefully into practice. It is rare to have an innovation work perfectly first time. Evaluations need to be undertaken, student concerns responded to, refinements made and the activity tried again. After a few cycles of this it is either dropped or it takes its place as a normal part of a course for a while, only to be modified again when circumstances change.

Almost all the examples reported in this section have undergone cycles of trial and evaluation and they have been subject to purpose-designed evaluation. They are discussed at length in order to give the flavour of self assessment in practice and to indicate the great importance of attending to the fine detail of implementation. Without persistence and a commitment to finding a way to make a good idea work effectively, some of them would never have turned into the successful practices which have been reported in professional journals.

## Chapter 6

# Self and Peer Marking in a Large Technical Subject

*David Boud and Harvey Holmes*

The chapter describes and discusses a method of incorporating self and peer marking in an undergraduate electronics subject with over 100 students. Although it is based on work which was undertaken some years ago, better examples of how to introduce self marking in a conventional class are rare. The use of self and peer assessment in a given subject requires a great deal of attention to the details of the procedure, especially if it is to be part of the formal assessment in the subject. The procedure described here requires the preparation of detailed model solutions and an extensive clerical procedure, but alternatives with a simpler clerical process are also possible. This example shows how evaluation data can be used to monitor the acceptance of a process over a three-year period.

A major difficulty in conducting large classes is that of ensuring that students get adequate feedback on their work to guide them in their learning. It is costly in staff time to give the specific and individual comments on work that are so useful in enabling students to resolve problems and overcome particular conceptual barriers to understanding. Increasingly, teaching assistance is hard to get, and the burden on the lecturer gets greater. It is desirable that procedures be found which allow students to gain feedback on their work, but at the same time do not increase staff loads.

This chapter describes an approach to the problem of marking which involves students assessing their own work and that of their peers. The aim of the procedure which was developed was to reduce the amount of time routinely spent by staff in marking a mid-semester examination, and to do this while simultaneously increasing the educational benefits to students taking part in the exercise. The marking method was developed in connection with the mid-semester test, since the educational benefits of feedback to the students should be particularly great at this stage of the course.

A procedure was developed to directly involve students in marking their own papers and those of their peers, and to encourage students to reflect on their own learning and consider their progress more carefully than is normally the case in such an examination. It was not expected that a single isolated activity would have a major impact on students' self assessment abilities, but that it would provide an opportunity to test the procedure within the context of a relatively traditional course and degree programme. It was intended to examine the reactions of staff and students, and to determine the acceptability of self and peer assessment methods in this context.

The following account starts by describing the electronics subject in which self and peer marking was used. Then the development of a particular method is outlined, paying particular attention to the important factors that determined the final form of the procedure actually used. Finally, the views of the students and staff are discussed.

## Background

The subject Electronic Circuits II was taken each year by about 100–150 third-year students majoring in electrical engineering. It was a core subject, one of a sequence dealing with electronics. The subject was taught over a 14-week semester, with two hours of lectures per week, and in alternate weeks either a one-hour small-group tutorial session or a three-hour laboratory session. The formal assessment for this subject was based on the following major components:

| | |
|---|---|
| Final examination (three-hour paper) | 50 per cent |
| Mid-semester test (two-hour paper) | 20 per cent |
| Laboratory work | 10 per cent |
| Tutorial work | 10 per cent |
| Project report | 10 per cent |

The mid-semester test was a two-hour closed-book written paper, taken in about the ninth week of the semester. Four questions were asked, and no choice was allowed. The questions were typically part theory, part problem solving.

## Development of the method

Assessment, as we have discussed in Chapter 2, has two major elements: the setting of appropriate criteria for performance in any given area, and the making of judgements of individuals with respect to these criteria. Within the context of a highly technical subject such as electronics, it was considered that it would be too demanding to involve students in both of these steps without substantial prior experience of self assessment in the discipline. So the study was limited to an investigation of self and peer marking with students using extensive annotated model answers as criteria for assessment.

The model answers were required mainly for reasons of consistency of marking, since the students doing the marking differed widely in knowledge and ability. These model answers were detailed solutions to the questions, with no steps omitted which probably would not also be omitted by examination candidates. They included discussions of the solutions and indicated possible alternatives. In some cases, they also gave additional or supplementary information which may have been of interest to some students. The preparation of these model answers, which usually ran to 10–12 pages of typescript, was a substantial effort that would not be needed for normal examinations. However, it was felt that they would be a major aid in the feedback process, as well as a help towards consistency of marking.

In order to make the marking scheme simple enough so that it could be applied with some degree of uniformity by many different and inexperienced markers, it was decided that the questions would be subdivided into subquestions of equal weight, and each subquestion would be marked out of five marks. In some papers, each question was divided into five such parts, in others into four such parts, so that each paper consisted of 16–20 equally weighted subquestions. It was found in practice that the formulation of examination questions with the constraint of a particular number of equal subquestions is hardly more difficult or time-consuming than without this constraint; the major effort goes into satisfying all the other requirements of good examination question construction, which still apply.

In an effort to ensure that all students applied the same criteria when marking, a four-page handout was issued. As well as describing in detail the overall scheme to be used, and giving a short discussion of the educational benefits of self and peer assessment, this handout also specified the marking criteria to be used. For each subquestion, the students were asked to mark as follows:

- two or less: inadequate understanding or very incomplete;
- three: satisfactory (pass), that is, sufficient understanding has been shown to indicate that there is a basically sound grasp of the subject, although details may need correction, and it may not be complete;
- four: good;
- five: very good – reserved for almost complete or perfect answers.

To increase the probability of a well-considered mark, the students had to give a detailed and specific justification of each mark in a separate column of the marking sheet (eg, 'only managed first step,' 'didn't know 'Ohm's law,' 'everything right,' 'complete except for neglecting $V_{CE}sat$'). In addition, various general instructions were given about marking; the main points being as follows:

- Marking should be over the full range of marks (0–5).
- The subquestions should be marked independently, since the final marks will be scaled to take into account the difficulty or ease of the test.
- Numerical or algebraic errors should not be heavily weighted, and should be counted only once (ie, in the part of the question in which they first appear, not in subsequent sections which they may also affect).
- Answers which are not given in the model solutions must be marked on

their own merit, possibly with reference back to the exact wording of the question or with consultation with the lecturers.

Also, hints about how to handle particularly good or particularly bad, irrelevant, ungrammatical, misspelled, or illegible answers were given. It was pointed out that the model answers were over-complete, and that full marks would be received for much less complete or polished answers.

Originally, when the idea was first mooted, it was intended to have only self marking. However, preliminary discussions with students left no doubt that such a scheme would meet with a great deal of distrust. Reservations were expressed that many students would not take the exercise seriously and would collude with each other or cheat, thereby gaining an unfair advantage. This attitude no doubt arose because the marks were going to be part of the formal assessment for the subject, and the students felt themselves to be in a competitive situation. (This was clearly shown in a later questionnaire.) If the results are not weighted in the final score, then the only people who would suffer from collusion or cheating would be the students themselves. However, in this case it was felt by the lecturers that the students would also not take the exercise seriously *unless* its results were going to be included in the final score. Hence, an attempt was made to reduce the opportunities for collusion or cheating. It is not possible to design a completely foolproof scheme of self assessment – if students really want to cheat, there is ultimately no technique that can foil this. There are, however, measures which can be taken to minimise the amount of cheating which can occur in the present scheme without detection by the staff. In this case, a scheme involving peer marking as well as self marking was developed. Also, provision for adjudication by the lecturers was added. These checks and balances added considerably to the complexity of administering the scheme, but were seen as essential if self and peer marking are to be tried in an environment where they are not usual, particularly if the result is to be used as part of the formal accreditation process.

The first time the scheme was tried (in 1978), the examination papers were distributed randomly and fairly openly to other students for peer marking. Although the students were not identified on the papers, this procedure left too much room for collusion and cheating, and there was some dissatisfaction on this account (see the student views in the next section). Accordingly, the procedure was tightened the next time. The complete process usually took about two weeks, but could be quicker:

1. The examination papers were collected and the front covers (with the students' names) removed. They were then given a code number and allocated in a predetermined quasi-random manner to other students for

peer marking[1]. A record was kept so that the locations of all papers was known.

2.  The students then marked the papers at home, using the model solutions and the marking instructions as a guide. Marks were entered on a separate marking sheet, not on the paper itself, and each mark justified, as already discussed.
3.  The papers and marking sheets were collected (usually at a convenient lecture). The papers were then redistributed to their authors for self marking, also on separate marking sheets.
4.  The papers and marking sheets were then returned to the lecturer, who allocated the final mark. If the two student marks differed by not more than 10 per cent, and if the lecturer's assessment was also not more than 10 per cent different from the self mark, the student received his or her own mark. Otherwise, the lecturer arbitrated and awarded a final mark on the basis of all three assessments.
5.  Finally, the papers and marking sheets were returned to the students, with all identification names and code numbers removed, so that even at the end, students would not be able to find out who marked their paper or whose paper they marked. At the same time, a questionnaire was distributed to the students to determine their response to the procedure.

This procedure is not totally cheat-proof, as there is a chance that students could receive their friends' papers for peer marking. Apart from this possibility, it would take a determined cheat to influence his or her mark by more than a small amount. If necessary, the procedure could be tightened still further, eg, by having the students mark the papers under examination conditions.

The reason that students received their own mark, if not too different from the other marks, was to encourage the idea of self responsibility in the marking. Obviously, there are other possibilities (eg, averaging of self and peer marks).

---

1   The redistribution cannot be purely random, since it can be shown that the probability that at least one student receives his or her own paper is

$$P_n = 1 - \frac{1}{2!} + \frac{1}{3!} - \frac{1}{4!} + \ldots + \frac{(-1)n+1}{n!}$$

where $n$ is the number of students in the class. This probability converges rapidly to $P_\infty = 1 - e^{-1} = 0.63212$ as $n$ increases.

At the first trial of the procedure there was no provision at all for a lecturer's assessment, but this was subsequently included to allow for the rare case of obvious collusion and excessively high marks. This acts as a deterrent, and was not needed for cases of collusion, although lecturers' assessments were used in cases where the peer and self marks were widely different. It was found that a quick glance through the paper was enough to determine whether the lecturer also needed to mark the paper.

## Results

The marks for the first and third trials of the procedure are summarised in Table 6.1. They had a good spread. The students considered both papers to be difficult and long, which explains the low average marks. The use of scaling, as in Ebel (1974), to obtain the final subject grades, allows for this effect.

One of the first questions likely to be asked is, how reliable are self and peer marking? It is only to be expected that there will be a tendency to mark oneself higher than an external assessor would, as one is aware of one's own intentions, which may not be apparent to others. This is shown in Tables 6.1 and 6.2 by the difference between the self and peer marks. The mean difference between the self and peer marks in 1979 was 3.4 (cf. Table 6.1). The standard deviation of this difference was 6.6, largely because of a small number of very large discrepancies. However, it can be seen from Table 6.2 that in 82 per cent of the cases in 1979, the difference between self and peer marks did not exceed 9 in magnitude. Apart from the systematic nature of

**Table 6.1** Mean and standard deviation of self and peer marks

| | | 1978 | | 1979 | |
|---|---|---|---|---|---|
| | | Respondents (n=59) | Total class (n=99) | Respondents (n=53) | Total class (n=94) |
| Maximum possible marks | | 100 | 100 | 80 | 80 |
| Self marks: | Mean | 45.8 | 45.5 | 34.5 | 36.5 |
| | Standard deviation | 13.6 | 14.4 | 12.3 | 10.4 |
| Peer Marks: | Mean | 40.6 | 41.4 | 31.2 | 33.1 |
| | Standard deviation | 13.4 | 14.3 | 11.6 | 9.5 |

The number of respondents shown in this table is the total of those returning the questionnaire, but the statistics in the respondents' columns are only for those students who both returned a questionnaire and reported their self and peer marks; a small number of students (9 in 1978 and 6 in 1979) did not reveal their marks on the questionnaire.

these differences, they are within the usual ranges of measurement error in examination marking (McVey, 1976). It is interesting that, as well as self markers who leniently viewed their own work, there were also a number of students who were very hard on themselves (cf. Table 6.2).

**Table 6.2** Discrepancies between self and peer marks

| | Number of students with the difference between self mark and peer mark in the range shown | | | | | |
|---|---|---|---|---|---|---|
| | **>20** | **19 to 10** | **9 to 1** | **0** | **−1 to −9** | **−10 to −20** |
| 1978 (n=99) | 4 | 21 | 46 | 3 | 20 | 5 |
| 1979 (n=94) | 1 | 14 | 51 | 5 | 21 | 2 |
| Total | 5 | 35 | 97 | 8 | 41 | 7 |

When the cases of large discrepancies between self and peer marks were examined, it was found that the main differences were usually in only two or three subquestions. They were often due to a misunderstanding by one of the students of either the answer given by the student, or the model answers. When arbitrating, the lecturer only has to check the sub-questions with large differences; usually, this can be done quickly, especially with the comments of both students to act as a guide. The marks awarded by the lecturer in such cases were usually slightly closer to the self mark than the peer mark, whether or not the self mark was the higher one. In 1979, the lecturer had to adjudicate in 26 of the 94 papers due to discrepancies of 8 or more.

The general impression of the remaining papers which did not have a large discrepancy between self and peer marks was that the total marks did not differ greatly from the marks which would have been given by the lecturer, which in most cases would have been closer to the lower of the two student marks than to the upper. There were often small discrepancies (1–2 marks) between the lecturer's and the students' marks for individual subquestions, but these tended to cancel out in the addition. In no such case was it considered necessary to award a final mark which was different from the self mark, ie, no cases of collusion in awarding unduly high marks were detected.

The conclusion from all this is that the scheme, with its various safeguards as already described, was as reliable as normal methods of marking. There was a systematic bias towards slightly high marks, but this is unimportant if appropriate methods of scaling are used. In this subject a modification of the scaling procedure recommended in Ebel (1974) was adopted.

As far as the validity of the marks is concerned, there is no reason to suppose that it was any less than with normal systems of marking, since the examination paper itself was very similar to a conventional one. Thus, self and peer marking is not a new method of assessment, such as multiple-choice testing, where the nature of the material tested is changed by the manner of assessment; it is merely a new procedure for marking. It could in principle be applied to most methods of assessment.

## Student views

On each occasion, a questionnaire was administered to students immediately after they received their self and peer marks. This sought to obtain the opinions of students in four areas: the idea of self and peer assessment, their views of the particular procedure used, their perceptions of cheating or collusion in the class, and their general attitudes towards the subject. The results from the first and third trials are tabulated in Tables 6.3 to 6.6. On each occasion, slightly more than half the class returned the questionnaire (cf. Table 6.1). The questionnaire was anonymous and the completed forms were not shown to the lecturers.

**Table 6.3** General attitudes toward the subject and course

|  |  | 1978 | 1979 |
|---|---|---|---|
| Compared to other subjects I am taking this semester |  | (n=59) | (n=53) |
| *60316: Electronic Circuits II is:* |  |  |  |
|     Above average in difficulty |  | 46 | 24 |
|     About average in difficulty |  | 11 | 27 |
|     Below average in difficulty |  | 0 | 1 |
|     Above average in relevance to me |  | 26 | 21 |
|     About average in relevance to me |  | 23 | 27 |
|     Below average in relevance to me |  | 7 | 4 |
|     Above average in interest |  | 13 | 19 |
|     About average in interest |  | 28 | 26 |
|     Below average in interest |  | 13 | 7 |
| I'm not interested in how much I learn in this subject, just | Agree |  | 8 |
| what results I get* | Disagree |  | 42 |
| The important thing in this subject is to get a pass in it* | Agree |  | 37 |
|  | Disagree |  | 13 |
| I would not be studying this subject if it were not compulsory* | Agree |  | 8 |
|  | Disagree |  | 45 |
| I wish to learn more about the material of this subject* | Agree |  | 42 |
|  | Disagree |  | 9 |

*These questions were only included in the 1979 questionnaire.

The views of students about the marking method should be seen in the context of their views of the subject as a whole (see Table 6.3). They regarded it as more difficult than other subjects they took simultaneously, but as more relevant to them, and more interesting. They wanted to learn more about the subject and were not taking it solely because it was a compulsory part of the course.

It can be seen from Tables 6.4 to 6.6 that, on nearly all items concerning the idea of self and peer assessment and the particular procedure, student opinion in 1979 was more favourable than in 1978. It is likely that this can be attributed to the much improved administration of the procedure in the second year.

It is apparent from Table 6.4 that the vast majority of students agree that the ability to be able to assess one's own performance is important, and to a slightly lesser extent, that the idea of self assessment is a good one. In 1978, they were more concerned about the high workload in the course as a whole than they were in 1979, and tended to rate the idea of self assessment more highly if they did not have such a high workload. They thought that self assessment was more demanding than external assessment. They also agreed that they should have had more opportunities for self assessment, and

**Table 6.4** Student views on the principle of self and peer marking

|  |  | 1978 (n=59) | 1979 (n=53) |
|---|---|---|---|
| The ability to assess one's performance is very | Agree | 48 | 49 |
| important | Disagree | 9 | 3 |
| Self assessment is more demanding than having | Agree | 47 | 40 |
| someone else assess me | Disagree | 10 | 11 |
| The idea of self assessment is a good one | Agree | 35 | 43 |
|  | Disagree | 21 | 43 |
| Self assessment would be a good idea if we didn't have | Agree | 41 | 42 |
| such a high workload | Disagree | 15 | 10 |
| We should have more opportunities for self | Agree | 30 | 33 |
| assessment | Disagree | 25 | 19 |
| Students should be more involved in assessing other | Agree | 30 | 30 |
| students | Disagree | 25 | 22 |

that they should have been more involved in assessing other students, but the results are less clear cut on these points.

As far as the procedure is concerned, the students strongly supported it (Table 6.5). They did not think that it was a waste of time, and they found it to be valuable in the assessment of both themselves and other students. In particular, they found that the exercise assisted them in making a realistic assessment of their abilities in the subject; that it enabled them to concentrate more on the value of the work done; that it made them more aware of what they needed to know about the subject, and that they benefited from having to consider their progress more carefully than usual. The exercise was found to be a useful preparation for the examination at the end of the course. A minority of students felt that they had learned from the other marker's comments about their paper. They still wanted to see some changes made in the procedure, but they thought that the rewards were sufficient with respect to the amount of time spent, and that the scheme was fair. Most students had no trouble in following either the marking scheme or the model answers.

As already mentioned, in the first year of operation there were some deficiencies in administration which provided an unnecessary opportunity for those who wished 'to beat the system'. When these avenues were covered in the second year, the perceived level of collusion diminished, as can be seen from Table 6.6. In the second year, students felt that the problem was less serious, although the small number of students admitting to collusion had not disappeared altogether. Because these questions probed a very sensitive area, it is difficult to judge how valid the responses were. The general magnitude of the problem indicated by these questionnaire responses was confirmed in discussions with students. A further tightening of the procedure was not regarded as necessary, especially with the provision for a lecturer's assessment.

Cross-tabulations of the questionnaire results revealed no significant relationships beyond the obvious ones due to the similarity of some questions. In particular, there seemed to be no clear relations between student marks and their views on self or peer assessment.

The questionnaire was actually more extensive than shown in Tables 6.3 to 6.6, as it had purposes beyond the assessment of the effectiveness of the procedure. One interesting additional result was that two-thirds of the respondents 'now realise what a difficult job examiners have'. Also, the parts of the process that were found most worthwhile by two-thirds of the students were preparing for the test and studying the model answers. However, marking their own papers was also found worthwhile by a small majority of the students, and marking the other person's paper, studying the differences, and taking the test were found worthwhile by a large minority.

**Table 6.5** Reactions to the specific procedure and views on self assessment

|  |  | 1978 (n=59) | 1979 (n=53) |
|---|---|---|---|
| I found assessing my own work to be valuable | Agree | 42 | 42 |
|  | Disagree | 14 | 9 |
| I found assessing another student's work valuable | Agree | 38 | 43 |
|  | Disagree | 19 | 9 |
| This exercise assisted me in making a realistic assessment of my own abilities in this subject* | Agree |  | 42 |
|  | Disagree |  | 9 |
| I benefited from the exercise by having to consider my own progress more closely than usual | Agree | 37 | 37 |
|  | Disagree | 19 | 13 |
| Having to justify my mark helped me concentrate more on the value of the work done* | Agree |  | 42 |
|  | Disagree |  | 10 |
| This exercise has made me more aware of what I need to know in this subject* | Agree |  | 41 |
|  | Disagree |  | 11 |
| This exercise was a useful preparation for the final exam in this subject* | Agree |  | 37 |
|  | Disagree |  | 15 |
| I learnt from the other marker's comments about my paper | Agree | 15 | 22 |
|  | Disagree | 37 | 29 |
| I found it difficult to follow the marking scheme | Agree | 13 | 6 |
|  | Disagree | 42 | 47 |
| I found it difficult to follow the model answers | Agree | 26 | 6 |
|  | Disagree | 28 | 47 |
| I would like to see some changes in the procedure* | Agree |  | 25 |
|  | Disagree |  | 23 |
| A similar (but improved) scheme should be used in other subjects | Agree | 30 | 34 |
|  | Disagree | 22 | 18 |
| I don't think the rewards were sufficient for the amount of time I spent | Agree | 27 | 14 |
|  | Disagree | 28 | 38 |
| The present scheme (of marking the mid-semester test) was unfair | Agree | 24 | 11 |
|  | Disagree | 29 | 38 |
| The whole exercise of self and peer marking was a waste of time | Agree | 12 | 5 |
|  | Disagree | 42 | 47 |

*These questions were only included in the 1979 questionnaire.

**Table 6.6** Perceptions of cheating or collusion among students

|  |  | 1978 (n=59) | 1979 (n=53) |
|---|---|---|---|
| Do you know of any collusion between students in marking? |  |  |  |
| None at all |  | 10 | 24 |
| I have heard rumors or gossip about it |  | 31 | 13 |
| I definitely knew it occurred |  | 16 | 15 |
| If you think it did occur, do you think it is a serious problem? | Yes | 28 | 17 |
|  | No | 28 | 32 |
| Do you know who marked your paper? | Yes | 17 | 12 |
|  | No | 40 | 40 |
| Do you know the name of the person whose paper you marked? | Yes | 21 | 9 |
|  | No | 36 | 42 |
| Did you collude with any students or groups of students in discussing or fixing marks? | Yes | 5 | 3 |
|  | No | 51 | 49 |

The additional free comments of the students were in general agreement with the impressions gained from the statistics of the answers in Tables 6.3 to 6.6. There were hardly any extremely negative opinions expressed. Most comments were appreciative or descriptive of the problems in the exercise, eg, the difficulty of marking one's own paper. Many comments were suggestions for changes in the details of the procedure. One interesting suggestion was that one hour should be set aside for group marking, with discussions on answers and different approaches to the answers. (This suggestion was subsequently adopted after the trials reported here.) Another was that formal collusion in marking could be beneficial, as discussions about answers and differences could be very rewarding. Several students suggested that the lecturer should check the papers first and cross out blank spaces, so that the answers could not be 'improved' during the marking process. Several also thought that the lecturer's mark should be more highly weighted in the final mark, or that the marks should be averaged, so that the self mark is not given such a high weight.

From discussions with students we believe that the foregoing conclusions about their views were valid for the whole class, although the questionnaire was returned by only 60 per cent of the students in 1978 and 56 per cent in 1979. It can also be seen from Table 6.1 that the respondents were a typical sample as far as marks are concerned. The views in these tables were also generally confirmed by the students in the fourth trial of the scheme in 1980.

## Staff views

From the point of view of the lecturers of this course, the most important aspect was that self and peer marking seemed to be fulfilling the educational objectives. In particular, it was giving students much better (and quicker) feedback than otherwise could have been provided. It also reinforced the material better than the usual methods of testing, as the students had to consider it several times more than usual (ie, when reading the model solutions, when marking the peer paper, when marking their own paper, and when considering the final results). In addition, of course, it gave them practice at self assessment, a basic skill they will need later in life. It gave reasonably reliable and valid marks, and did all this without disrupting normal teaching. Student satisfaction with the method was also gratifying.

The nature of the work required of the lecturer is quite different from that needed with conventional testing methods. The basic setting of the examination paper is similar, but thereafter it differs: model solutions must be prepared, and the whole process must be administered. The preparation of the model solutions must be done carefully to avoid ambiguities and to cover all likely solutions. Administration of the process also requires care, and involves a large amount of clerical activity, as detailed presently. The effectiveness of self and peer marking is obviously very procedure-sensitive, so that the lecturers have to pay particular attention to the details of the process; however, the procedure as was finally developed was relatively insensitive to disturbances. Instead of only one deadline, there were several deadlines to be met by either staff or students. However, it was the view of the subject lecturers that their activities in self and peer marking were much more congenial and varied than those in conventional marking (in this case with about 100 papers). The preparation of the model solutions could even be quite satisfying, and could have later pay-offs as well (eg, they may be useful in a textbook or as tutorial problems). Even when the lecturer had to mark a student's paper, the marking was easier than with conventional marking, as already discussed.

The amount of work involved for lecturers can be quite different with self and peer marking. The main differences are the preparation of the model solutions and the clerical work (giving code numbers, quasi-randomly preassigning peer markers, handing out and collecting papers twice, sorting them, recording marks, removing identifying names or code numbers from the papers or the marking sheets, and checking marking sheets). The lecturers also have to mark parts of those papers with large discrepancies between self and peer marks, and at least look through the others to check that nothing untoward is occurring. Some of these activities are also needed with conventional marking, but the amount of clerical work is certainly greater with this procedure. The clerical work could be greatly simplified if a computer were used to aid the sorting, coding and recording activities, but this was not done. It could also be simplified if the procedure were changed, eg, by having students mark the papers under supervision and discuss responses with tutors (Feletti, 1980).

With the scheme described, the workload for the lecturer is higher because of the model solutions, but the incremental time per student is much less than with conventional marking. In 1979, a rough diary was kept of the time spent by the staff on the mid-session test, and an estimate made of the time that would have been needed for normal marking. The figures are not precise enough to be repeated here and would vary greatly, depending on individuals and the subject, but they indicate that for the class of 94 students, the time spent administering the scheme and preparing the model answers was about 75 per cent of what would have been needed for conventional marking. The staff time required in the first year of running such a scheme as this would, of course, be higher due to the need to compose instruction sheets, etc. For very small classes conventional marking would require less time, but the advantages of self and peer marking would increase with the size of the class. It is difficult to estimate the crossover point at which self and peer marking becomes more efficient in terms of staff time, as this depends strongly on such factors as the exact procedure used, the nature and length of the examination paper, and the relative efficiencies of lecturers in performing the various tasks involved. On the basis of the times estimated in 1979, we would expect the crossover point for class sizes to lie in the 20–60 range in most cases.

## Conclusions

It is possible to devise schemes with self and peer marking which work in technical subjects such as electronics. These can have a high degree of student acceptance and a number of educational advantages, particularly good feedback to the students, increased reinforcement, and practice at self assessment. Marks can be reliable and valid and the procedures can fit into conventionally taught courses.

The procedure which was adopted is only one of many that could be tried in technical subjects. It can be varied in many ways, several of which were mentioned above. The main problem with injecting an element of self or peer marking into a traditional system is to overcome the initial distrust of the students. It would appear from the comments of the students that self or peer marking could be used in almost any situation, provided that the instructors are prepared to mark as well. In the procedure described in this chapter we tried to avoid this need, but in the end had to compromise by having the instructors mark in exceptional cases. However, the marking in these cases is easier than normal because of the guides provided by the students' marks.

The use of self and peer marking seems to be very sensitive to the procedural details, especially if it is used in an isolated subject, and if the result is to be used as part of the formal assessment in that subject. It is essential that a lot of thought be given to these details, otherwise the results may be worthless. The procedure described here has several checks and balances built in, including peer marking, coded papers, teacher marking if necessary, etc. These extra components in the procedure added considerably to the complexity of administering it, but made it a relatively robust scheme, which is unlikely to go drastically wrong.

The nature and amount of the examination load on staff is substantially different when self and peer marking is used in technical subjects. It requires much more preparation before the examination, especially the preparation of detailed model solutions. It also involves additional clerical work, although the use of a computer or changes to the procedure would greatly reduce this. On the other hand, routine marking is eliminated, and the model solutions may later find other uses. For small classes the net load is higher than with conventional marking systems, but for large classes it is less. This is probably one of the few educational innovations that can reduce staff load in large classes as well as have educational benefits.

## Chapter 7

# Self Assessment using Provided Criteria in Engineering Design

*David Boud, Alex Churches and Elinor Smith*

Teaching and learning in a design subject is quite different from more analytical aspects of courses, but the development of self assessment skills is no less important. This chapter reports on the development and evaluation of a strategy in which students are provided with criteria to use in a self-assessment exercise. Although the work described here was completed some years ago, the chapter presents a good example of the use of self marking in the initial stages of a subject before students are able to articulate criteria of their own. A particular feature is the inclusion of staff assessment of the quality of the students' self assessment exercise.

The development of skills in engineering design is a fundamental and important part of any engineering course. However, the demands of teaching design differ in many respects from those involved in the more analytical, engineering science aspects of courses. In design, there is an emphasis on synthesis rather than predominantly on analysis; students need to become aware of the importance of considering design as an iterative process with many possible solutions rather than a tightly constrained problem with one single solution; and the subtle and complex appreciation of 'good design' needs to be developed.

We realised the importance of students being able to assess their own work and monitor their own performance throughout the design process. We believed that students need to develop an awareness of their own learning and be able to check for themselves whether they are proceeding in the desired direction. They should know the limits of their own knowledge and be able to seek assistance when necessary in an informed and discriminating manner.

Considerations such as these led us to explore ways of introducing students to formal self assessment in the early parts of their course programme. The self assessment exercise fitted well into the second-year design course. The process of design is open-ended and demands decisions which are largely intuitive in the early stages and which cannot be fully evaluated until much later in the process. The thought processes are in many respects the antithesis of those followed in analytical subjects. The result is that designers need continually to assess and re-assess their decisions as the work proceeds.

In introducing self assessment to the course, we were primarily concerned with developing students' skills in assessing their own work, rather than with using self assessment as a grading device. However, in the context of a very heavy course load it was thought that students would not take seriously the exercise that we were to introduce unless it counted as part of the overall assessment. This view was supported by students and after some deliberation 4 per cent of the marks for the subject were allocated to the exercise. These marks were to be awarded for effective self assessment rather than for performance on a design task *per se*. This chapter describes the form of self assessment used and analyses the responses to the self assessment exercise by staff and students. It discusses the need for development of self assessment procedures in engineering courses.

## Course context

In second-year design, during the years surveyed, students were given lectures on design practice and theory and, in the first half of the course, were asked to design a range of machine components. The second half of the course was devoted to a major design project – the design of a machine assembly – plus a design-and-build project (Churches, 1982; Churches *et al.*, 1986). The design of the machine assembly was used as the basis for the self assessment exercise. Students spent three hours per week class contact in design and the machine assembly part took place over 10–12 weeks. In two of the years surveyed, the design project was a mechanical drive for a hydraulic piston pump and, in the third year, a drive for a punching press. All three projects involved the students in a conceptual layout, followed by detailed calculations of cyclic work, energy storage and power requirements, leading to motor selection belt drive specification, and the design of the flywheel, shaft, bearings, etc. For most of the students, this was their first attempt at designing a machine assembly in which design decisions needed to be made at different hierarchical levels as well as in a logical progression within each level. To assist them in deciding the design sequence, the task was split into sections and, to help with scheduling, target dates were set for when each section had to be submitted for marking by the class tutors.

Students were told that the project would be followed by a self assessment exercise which would count towards their final mark in the subject, but the exercise was not distributed until the design project had been virtually completed.

## The exercise

The exercise provided a set of factors to be considered in judging a design exercise (criteria) and asked students to assess (judge) the extent to which they applied each factor in their design. They were asked to make a written statement about each factor and to award themselves a mark out of ten on each. Eleven factors were provided and students had the opportunity to add two more of their own and assess themselves with respect to them (see Figure 7.1). In addition to the self assessment, the students were asked to complete a brief questionnaire which sought their views about self assessment and the worth of the exercise. These were handed in anonymously at the same time as their self assessment exercises, and guarantees were given that these would not be analysed until all marking had finished. Although there were minor variations from year to year, this procedure was followed for three successive years. All enrolled students were given the exercise, the response rate over the three years being relatively constant at 75–85 per cent. In the light of student comments, the instructions were clarified and the factors made more explicit from one year to the next, but the basic process remained unchanged. It is important to note that the course in which the self assessment exercise was introduced had been taught in a similar fashion for several years previously and that the introduction of self assessment was made in such a way as to minimise disruption to other aspects of teaching.

## Evaluation

The main aim of the evaluation was to ascertain whether the self assessment procedure adopted was acceptable to students and to gather information which would enable self assessment exercises to be designed effectively (see Figure 7.2). If self assessment is to be introduced in courses of this kind it must be done in such a way that it is considered to be of benefit by those for whom it has been designed and is acceptable to the staff who are responsible for implementing it. The evaluation of the self assessment exercise was kept simple so that it would not intrude upon the students' time. It was intended to be formative and indicative of students' reactions: more sophisticated

*Procedure*
Some of the factors to be considered in judging a design exercise are listed below. We want you to consider each one in turn and assess the extent to which you applied each factor in the design of the mechanical drive. After each factor there is a space for you to make your comments and to assign yourself a mark out of ten which represents your own assessment of your own performance in that particular aspect of the design project. We will be judging your completed self assessment in terms of the accuracy of your appraisal and the *evidence* which you cite for your judgement. A mark by itself will not be considered: you *must give your reasons why you think that you deserve a particular mark.*

*Strategy of design*
In this section of the self assessment exercise, we consider the ways in which you tackled the design task. You probably began by developing a design concept for a complete mechanical drive. Once a design concept has been proposed, the task can be broken down into a number of major stages (or components). Most of these stages contain a number of minor stages within themselves which require a logical approach. What is your assessment of the way in which you organised most of your work within the section of the project dealing with:

(1)  developing a concept for the complete mechanical drive?
Comments:*                                                    Mark (max 10)

(2)  the form and layout of each major component, eg, clutch, bearings, belt drives, shafts, etc.
Comments:                                                     Mark (max 10)

*Quality of assumptions*
At various points in the design it was necessary to make assumptions in order to simplify calculations, to define conditions of usage, etc.

What is your assessment of:
(3)  the extent to which you were able to make realistic assumptions, that is, assumptions which are not likely to be grossly in error in terms of estimating a likely value of some variable, or predicting the conditions of use?
Comments:                                                     Mark (max 10)

(4)  the extent to which your assumptions were conservative that is, erring on the safe side?
Comments:                                                     Mark (max 10)

*Correctness of calculations*
(5) Within the design strategy and assumptions you used what is your assessment of the extent to which your calculations were correctly worked through and checked for errors?
Comments:                                            Mark (max 10)

*Decisions*
(6) During the design you had to make a number of decisions, that is, choices amongst various possibilities, eg, location of fly wheel, location of clutch, belt drive vs chain drive vs gears, number of stages of speed reduction to be used, type of bearings, etc. What is your assessment of your ability to make appropriate decisions in the project, ie, decisions which lead to a successful design?
Comments:                                            Mark (max 10)

*Quality of final design*
Looking back on your design now that it is finished, what is your assessment of its overall quality?

(7) With respect to its performance; that is, will your mechanical drive work well and give little trouble?
Comments:                                            Mark (max 10)

(8) With respect to ease of manufacture; that is, can it and components be made and assembled simply and cheaply?
Comments:                                            Mark (max 10)

(9) With respect to the use of materials; that is, were the appropriate materials and process chosen for each part?
Comments:                                            Mark (max 10)

*Project presentation*
To what extent was your design presented clearly and neatly and with sufficient details so that another engineer could check the work?

(10) With respect to the written work and calculations
Comments:                                            Mark (max 10)

(11) With respect to the drawings?
Comments:                                            Mark (max 10)

*Other factors of importance*
You now have the opportunity to propose other important factors which you consider be used to judge design projects of the kind which you have just completed in this course, and rate your work with respect to them. Please be specific.

(12) Factor 12
Comments:                                                                 Mark (max 10)

(13) Factor 13
Comments:                                                                 Mark (max 10)

*Overall assessment of performance*
(14) Considering your performance as a whole, how well do you consider that you have performed in the project?
Comments:                                                                 Mark (max 10)

*A space of 50 mm was included after each item for students to write a descriptive assessment.

**Figure 7.1** *Student self assessment exercise in engineering design*

evaluation procedures could be used once self assessment was accepted as a useful component of the course.

The main areas in which benefits were sought from the self assessment exercise were in the development of students' attitudes towards their work. These are difficult to assess directly, so the greater part of our evaluation arose from answers given to the short questionnaire. However, as shown in Figure 7.3, it was possible to compare students' assessment of their work with lecturers' assessment of the same work, for the three years surveyed. Students in each year received detailed feedback from the early sections of the project which had been marked promptly and returned so that corrections could be incorporated in the later sections of the work. The final submission comprising detail and assembly drawings, etc. had not been marked when the self assessment exercise was handed in.

The student marks were derived by averaging their self-awarded scores on each of the 11 factors. These are compared in Figure 7.3 with the overall mark awarded by the lecturer for the design project. While these marks were given partly for correct analysis and partly for what the lecturer considered to be 'good design', they were not derived by considering each of the 11 factors explicitly. In the strictest sense, therefore, the two sets of marks are not directly comparable. It was not expected that students' marks would be consistent with those of staff at the second-year level: students are learning about how to apply new criteria to their work and they have little experience at this stage on which to form their judgements. One of the purposes of the exercise was therefore to increase students' performance in this important area. The histograms for 1981 and 1983 (Figure 7.3) were roughly

*Comments on the exercise*

The formal part of the exercise is now complete. We would appreciate your comments on the self assessment exercise so that we might take them into account when planning self assessment procedures. This page* will be removed and will not be considered until after your earlier assessment has been examined. Please respond under the following headings:

*Ease with which the instructions were understood?*

*Did you think that this exercise helped you pinpoint your strengths and weaknesses?*

*Was the self assessment exercise a worthwhile learning experience?*

*If a similar method were to be used on future occasions, what changes would you suggest to the procedure?*

*Other comments*

*The questions were set to fill one A4 page

**Figure 7.2** *Student survey of self assessment exercise*

symmetrical, the most frequent outcome (mode) being that students and lecturers awarded the same mark, within 2.5 per cent. In both these histograms the mean fell within the same range, with lecturers on average awarding very slightly lower marks (0.2% and 1.8% respectively). The standard deviations of 10% and 12% for the two years indicate that, in roughly 30% of cases, the discrepancy in marks exceeded these values. In 1982, the histogram was significantly skewed, such that lecturers awarded more marks than students. In this histogram the mode occurred at 10 per cent L>S and the mean at approximately 3.9 per cent L>S. The questionnaire sheet which was returned with the self assessment exercises provided information about whether students considered self assessment to be a worthwhile learning exercise, how the instructions could be improved, whether the exercise helped pinpoint strengths and weaknesses and, if a similar method were to be used on future occasions, what changes could be suggested. The questions were deliberately posed in an open-ended form to enable students to respond from their own perspective using their own words. Their responses were content-analysed and the major categories of response were identified.

Details of the number of students enrolled in the subject in each year and the percentage of students who handed in the self assessment exercise and questionnaires are given in Table 7.1.

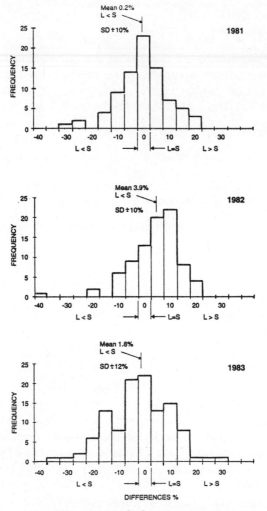

L = Lecturer's assessment ; S = Student's assessment

**Figure 7.3**  *Comparisons of students' and lecturers' assessments*

Not all students answered every question, hence the percentages of respondents for particular questions are shown in Tables 7.2 and 7.3.

Within the student group which responded to the questionnaire, the results of the evaluation were fairly consistent over the three years. When asked whether they felt the exercise was a worthwhile learning experience, over 70 per cent of respondents each year thought it was (see Table 7.2).

**Table 7.1** Student enrolments and percentage respondents for the three years surveyed

| | Year | | |
|---|---|---|---|
| | **1981** | **1982** | **1983** |
| Total enrolment | 94 | 98 | 150 |
| Total respondents (%) | 79 | 86 | 75 |

**Table 7.2** Responses to the question 'Was the self assessment exercise a worthwhile learning experience?'

| | Year | | |
|---|---|---|---|
| | **1981** | **1982** | **1983** |
| Respondents (%) | 79 | 86 | 75 |
| Yes (%) | 76 | 77 | 72 |
| No (%) | 22 | 14 | 21 |
| Undecided (%) | 3 | 8 | 6 |

**Table 7.3** Responses to the question 'Did you think that this exercise helped you pinpoint your strengths and weaknesses?'

| | Year | | |
|---|---|---|---|
| | **1981** | **1982** | **1983** |
| Respondents (%) | 74 | 77 | 75 |
| Yes (%) | 67 | 71 | 72 |
| No (%) | 33 | 24 | 18 |
| Undecided (%) | – | 5 | 11 |

Positive comments from students included:

> Yes – uses best method of learning – through own experience and mistakes.

> It was worthwhile in the respect that I was able to determine how I thought I performed. It was a worthwhile exercise; now I can use this approach on more assignments and maybe improve.

> It gave me the opportunity to assess myself, an activity which I will be doing a lot of as a professional; after all there won't always be tutors around to do it for you.

> This exercise made you look back at the design critically and this must help in learning and understanding.

Of the students who did not find the exercise worthwhile, the following comment was probably the most pertinent:

> It merely increased my frustration as it represented another exercise set for design that prevented me from studying other equally important subjects – as it has done throughout the year.

The students were also asked whether the exercise helped them to pinpoint their strengths and weaknesses. Again a large percentage of the students from all three years said that it did (see Table 7.3).

Positive comments from students included:

> Yes, marks are only a reasonable guide, self assessment gives you a critical evaluation of your design, especially your weaknesses.

> Yes, it does help, because it gives me a chance to look at myself!

> As engineers we need to know our strong and weak areas so we can develop the weak areas.

Some negative student comments were:

> Self assessment is difficult, especially in the absence of a frame of reference.

> No, I feel that the comments [written by tutors] at the end of each section of work were more helpful.

The students were asked to comment on any changes they would like to see made to the exercise in the future. Table 7.4 shows the main categories of comments by the number citing them per year. It should be noted that as students had to provide these suggestions, it is likely that the figures underestimate the number of students holding these views.

Table 7.4 shows that approximately 14 per cent of students in each year felt a need for more specific questions, a typical comment being:

> I would like to see the questions directed more directly to the specific sections and the problem [that] would have to be overcome in those sections.

Modifications to the factors were made in 1982 and 1983 with the intention of making them more specific. That this did not diminish the number of students expressing this view suggests that a more profound change than this was desired.

A self assessment exercise following immediately after each section of the

**Table 7.4** Student comments on possible changes to the self assessment exercise

| | Year | | |
| --- | --- | --- | --- |
| | **1981** | **1982** | **1983** |
| More specific questions | 10 | 12 | 16 |
| Use multiple-choice type questions | 1 | 1 | 3 |
| Leave more room for answers | 4 | 2 | 4 |
| Prefer a self assessment for each section of project | 1 | 14 | 2 |
| Need more time to do exercise | 5 | – | 7 |
| Change from specific mark to grade | 1 | – | 3 |

project was a popular suggestion in 1982 (16 per cent) but received little support in the other years. One comment was:

> In my opinion more could be gained by having the students do self assessment of the previous week's work as the project progresses. This makes students more aware of their own faults.

In the section requesting other comments, students' replies sometimes dealt with aspects of the design project and were not relevant to the self assessment exercise. The following comments were amongst the most illuminating:

> I think the exercise could have been more worthwhile if we were able to discuss deficiencies with the tutors instead of doing the exercise alone at home.

> Not only is self assessment good for the students, I feel that academic staff can have a picture of the problems, weaknesses of students in this design process.

> I think self assessment is worthwhile in all learning experiences rather than just doing and getting marked; it gives a sense of involvement.

Also during the exercise the students were given the opportunity to propose any additional important factors which they considered should be used to judge design projects of the kind they had just completed. The factors they suggested were grouped into fairly broad categories, as shown in Table 7.5. The responses were quite numerous, averaging more than one suggestion per respondent in each year. The authors believed that most of the factors listed by students had been covered in the exercise, the exceptions being the last two in Table 7.5. These figures suggest that, for a significant number of students, the wording of the questions had not conveyed the meanings intended.

**Table 7.5** Other factors which students felt were of importance and which they considered were not covered in the self assessment exercise

|  | Year | | |
|  | 1981 | 1982 | 1983 |
| --- | --- | --- | --- |
| Creativity and initiative | 10 | 18 | 27 |
| Demonstrated understanding of underlying theory | 7 | 14 | 26 |
| The physical characteristics of the final product | 19 | 19 | 8 |
| Practical considerations eg, cost, markets, etc. | 5 | 7 | 25 |
| Efficient use of time by designer | 11 | 16 | 21 |
| Organisation of project and report | 12 | 13 | 18 |
| Other specific features eg, safety, simplicity | 16 | 6 | 8 |
| The time and effort put into design and report | 13 | – | 9 |
| The amount of practical experience of each student | – | – | 7 |

In each year surveyed, three senior lecturers were involved in lecturing and tutoring the classes, as well as three tutors. All staff members strongly supported the concept of self assessment and their positive attitude to the exercise was undoubtedly one of the reasons for the high level of student acceptance. The staff recognised that such an exercise had benefits in improving design skills and as one small step towards achieving professional maturity, as well as having benefits in 'learning how to learn'. The following comment by one staff member (not one of the authors) is typical:

> The developing awareness of the possibility of, and the necessity for evaluation of one's own strengths and weaknesses is a valuable addition to the professional attitudes of the students who take this exercise seriously.

## Discussion

By the end of the course and the self assessment project, most students could see that their design methods had not been particularly effective. Most could see a quicker and more effective strategy for that design in the light of experience gained during the project. Fewer could see how to extrapolate their new knowledge and methods to other design problems, although most could see that in practice this would be required. How, or whether, self assessment is effective in helping students to develop a generalised design strategy is a question which has not yet been addressed. However, students did find the exercise useful in clarifying and identifying specific deficiencies which they can address in later parts of the course.

The fact that not all students responded to the self assessment exercise and questionnaire is attributed to the timing of the exercise, which was issued during the last week of semester. By this time, in a continual assessment subject, students already have an accurate assessment of their standing in the years' work. There was little incentive for those with a 'credit' grade to spend time working on the self assessment exercise. It is difficult to estimate what might have been the approval rate of the exercise had all students responded. Certainly, the group which did not respond might be expected to have a lower approval rate. However, at the very worst, it is clear that well over half the class in each year found the exercise a worthwhile experience.

We have been unable to find any reason for the discrepancy in the 1982 histogram of student vs lecturer assessment of the design project (Figure 7.3). One staff member was absent on study leave that year, but all staff members had worked on the course for several years and a remarkably uniform standard of marking had evolved. So far as is known, the self assessment exercise was presented to the students in the same manner as previously, although by a different staff member. However, it is possible that students responded to subtle cues, of which the staff were unaware, implying that it would be more profitable for students to under-rate their work rather than risk any suggestion of over-rating.

It was gratifying to find that students in an engineering course responded positively to a self assessment exercise. We were also pleased to find that, despite its obvious limitations, students regarded it as a worthwhile learning exercise which helped them to pinpoint their strengths and weaknesses. Looking back, the main limitations of the exercise were:

- The activity was retrospective. Students were not encouraged by the structure of the exercise to monitor their own progress during the conduct of the project, although there were exhortations from staff to this end.
- It was individualistic. Students worked alone to identify their own strengths and weaknesses. The self assessment activity did not engage them in discussing criteria with their peers or with staff to arrive at a common judgement. Thus students added criteria of their own which staff believed were already present in the list provided.
- Criteria were provided. Students were not required to go through the process of determining what criteria (factors) were appropriate. Involvement in the development process helps to forge a commitment to these

criteria, as has been evident in self assessment exercises in other subjects (Boud and Lublin, 1983).

These limitations occurred almost entirely because self assessment was added in a piecemeal fashion to the course after it had already been planned.

The desirable features of future developments in self assessment within the design area are:

- Introducing it at a time when other changes are planned for a course.
- Making it an integral part of the learning process rather than something which might be seen as an adjunct to the main activity of design.
- Involving students in discussing and clarifying criteria during the design process. This would act to make the criteria explicit and to increase student commitment to them.
- Providing opportunities for students to compare their judgements with those of staff and to discuss these with them.

Some of these features have already been incorporated with success into courses in other subjects.

For many second-year students, the self assessment exercise was their first attempt at assessing their own or another person's work and some found it difficult. It needs to be borne in mind that the second-year exercise was not given until halfway through the course, by which time university study habits and expectations have become quite well established. If self assessment is to be pursued as a learning mechanism in the design area, it may be desirable to introduce the process early in the first year of the course.

## Conclusion

The results obtained have demonstrated the potential benefits, and some pitfalls, of applying self assessment to a professional engineering course. Our approach was a simple one, adding a self assessment exercise at the end of an existing design course. There are further benefits to be gained in a closer integration between self assessment and the course material and in reinforcing the self assessment concept throughout the four years of a course. The approach adopted here is an example of the first step which might be taken in exploring the use of self assessment in an area where criteria are complex and in which students may need to gain experience in applying provided criteria before developing their own.

# Chapter 8

# Involving Self and Peers in the Assessment of Class Participation

*David Boud and Alan Tyree*

This study uses a combination of self and peer assessment in judging class participation. Criteria are individually determined by students as part of the exercise. It illustrates the use of self and peer assessment in the context of the teaching of law, although the basic method could be used in any subject area. A feature of this example is the use of a technique which involves rating on a self-normalising scale to avoid grade inflation.

The quality of a lawyer's work is, for the most part, judged by fellow lawyers. This is a position which the legal profession shares with the other professions. It is a position which all of the professions guard jealously, although one which has come increasingly under attack by the wider community in recent years. This 'internal' assessment is generally on an informal basis, the criteria and standards used being inarticulated. It is only when something goes terribly wrong that the lawyer is subjected to a formal assessment.

The situation of the professions thus differs markedly from that of many other forms of employment in two ways: first, that most assessment is by peers rather than by those in a supervisory capacity; second, assessment is not usually of such a form that it will tend to improve the day-to-day or long-term effectiveness of the lawyer's work. It is of an ill-defined nature which is more related to maintaining the professional image rather than the raising of standards.

This structure of the profession has implications for individual lawyers. The lack of effective external assessment directing day-to-day work means that the ability to define goals and to self assess progress toward those goals must be better than those of most non-professionals. Lack of the self-assessing ability may eventually produce effects which will meet the adverse assessment of the person by his or her peers, but such peer assessment may be too late to have the necessary corrective effect. In the extreme, a lack of ability to assess one's own performance will bring failure in formal assessment along with its usually unpleasant consequences.

The ability to assess oneself accurately is of further importance to lawyers at the most basic level of practicability: lawyers never have enough time. The ability to self assess can help a lawyer make optimal use of the time available. If it is accepted that the ability to assess oneself is a desirable trait in a lawyer, we must ask what is the responsibility of those in legal education to develop and stimulate that skill in law students. Is it possible to teach self assessment skills? If it is, should it be a clearly defined aim of legal education? These are broad questions for which there are no definitive answers; but we will argue below that some legal skills have a component of self assessment and that a clear appreciation of this could help sharpen the definition of the objectives of early legal education courses.

## Student ability in self and peer assessment

We decided to investigate students' ability to make assessments of themselves and their peers in a one-session (15 week) first-year class entitled 'The Legal System' taught by the second author at the University of New South Wales. The class size was 28 and was taught in the 'Socratic' fashion. The course had the usual aims for such a course and was structured around the development of consumer protection through common law and the legislative process.

Admission to the law course was restricted; students were admitted on the basis of their marks in a state-wide examination (the Higher School Certificate). There were, in addition, a few places allotted to mature-age students and a special programme for the admission of Aboriginal students. One of each of these special categories participated in this experiment.

The experiment was limited to the assessment of class participation. This is an important part of the assessment process in law at New South Wales and has been the subject of other studies (Armstrong, 1978; Armstrong and Boud, 1983; Hayes and Hayes, 1973). Class participation accounted for a large part of the overall mark in the legal system course, being 20 per cent of the final mark for the course.

As a means of examining students' behaviour in self and peer assessment, class participation had other appealing characteristics. Although it is a relatively small part of the overall input of a student into the course, it is a very public part. There was no need for the students to read the work of others or, indeed, to prepare in any special manner for the exercise.

The two aspects of students' ability to make assessments were considered: establishing appropriate criteria for assessment; and rating by students of themselves and their peers in terms of these criteria. Students were required to think carefully about the aims of the course and the role of class participation in the course before determining the criteria they would use.

A series of instructions was provided for each student. These gave guidelines for constructing assessment criteria, and focused the attention of students on the need to establish priorities and to have clearly written criteria. Once the students had constructed the criteria they would use, they made an assessment of both their own performance in class and that of the other students in the class.

The choice of a suitable scale to use for rating was the subject of some debate between the authors. The simplest method was to use a ten-point scale with students giving a mark out of ten on each criterion. This was familiar and easy to use but it suffered from two main drawbacks. First, a mark of, say, five has certain connotations independent of the criteria being used. That is, it is regarded as a bare pass and the student receiving it can be thought to have bare-pass qualities. Second, there is the possibility of the entire class using a very small band of marks. This would lead to a lack of discrimination between students, causing difficulty in interpreting the results of the exercise, or possibly to the inflation of grades, as has been reported elsewhere (Huntley, 1976).

An alternative to the ten-point scale was to use what is called a self-normalising scale. With such a scale marks are allocated so that the full range is used and equal numbers of students appear above and below the average for the class. This scale has two advantages. First, no grade inflation can occur because no matter which students are involved the average for the class is defined in advance. Second, it is more valid to compare the marks of different students as there will be less variation in the method of marking. The main disadvantage is the strangeness of the method. Most students and teachers know, or think they know, how to use a ten-point scale even though they might not use it in an identical fashion, but when the method is substantially varied they need special instructions. There is also the significant drawback of comparing students with respect to each other rather than making an assessment with regard to explicit standards of competence.

As part of the study it was decided to use both types of scale and to compare the effects. Once students had established the criteria they were to use, they were asked to mark themselves and their peers using Method A: the scale 1, 2, 3, 4, 5, 6, 7, 8, 9 , with 5 as the pass mark; and Method B: the scale −2, −1, 0, +1, +2, with the rule that there should be equal numbers of students above and below the mean of 0. Method B thus approximates to a normalised scale.

The sequence was as follows:

1. Students listed all the criteria which they thought were important in assessing class participation.
2. They clarified these and elaborated on them as necessary.
3. They selected the three criteria which they considered to be the most important.
4. They rated themselves and other members of the class using each one of these three criteria in turn on both Method A and Method B.
5. Independently of the students the teacher used the same scheme to produce equivalent sets of marks for each student.
6. Finally, students gave their written comments about the exercise.

At the end of the exercise, which took approximately one hour of class time to complete, the following marks were available for each student on each criterion using both methods:

- Self mark (mark given by himself or herself)
- Peer mark (average of marks, given by the other students)
- Teacher mark (mark given by the teacher)

## Results

Twenty-five students were present in the class when the experiment was conducted. Although all students had been told about it in advance they did not know at what time it would take place. Ratings were obtained from all 25 students for Method A and from 23 for Method B. Two students had completely misunderstood the instructions for Method B and their results could not be used, and 11 others had not adhered to the rule of equal numbers above and below the mean. Some of these students tried to justify their non-observance of this rule, one commenting, 'everyone should consider themselves "above average"'!

### Criteria

The students produced a total list of 148 criteria, an average of 5.9 per student with a range from 5 to 8. These criteria were subsequently classified under the following headings:

1. Characteristics of an individual's contribution
   Cognitive: logic, objectivity, knowledge, creativity.

Expressive: clarity, fluency, conciseness.

Affective: enthusiasm, interest.

Contribution to the process of learning: recognition of the responses of others, constructive criticism, contribution to group climate, relevance.

2.  Inferred preparation: amount, consistency, timeliness

3.  Attendance.

This part of the exercise was received very favourably by the students. One student commented:

> This is an excellent exercise, for it makes one aware of what a good student should do.

Another wrote:

> These steps allowed those of us involved to suggest whichever factors we wished and express them in whatever way seemed to us the most appropriate. This lack of rigidity is excellent and may allow us to present to staff factors for judging performance which previously they had not considered.

The latter comment was quite accurate. The factors which were outlined by the students were all relevant in the view of the teacher and provided a considerably broader list than the one that was initially generated.

The main dissatisfaction with this aspect of the exercise was that having specified a series of important criteria they only had an opportunity for three of these to be used for assessment. This view was expected, but was considered by the authors to be an inevitable consequence of the need to limit the exercise to a manageable scale. A significant criticism was voiced by another student:

> I think the factors would be better arrived at by class discussion because one person is liable to miss out on an important one, or word it poorly. Once decided on, they should all be used.

If a procedure similar to the one we have used under experimental conditions were used for student assessment then considerations of parity and fairness would provide strong arguments for a common set of criteria. However, there is a limitation in this for, no matter how well-worded a given criterion might be, it would always be subject to multiple interpretations, and thus an apparently common scale would, in practice, not be assessing the common factors for which it was designed. (Nevertheless, in subsequent studies in law, criteria which were elaborated and discussed in class were used. This approach was particularly commended by students. See Chapter 15 for details of how this was done.)

## Ratings

For convenience in presenting the results, only the mark obtained by averaging over the marks on the three criteria is shown.

Comparisons between the marks given to each student by themselves, their peers, and their teacher are shown in Table 8.1. Product-moment correlation coefficients were calculated for each comparison for both methods. The main features of these results are as follows:

- Students tend to rate themselves more favourably than they are rated by their peers.
- Students rate themselves less favourably than they are rated by the teacher using Method A, but this is completely reversed when Method B is used.
- Peers are much harsher in their ratings than the teacher when Method A is used, but using Method B this is reversed and the peers are somewhat more lenient than the teacher.
- In general, on both methods there is a very high level of agreement between the marks given by peers and those given by the teacher.

**Table 8.1** Comparisons of students marks

|  | Method A | Method B |
|---|---|---|
| *Comparison of self and peer ratings* |  |  |
| Number of students with marks: |  |  |
|    self higher than peer | 17 | 16 |
|    self lower than peer | 8 | 7 |
|  | 25 | 23 |

$r_A = 0.51^{**}$, $r_B = 0.60^{**}$

|  | Method A | Method B |
|---|---|---|
| *Comparison of self and teacher ratings* |  |  |
| Number of students with marks: |  |  |
|    self higher than teacher | 9 | 17 |
|    self lower than teacher | 16 | 6 |
|  | 25 | 23 |

$r_A = 0.46^{*}$, $r_B = 0.55^{**}$

|  | Method A | Method B |
|---|---|---|
| *Comparison of peer and teacher ratings* |  |  |
| Number of students with marks: |  |  |
|    peer higher than teacher | 4 | 16 |
|    peer lower than teacher | 21 | 9 |
|  | 24 | 25 |

$r_A = 0.75^{**}$, $r_B = 0.83^{***}$

The asterisks indicate the statistical significance of each correlation. (* = significant at .05 level, ** = significant at .01 level, *** = significant at .001 level.)

One of the difficulties of comparing sets of marks is that different people tend to use different parts of the same scale on which to rate. It is quite common for different tutors to give the same piece of work widely differing assessments. A statistical device can be used to modify sets of marks so that different markers appear to produce the same mean mark and the same spread of marks. This then enables direct comparisons to be made between the marks received by a particular student from different markers. This procedure is known as producing a normalised score.

Now if the students had correctly interpreted our instructions for Method B the calculation for the normalised B scores should leave their results effectively unchanged, for what the normalising procedure does after the marks have been given is essentially the same as what the 'self-normalising' Method B aimed to do.

Table 8.2 presents the same comparisons as Table 8.1, but in terms of the normalised scores. The correlations are unchanged as this procedure has no effect on them. The fact that the results of normalising the B scores *does* show a considerable shift is evidence of the degree to which students failed to follow our instructions.

When the normalised results are considered the findings become clearer:

- Students tend to rate themselves more favourably than they are rated by their peers.

**Table 8.2** Comparisons of students marks using normalised scores

|  | Method A | Method B |
|---|---|---|
| *Comparison of self and peer ratings* | | |
| Number of students with marks: | | |
| self higher than peer | 14 | 14 |
| self lower than peer | 11 | 9 |
|  | 25 | 23 |
| *Comparison of self and teacher ratings* | | |
| Number of students with marks: | | |
| self higher than teacher | 10 | 9 |
| self lower than teacher | 14 | 14 |
|  | 25 | 23 |
| *Comparison of peer and teacher ratings* | | |
| Number of students with marks: | | |
| peer higher than teacher | 15 | 11 |
| peer lower than teacher | 10 | 14 |
|  | 25 | 25 |

The normalised score is calculated from the formula $z = \dfrac{x - X}{s}$ where $x$ is the original mark, $X$ is the original mean mark, and $s$ is the standard deviation. The normalised score is known as a 'z-score'.

- Students tend to rate themselves less favourably than they are rated by their teacher.

Our other finding remains unchanged:

- There is a very high level of agreement (ie, correlation) between the marks given by peers and those given by the teacher.

The difference between distributions of the results using the two methods is an important finding. The kind of rating scale used can have a profound effect on the results even when the criteria used are unchanged. If this finding is duplicated in further studies, it could lead to a reassessment of the previous work that has been done on self and peer assessment. If the finding that students rate themselves more or less harshly than the teacher can be so easily reversed then the acceptibility of self assessment could be simply influenced by the choice of an appropriate scale.

Student preferences for Method A or Method B were very polarised. They seemed to appreciate the issues involved in using the different scale, but plumped for one or the other. Nine students gave a clear preference for Method A and six for Method B, but some of these appeared to be voting against the alternative. For example, one student wrote of Method B:

> Horrible! It is quite unfair to give someone −2 simply because someone else has scored +2. The mathematical logic of this section is not appropriate when applying to classes.

This student is making the point that there are more issues to be considered when making a choice of a rating scale than simply the logical ones. Assessment is an emotive subject and procedures need not only to be scrupulously fair, but they must also be felt by students to be fair. Marks have, unfortunately, an association with status and nobody seems to want changes in status for purely logical reasons.

## Conclusion

While this study was conducted in the area of law, the major outcomes seem more widely applicable. The most gratifying results were the positive responses from the students. They felt that they had participated in a worthwhile learning experience. Our reading of the criteria which they constructed for the purpose of assessment led us to the same belief.

We have already discussed the numerical results of the experiment. We note that the correlations between each of the combinations of assessors is good, but students seem to have used a different part of the 'standard' scale than did the teacher. It was in anticipation of this problem that the 'self-normalising' scale was introduced. However, a significant proportion of the students found this scale to be objectionable. Using normalised scores from the 'standard' scale for the purposes of comparison would seem at least as satisfactory as attempting to construct a more sophisticated method of marking.

As always, a study of this sort raises more questions for consideration. The results of the students' participation was *not* a part of the formal assessment of the course, a fact which was known to the students at the time of the exercise. Would it make any difference to the comparative results? Furthermore, it might be hoped that more advanced students would have gained greater facility in the self assessment process, even if by 'greater facility' we mean only that the students have a more accurate assessment of the teacher's expectations. This issues are discussed at greater length in Chapters 12 and 13.

We believe that the questions raised in the preceding paragraph are not independent, but may be influenced by an underlying factor. We conjecture that in a climate of greater competitive tension the agreement between the self/peer/teacher assessment could be expected to deteriorate as self-preservation instincts come to the fore as conscious or unconscious motives in the assessment procedure. If this conjecture is correct, then including the experiment as part of the formal assessment procedure would decrease the observed agreement.

But a decrease in the observed agreement should not, *in itself,* be grounds for rejecting the use of self and peer assessment as a part of the formal assessment process. If the educational benefits of such an exercise are great enough, we should be prepared to modify the assessment procedure in such a way that it is compatible with our educational goals.

# Chapter 9

# Using Self Assessment Schedules in Negotiated Learning

This chapter focuses on the use of a self assessment schedule. The aim of the schedule is to provide a comprehensive and analytical record of learning in situations where students have substantial responsibility for what they do. It is a personal report on learning and achievements which can be either for students' own use or as a product which can form part of a formal assessment procedure. It is qualitative and discursive.

The issue which the use of a self assessment schedule addresses is that of finding an appropriate mechanism for assessing students' work in self-directed or negotiated learning situations which takes account of both the range of what is learned and the need for students to be accountable for their own learning. Almost all traditional assessment strategies fail to meet these criteria as they tend to sample a limited range of teacher-initiated learning and make the assumption that assessment is a unilateral act conducted by teachers on students. The schedule provides a vehicle for learners to reflect on their learning and give a public account of what they have learned. It consists of a framework which focuses attention on the goals and criteria of learners, elicits evidence of achievements and provides an opportunity for learners to make their own judgements about how successful they have been in meeting their goals.

This account describes the idea of the self assessment schedule and how I came to use it in my own teaching. It also relates the idea to other activities in negotiated learning, discusses the reactions of staff and students, and explores the problems and difficulties which may be encountered in its use. The use of a self assessment schedule as presented here is something more than an item to be added to the assessment repertoire. It raises issues about judgement and learning which are seldom confronted in most discussions of assessment: how can assessment contribute to reflection on learning, and to what extent can assessment help students make sense of their courses?

## How did a self assessment schedule come to be used?

For the past 20 years I have been teaching courses which have involved a high degree of collaboration between staff and students in their design and conduct. These have been postgraduate classes in science education, educational research and adult learning, ranging in size from eight to 24 students. They have been conducted in four higher education institutions in two countries: Australia and Canada. What they have in common is that all were based on the idea that students bring a great deal of knowledge and expertise to a course and that courses at the postgraduate level should treat students as co-learners who have much to contribute as well as much to learn.

The particular approach to teaching I adopted was one in which the aims and objectives, the content and programme of activities, and the evaluation and assessment were negotiated between staff and students in the context of what Heron (1974) terms 'a peer learning community'. In a peer learning community, staff and students learn from each other and each person is responsible for intervening at any stage in the process of the class to express their needs and interests. The course is designed around the particular needs and experience of the group and addresses both what the staff member considers important as well as what students wish to explore. In any given institution there are usually limits to students' full involvement in this process deriving from the exigencies of a required syllabus and assessment policy. In my teaching, I have moved as far in the direction of full participation as I felt able consonant with the views of students and institutional regulations. In three of the institutions the ultimate constraint was the requirement that students be graded.

## What issues were considered?

In thinking about what forms of assessment I might use, three considerations were to the fore. These reflect some of the issues discussed earlier in Chapter 4. First, forms of assessment which are fully defined by teachers are not appropriate for all forms of learning. This is clearly the case when the prior experience of the learner and the linking of this to new knowledge is central, but it can also apply more widely. Some forms of learning are inherently inaccessible to teachers, or may only be partially accessible, and these are no less valid than those areas on which it is possible for students to report publicly.

Second, there is a continual tension in assessment practice between coverage of objectives and depth of assessment. Often the only way to explore a wide range of learning is thought to be through multiple-choice tests, but these tests have considerable limitations in the kind of objectives which can be assessed and the high level of skill required to test higher order cognitive objectives. Forms of assessment which have higher validity than multiple-choice testing, such as project reports which involve the integration of knowledge and experience, also tend to only partially cover the range of learning.

Finally, it is common for only the products of learning to be assessed. Not all learning is manifest in a final product. Learning processes tend to be ignored in assessment and this contributes to the poor value assessment has in improving learning.

## What is a self assessment schedule?

The self assessment schedule is one solution to these difficulties. It is a document that students prepare towards the end of a course in which they summarise their learning and make judgements about it. Various headings under which they can do this are suggested to them. These do not represent subject content areas, but aspects of planning for learning. They are:

- *Goals.* This includes both those goals identified at the beginning of the course and those which emerged during it. It includes those common for all participants and those unique to the individual. It also includes goals relating to the process as well as the outcomes of the course.
- *Criteria.* This represents the yardsticks against which it is possible to judge whether the goals were achieved. Some goals might simply be at the level of awareness of ideas, whereas others might have more demanding standards. For example, in a course on adult learning, one student might be content to be aware of a range of approaches to the analysis of learning styles, whereas another will want to have sufficient knowledge and skill to apply learning styles inventories with given learners and use this information to generate alternative learning options.
- *Evidence.* Students indicate what evidence they have for the pursuit and attainment of their goals. Items might include reference to papers written, notes on readings, extracts from learning portfolios and accounts of work within their peer group. Evidence will also include statements that they have received feedback from peers and others with whom they have had contact.
- *Judgements.* This includes reports of what others have said, qualitative

analyses of the extent to which objectives had been met, and comments about the appropriateness of the criteria which have been used.

- *Further action.* Finally, students indicate further action to pursue their objectives, both to extend them and to address those aspects which they felt that they had not pursued sufficiently within the confines of the given course.

Although the headings are specified, the form and level of detail is not. There are as many different interpretations as there are students who have used it. See Figure 9.1 for typical instructions to students.

## In which contexts has it been used?

In some situations I have used this as the only form of assessment, but more commonly I have combined it with other assignments and with an exercise in which students propose a grade for themselves. An example of this is in a Masters course, 'Researching educational practice'.

In this course, students establish goals for themselves and negotiate a set of goals which they pursue as a group. They keep a detailed record of their learning in the form of a portfolio (Bawden and McKinnon, 1980; Walker, 1985). The portfolio is for the compiler's eyes only, but evidence is drawn from it for use in the self assessment schedule. Each student also submits an assignment consisting of a proposal to research some aspect of their own educational practice based on a particular model or approach to research. A checklist for evaluating proposals of this kind is generated by the group during one of the classes (using the process described in Chapter 15). Each person then prepares a detailed and descriptive assessment of their learning in the form of a self assessment schedule. This includes an appraisal of the research proposal as well as consideration of any other learning relevant to the subject whether or not it was formally part of the course. As each person contributes to the design and conduct of at least one session, an appraisal of that is included also.

A few weeks prior to the end of the course, a session during which students receive qualitative feedback from their peers is conducted and information from this is used as part of the schedule as the student chooses. Students form learning partnerships during the course (Robinson, *et al.*, 1985; Saberton, 1985) and normally students in the partnership would show a draft of the final schedule to each other for comment before it is submitted.

All of the above aspects of assessment are a part of assessment for learning, rather than assessment for accreditation, and have a potentially beneficial influence on students' experience of the course. However, in most instances,

---

*Self assessment schedule*

A self assessment schedule is a document which records your goals and achievements in a given area and judgements about them. It is a statement which needs to contain sufficient information in it to enable someone who is familiar with the general area of the subject to ascertain what learning activities the author has engaged in and what he or she has learned. While the schedule itself is a summary, brief attachments may be appended to indicate, for example, scope of reading.

It may be presented in whatever form is considered appropriate (eg, lists of items under each goal, tabulated in a chart, etc). Whatever else it includes it should address the following:

A.  Specify the *goals* you are pursuing in this subject. These will include your initial goals, those which emerged during the course, and those which have been agreed by the class or your working group. Be as detailed as possible and list all your sub-goals.

B.  Indicate the *criteria* which should be applied to judge the extent to which these goals have been met. That is, what are the appropriate standards to be used for assessing your goals in this subject? (ie, what is the yardstick against which you are assessing yourself with respect to each of your goals?) Include both your own and any agreed as common criteria.

C.  For each of the goals specified above (in A), and for each of the criteria indicated (in B) list the *evidence* which you have which relates to how well you have met each one. The main evidence on which you will draw will be your research proposal and outcomes from your reading and study in the subject matter area, but you may include other items if you wish. Do not make any judgements at this stage, just indicate the information which you have available which enables you to make a judgement about your performance/achievement. (The evidence may take the form of items from your portfolio, other pieces of work, comments from peers, etc.)

D.  For each of the items listed above give your own *judgement* on the extent to which you have been successful in achieving what you have intended to achieve with respect to the criteria you have set and the evidence at your disposal. This should be a qualitative judgement based on your own criteria and should not refer to marks or marking criteria.

E.  For those goals which you believe you have not met sufficiently, indicate what you would need to do in order to meet them, ie, *further action*.

**Figure 9.1**  *Typical instructions to students*

the institution also requires grades to be generated. Over the years I have used a number of approaches to this tricky task. It is always a strain on both staff and students for cooperative learning to take place in conjunction with grading. However, in most situations there is no alternative acceptable to the institution. In the case of 'Researching educational practice', grades have most frequently been generated by the following procedure.

Satisfactory completion (ie, a pass) is based upon:

- contributions to class learning,
- submission of a self assessment schedule,
- submission of a research proposal and completed evaluation checklist.

The level of grade awarded is dependent on the quality of the proposal assessed according to the criteria agreed by the class for the checklist and the published grading policy of the school.

Each person awards themselves a mark together with a justification for it based upon the evidence submitted in the light of the school's grading policy. Independently of this, I make an assessment of the evidence available without knowledge of the student's proposed mark. If the two proposed marks fall within the same grade band (there are four passing grade bands and one failing one), the student receives his or her own mark. If they do not fall within the same band, a discussion takes place during which each party justifies their grade. Agreement generally results, but there is provision for final arbitration by a third party if needed. A member of staff familiar with the subject is nominated at the beginning of the course and in the case of a dispute, this person receives all documentation and on the basis of this alone makes a determination unconstrained by any previous grades. Resort to this step is very rarely made.

A number of variations on this procedure have been used. The level of agreement between staff and students has changed, but the general principle adopted is that the acceptable level of disagreement should approximate to the normal error which might be expected between markers on the given type of assignment. Typically for an essay-type assignment this would be +/– 5–10 per cent. On some occasions, I have attempted to grade the schedule itself and contributions students make to the class, but these are difficult and inappropriate tasks in this circumstance. The schedule is an idiosyncratic document and there are dangers of undermining the cooperative nature of the course in so doing. Figure 9.2 shows the guidelines provided for students in 'Researching educational practice'.

## How have students used it?

The idea of a self assessment schedule and, indeed, self assessment in general, is a novel one for most students. While there are few difficulties in

**Guidelines for assessment**

*Principles*

Assessment for learning:

(a) All students will keep a detailed record of their learning in the form of a portfolio. The portfolio itself is for the compiler's eyes only, but it should be kept in such a manner that evidence can be draw from it for assessment purposes.

(b) Each person will submit a research proposal of around 3,000 to 4,000 words for some aspect of their own educational practice which represents the application of a particular model or approach to research/evaluation.

(c) As part of one of the classes a checklist for the evaluation of proposals for researching educational practice will be discussed and prepared.

(d) Each person will prepare a detailed and descriptive self assessment of their learning. This will include an appraisal of the paper using the checklist and consideration of any other learning relevant to the subject.

(e) Each person will contribute to the design and conduct of at least one session, an appraisal of which should also be included in the self assessment.

(f) In so far as it is practicable there shall be an opportunity for students to receive feedback from their peers as they wish prior to the submission of (b) to (e).

For marking:

(g) Satisfactory completion of the subject (ie, a passing grade) is based upon:
   • Contributions to class learning primarily in the topic area chosen.
   • Submission of a self assessment schedule which documents and makes judgements about learning and contributions to the class with respect to the specified headings (A to E) in the self assessment schedule.
   • Submission of a research proposal and completed evaluation checklist.

(h) The level of grade awarded will be dependent on the quality of the research proposal assessed according to the criteria agreed in the checklist and the published grading policy of the School of Education.

(i) It is expected that each person will award themselves a mark together with a justification thereof.

(j) The lecturer will make an independent assessment of the evidence presented and arrive at a mark prior to reading the proposed mark.

(k) If the student proposed mark and the lecturer proposed mark do not fall within the same grade band there will be a discussion between lecturer and student during which justification of marks will be considered. If the marks fall within the same band, the student will receive his or her own mark.

(l)    If a mark cannot be agreed the Subject Assessor shall make a final determination unconstrained by the original proposed marks and based solely on the original documentation provided by the student.

*Self marking*
On a separate sheet at the back of your schedule indicate a percentage mark you would award yourself for your performance in this subject and the grounds on which you give it. You should take into account the criteria and evidence you have assembled, any feedback you have had from your peers and the grade distribution which applies in this School for work at a Masters level. The grade distribution gives an indication of the maximum number of students in the class who might achieve grades higher than Pass. To justify a grade higher than Pass you would need to indicate ways in which your achievements are significantly greater than most most students in the class. On completion of the final draft of your self assessment schedule submit your research proposal and checklist, self assessment schedule and the mark (and justification) separately.

*Sequence of activities*
The following sequence is proposed:

1.    Peer feedback session. In the light of the handout on `Giving and Receiving Feedback' students give each other feedback of a type which they define for themselves. Week 11.
2.    Preparation of checklist (criteria) for assessing research proposals. Class exercise, Week 11.
3.    Preparation of draft self assessment schedule, following the guidelines overleaf.
4.    Seeking comments from others. Draft schedule is shown to at least one other student in the class and comments are received from them. By Week 12.
5.    Revise self assessment schedule, as needed.
6.    Submit self assessment schedule and paper. By Week 13.
7.    Moderation of self assessment and adjustment of grades, if necessary.

**Figure 9.2**  *Example of student assessment guidelines*

accepting self assessment in principle, the prospect of engaging in a self assessment which forms a central part of the course is one to which some students react with caution. However, once they experiment with it, they start to see its value. The majority of students have been initially supportive and become enthusiastic having been through the process of constructing a schedule. There is much more concern about the self grading aspect of the course I have described than there is about qualitative self assessment, mainly because of students' prior experience of assessment in norm-referenced situations.

Some students are highly analytical and present their schedule in a tabular form for each objective, others adopt a narrative or free-form approach. With encouragement, students are clearly able to make it their own. However, the range of options for its use are not always apparent to them and it is useful, near the time at which they are to prepare their first draft, for some of the alternative styles to be discussed.

## What is the self assessment schedule useful for?

The greatest value of the schedule appears to be the prompt that it provides for students to reflect on their learning and think about the applications of ideas in their own situations. It is common for them to report that they only start to become aware of what they have learned when they looked back on the course in a systematic fashion as a prelude to completing the schedule. Indeed, it seems especially important in a course which has objectives which emphasise the process of learning for this kind of reflection to be promoted. Part-time students are often under severe pressure in their studies and the opportunities for them to stand back and think about what they are doing are limited. The schedule is a mechanism which encourages this activity and legitimates it as a normal part of the course.

Certainly, it is not a panacea which will remedy faults of assessment systems. It does, though, address some of the difficulties encountered by other approaches. It recognises emergent objectives, it focuses on processes as well as products, it engages learners in making judgements about what it is appropriate to learn as well as what they have learned, and it encourages a reflective approach to coursework. It does not cope with the problem of self assessment of areas and domains of learning of which the student is unaware.

## Student responses

Each year, I have collected the views of students about the course in general and the use of the self assessment schedule in particular. It is often difficult for students to separate out one aspect of a course which has many novel features. In this case it is particularly difficult to separate views on the self assessment schedule itself from views on the generally more contentious aspect of self grading. In the quotes which follow, I have attempted to highlight common responses and give a flavour of student views. (The reference at the end of each quote is to the name and year of the course[1]):

Overwhelmingly, students find the use of the schedule a useful, albeit demanding, exercise which helps them focus on their learning:

> I like it. Very confronting, yet also comforting, i.e. being in control of one's own process. REP88

> A very important learning tool for me. I really struggled with it but feel this process will prove to have been very helpful to me for future courses and direction. BP84

> Tends to force you to clarify your intentions. BP84

> Very difficult process but worthwhile – made me think more critically about what I had gained from the course, and also to a certain extent, what I hadn't achieved (that I had expected I should!) REP88

> This is an essential skill in life. We are so often assessed by our superiors and we assess the ones below us. This self assessment procedure is practical, revealing and makes us conscious of our direction in study and work. The 'self assessment' technique is the most valuable thing I've learned in the course. AL86

One of the valuable aspects is the way in which completion of the schedule acts to help students review learning which is not always apparent:

> I find it absolutely critical to a learning experience – one consolidates learning which is very affirming – one clearly sees what one has accomplished and what is still possible and/or required to fulfil needs. MP84

> Excellent closure on my learnings! I had no idea that I had accomplished as much, until ... the self assessment sheet procedure. BP84

Although the exercise appears at first sight to be an intellectual one, it drew a number of students into their personal experiences, emotions and feelings. Perhaps this is one of the reasons that there seems to be an initial reticence about engaging in the activity:

> Excruciating! And almost too big of a block for me to get over/around. What it added to my understanding and to my awareness of what learning had taken place was a sense of form. The outline for the s/a schedule was clear and concise, but its cogency masked the depths I'd

---

1 MP – The Maturation Process and Adult Learning, OISE, Toronto
  BP – Basic Processes in Facilitating Adult Learning, OISE, Toronto
  AL – Adult Learning, UNSW, Sydney
  REP – Researching Educational Practice, UNSW, Sydney.

> have to dredge in order to satisfactorily analyse myself, the course, the contents and the process and the procedures. MP84

> I found this challenging and useful. It helped me with organising how I get my students to do this. Highlighted the need for me to improve my discipline of keeping a portfolio regularly. REP88

They report a high level of uncertainty and frustration at first during the process of preparation, but the same students express great satisfaction when it has been completed. They feel that they have engaged in significant learning:

> I procrastinated a great deal before finally launching into the task of doing my self assessment.... Intellectually, I understood the rationale for doing it – particularly since much of the material I would cover would be cognitive or skill-oriented, but because there was such a large amount of affective content which could not be separated from the other stuff, I hesitated. Nevertheless, I did get started, and once involved, I found my energies to be really focused and I was amazed at how motivated I became as I went over some of the material in the portfolio. This exercise has been really useful for me as it has forced me to view the learning experience from a more objective perspective and it has enabled me to tie up many of the loose ends and conclude the experience of the course. Another outcome of the exercise that I hadn't anticipated, was the change in my affective state. I was left feeling extremely fatigued, but with a great feeling of calm, as though I had wrestled with some of the 'negative' feelings that had developed during the last few sessions, eg, anxiety, alienation, anger, hurt and had laid them to rest. MP84

> Difficult to begin, but once I got started I enjoyed it – it helped to clarify and elaborate on my goals – which helped me to realise what I had accomplished as an individual and as a class member. MP84

> I enjoy doing them – makes me reflect and analyse what I really have learned and gained from courses. REP88

In discussion of completed schedules, students often say that they wish they had added items or that they would tackle it differently the second time around. Students who use a schedule in a subsequent course often report higher levels of satisfaction about what they have achieved:

> I feel more confident in writing out the schedule this time. Perhaps the goals are clearer and the evidence more obvious. REP86

> I found it valuable this time, probably because I'd had time to think about it after trying to do it for Adult Ed. REP88

Establishing criteria was one of the most difficult aspects:

It is extremely useful for me, as I tend to see any negative in regard to a goal, as the total experience, and by establishing criteria for a goal, I have not been able to allow a negative to overshadow the many positives of the whole experience. Establishing criteria is a good skill to learn and is very applicable to assessing professional competency. REP88

The suggestion you gave on the sheet was the main reference on which I wrote my self assessment schedule. The procedure laid out was clear and precise. Difficulties occurred when I wasn't too sure about 'criteria'. AL86

The goal of encouraging reflection seems to have been met:

Rather difficult to do. One is tempted to give what appears to be the expected. To do it honestly (which is really what is expected) is truly a reflective process and an introspective exercise. It had the effect of organising my thinking about the course and preventing my feelings from being the sole influence. BP84

Extremely difficult, but a worthwhile activity as it made one reflect back over the learning which had taken place. REP88

Some students objected to the use of the schedule which links it with self marking:

Didn't like the mark aspect, but could see some value. I learned a lot about myself. I rebelled against validation once. I learned with my own self evaluation. I'm constantly self evaluating so just wanted the traditional 'mark' – wish I didn't need a mark – a necessary part of this course – forced me to structure my evaluation. I learned that I need to give my 'evaluations' more concrete traditional evidence of my work learning. It made me remake a commitment on paper – my writing is not detailed enough. BP84

A few students do it because it is required and feel no commitment to it and invest little of themselves in it:

What happened was it made me get a learning partner . . . I didn't focus my attention too much here. I was busy with some of my goals and felt I did this just because it was a requirement. BP84

One student believed that there was a danger that the formal role of the schedule may detract in some circumstances from its benefits:

Very effective because it forces one to look at real learnings. Can be difficult for someone else to appreciate because it is such a personal thing. A person may feel pressured because of evaluation and may not be really honest with feelings. BP84

Comments from earlier years led to modifications, especially more emphasis on what criteria are and how to ease entry (see the section in Figure 9.3 on 'Some tips'). More time is now spent in class on discussing the schedule, what forms it can take, examples of the kinds of approaches others have adopted, and the importance of separating the grade-generation component from the formative exercise of preparation of the schedule.

## From the teacher's perspective

Hardly any students found the combination of self assessment and self grading an easy exercise, no matter how they interpreted the task. It seems as if any serious reflection on learning, and this is what students mostly engaged in, is hard-won. The least demanding strategy was simply to treat it as another assessment requirement and conform to the apparent require- ments of the tutor. That so very few took this approach is a tribute to these students' desire to learn and make sense of their learning. In general, they had been successful in getting ownership of the course and its assessment procedure. All were busy people, the majority with jobs and families to support. They appeared to be intrigued by the process and found sufficient in it for themselves to persist in making, sometimes quite ruthless, assessments of their work.

On a practical level, certain kinds of information in the self assessment schedules of some students can tend to be omitted. Typically, these omissions include information about reading and its relation to the learner's goals. It is especially noticeable when it is apparent that the students concerned have read widely. There is always the possibility that anything for which there is not a direct prompt in the instructions will be omitted. A few students in each class do not seem to be able to go beyond the limit of the instructions and make the schedule their own (not surprising perhaps, given the overall context of courses in higher education). There is a tension between spelling out everything in detail and thus satisfying the need of the lecturer for completeness in the schedule, and leaving the instructions deliberately open and hoping that students will use it creatively. The choice depends on (and mirrors) the nature of the context. Some learners are naturally more self reflective or self critical than others, some are more willing to share their learning than others. In some situations, it may be important for the self assessment schedule to be exhaustive, in others it may suit the overall goals for it to be more open-ended.

The process described is one which taps into an aspect of higher education which is seldom explicitly considered: the overall making sense of an

---

*Some tips*
(a) Don't wait until near the end of semester before you start to think about what your schedule might include. As you keep your portfolio, mark items which you want to refer to in your schedule. When the time comes to prepare your schedule it should mostly be a matter of writing it out in a coherent form on the basis of the various bits and pieces which are dotted around your portfolio and making some final judgements on what they all add up to.

(b) Let yourself be open to goals which you had not considered when you started. If you find that the subject is not what you expected make sure you either attempt to modify it to suit you, or re-appraise your goals sooner rather than later.

(c) The schedule need not be long, the length depends on how much detail you include and the style of presentation. Some people can fit everything on an A3-size chart, others might take 6–10 pages. There is no standard format; its form should be a reflection of what you find most comfortable to do.

(d) Some people get stuck on the idea of criteria. Put simply, criteria are the indicators by which you judge whether you have achieved what you wished to. For example, if one of my goals in taking the subject was to find out enough about different models of evaluation to be able to make a sensible choice in planning a review of the curriculum in my department, my criteria might include a statement of this and also break it down into parts: 'Knowledge of at least three evaluation models which have been used for curriculum evaluation including strengths and weaknesses of each, identification of what expertise is required to use them, and pitfalls to avoid in implementation'.

(e) If you are giving someone feedback on their schedule (this also applies to your own review of your work), it is often helpful to look at the consistency between goals, criteria, activities, evidence and judgements. For example, does the evidence relate to the goals, are the judgements based on the evidence cited? Even though you cannot comment on the substance of what is written, you can usually say something about how it hangs together and the general picture it portrays.

**Figure 9.3** *Tips for students in using a self assessment schedule*

educational experience. There is a great deal of research in higher education which suggests that students can do extremely well on conventional examinations, but fail to comprehend quite basic concepts (Marton *et al.*, 1984). One of the reasons for this is, perhaps, the nature of the assessment tasks (eg, Ramsden, 1988a). If students believe that they can successfully complete the required assessment tasks without a full appreciation of key concepts, then many of them will do so. The use of self assessment and the act of reviewing learning for a course does not, of course, ensure that students will apprehend key concepts, but it does give them the opportunity to review their own understanding and it can prompt them to return to ideas and seek to make sense of them.

## Problems and difficulties

There is a continuing problem in negotiating an assessment procedure in a course with external limitations on grading. There is always a tension between proposing and advocating a particular form and adopting a fully negotiated assessment strategy. The latter takes a great deal of class time, partly because of the anxieties many students have about assessment in general and their need for reassurance.

One year I attempted to fully negotiate the assessment process from first principles, but students became frustrated with the proportion of the total time available which was occupied by the discussion. In a limited timescale of 2x14 hours some compromise on negotiation of both curriculum and assessment procedure is necessary and groups have to be encouraged to limit the class time spent discussing assessment and to give the opportunity for students who are not satisfied to discuss particular issues outside the class. This leads to subsequent class time being spent only on assessment issues about which students feel strongly.

Students who do discuss matters individually with me (perhaps about one in ten) tend to have one of two concerns. Some doubt their ability to assess themselves: they are often people who have been successful in plotting a path through the conventional assessment system and have been surprised by how easy this has been for them. They are then confronted with the prospect of making their own judgements and they are anxious about what they might find. Their personal standards are high and they are worried about discovering that they are wanting in important respects: they fear that they will be exposed as not being competent. In this case, reassurance is required and expression of confidence in their ability to tackle the challenge, to encourage them to produce a first draft, is needed. Having started, they generally discover that they have accomplished much and are pleased to document it.

The second group have objections to the notion of self grading, arguing that grading is the teacher's responsibility and that it is irresponsible or unethical to hand this over to students and is a way of getting out of work. Depending on the particular emphasis of this criticism, it might be necessary either to start pragmatically by pointing out that this system involves the staff member in more work in that he or she has to do all the marking they would do otherwise and that far from opting out, they act as a moderator of self assessment, challenging interpretations and grades which do not appear justified. Alternatively, it might be appropriate to go back to first principles and discuss the nature of learning and assessment and the mutual responsibilities of teachers and students, leading to the conclusion that both have a role and that the conventional distribution of responsibilities is not intrinsically more educationally sound than the one in which we are engaged. There is one aspect of this second class of objections to which I am sympathetic. There is a contradiction to be found in having self grading moderated by a staff member in a situation in which the assessment policy of the school is unilaterally decided by staff. Most students found the required norm-referenced grading distribution to be educationally unsound. Unfortunately, neither I, nor the students, were successful in pursuading my colleagues of this point of view.

## Scope for wider application

The approach described is one which, acknowledging the contradiction, works quite satisfactorily in several contexts, and I am sufficiently convinced of its value to use it in almost all courses. Since I have moved to an institution with a different grading policy, the contradictions have disappeared! It suits circumstances in which a significant degree of responsibility is taken by students for the course and their own learning. Of course, it could be used in conventional classes, but it would then be another task to be completed and its potential for encouraging reflection and integration of learning might not be realised. Unless students have made a commitment to learning, as distinct from completing the course, they will turn anything into an exercise to be disposed of as easily as possible. The form is not the most important aspect of this innovation: it is the intentions and the appropriateness of context.

# Chapter 10

# Using Self Appraisal with Peer Feedback in Professional Development

*David Boud and James Kilty*

This chapter describes a series of workshop activities which have been used for self appraisal with university teachers. It presents a process which has been designed to help members of various professional groups monitor their own effectiveness in conjunction with their peers. The self appraisal process is one way of initiating a programme of professional development which is defined by the participants. Individuals define criteria of competence for their work, monitor their daily professional activities, review their performance and make plans for modifying their practice in the light of their appraisal. The chapter is written from the point of view of someone who may act as a facilitator for a self appraisal group and discusses issues in facilitating the process.

There are many ways to initiate staff development activities in institutions: through workshops or courses, through course development, through professional involvements or through administrative edict. Approaches which are based upon staff identifying their own needs are usually the most productive and present the greatest chances for long-term development.

The self appraisal workshop is one way of systematically initiating a self-defined programme of professional development. Unlike many other workshops, its content is not determined in advance although it is organised around an explicit process. It is an approach which provides a forum for individuals, in consort with their peers, to identify and engage in activities which they perceive as necessary and important for their own development. A self appraisal workshop may take any area of professional practice as its starting point. In connection with teaching it could focus on teaching skills, counselling, assessment, interpersonal relationships, etc. In the research area it could relate, for example, to research skills, funding, management of projects, relationships, or reporting. In administration, it could deal with organisational skills, committee work, chairing meetings, planning, or working with people.

The procedure outlined here has evolved from our experience over a number of years with a variety of professional groups and in a range of settings in order to meet the needs of experienced and relatively independent practitioners to appraise the quality of their practice. These have included doctors, dentists, managers, group facilitators, counsellors, teachers, trainers, clerics and students (eg, Heron, 1981). We have used it most extensively with teachers and staff developers in higher education.

## Rationale for professional self appraisal

Freedom to practice as one judges appropriate is one of the traditional foundations upon which academic life is built. Such autonomous professional practice brings with it the corresponding responsibility to monitor and maintain and improve the many and varied aspects of that practice. Engaging in the appraisal of one's own practice is thus particularly compatible with the self-determining nature of an academic, and is a form of research inquiry which is in accord with the ethos of universities. It is, however, a challenging activity. Self appraisal is usually carried out unsystematically or in a guarded way, especially when others are involved, and it can be relatively superficial. Peer appraisal is rarely carried out face-to-face. Where it is, it is often in a situation of hostility when something has gone wrong. The workshop described in this chapter was therefore developed to provide a systematic way of supporting participants in the process of self appraisal. In it, colleagues adopt a collaborative rather than an adversarial role within a context of mutual inquiry.

The content of the workshop is not predetermined, but chosen by participants in the light of their own needs and interests. The process is described here in terms of 19 stages, but the number and order can be varied with discretion. The activity of the workshop engages participants in defining criteria of competence and associated standards in any area of everyday practice; monitoring their activities in daily professional life; and reviewing their individual performance with others who are also involved.

The workshop aims to:

- introduce a strategy for the appraisal of performance which can be engaged in by peers as an on-going practice;

- provide an opportunity to reflect upon and review any area of professional competence;
- encourage individuals through this self appraisal to identify ways in which they might improve aspects of their own practices, selected by themselves;
- enhance the possibility of this improvement through the supportive scrutiny of peers;
- foster and develop support systems for individuals interested in self directed improvement by decreasing the loneliness of practice in isolation.

## Practicalities

The length of the workshop may be varied according to circumstances. However, the version which we have most commonly used requires two sessions of approximately three hours separated by approximately seven to ten days. The intervening period allows participants to engage in monitoring their own practice between sessions.

A degree of heterogeneity in the experience and background of participants enables a wide range of criteria and methods to be generated. When participants come from the same institution, we have found is easiest to start with those who do not work closely together and whose work does not directly affect that of others present. In this case, eight to ten members is a reasonable upper limit. When members are close colleagues, more than five is likely to require a lengthy closure time. When members are from different departments or institutions, the number will be limited only by the personal preference of the facilitator or the number of participants available who can facilitate small group work.

## The workshop process

The following sequence presents the stages we have commonly used, with some commentary about each. We have adopted a prescriptive approach in order to emphasise key elements. Those experienced in facilitating groups will be able to identify many variations on these themes.

*1. Initiate self appraisal group (approx. 30 mins)*

There are many ways in which a self appraisal group can be formed. It is preferable for a group to come together in response to a set of commonly felt needs. Our starting point has usually been either a desire by a group to engage in a self appraisal exercise or a problem area which has been identified and which might be approached by such an activity. It has also been initiated as part of an ongoing professional development programme and as a conclusion to a series of workshops on another topic.

We have made certain principles explicit from the start. Attendance is voluntary and participants are free to opt in or out of the activity. In staying, participants are asked to commit themselves to:

- reflecting on their own practices with the assistance of others;
- engaging in self appraisal of an agreed area of practice and to share as much or as little of that experience as they feel appropriate;
- attending all the scheduled meetings.

In some cases a detailed briefing circulated in advance is appropriate but in many workshops a simple outline of the basic idea of self appraisal is quite sufficient. However, we have found that plenty of time needs to be devoted at the start to explanation and discussion of the principles, before launching into the stages which follow.

## 2. Select an area of practice to appraise

The areas which will be the focus of activity can be elicited from the group and negotiated on the spot or they may already have been agreed in advance. The group as a whole might agree on a common area on which to work or individuals may select different ones. We have found it simpler in the first instance if a common area is considered. Once participants are familiar with the self appraisal process, it is possible for different participants to select quite different areas of their work to focus on. Examples of areas which have been selected include: lecturing, the management of time, consulting with students, and group leadership.

## 3. Agree on criteria of competent practice (approx. 45 mins)

Once the area to be appraised is decided, we pose the following questions to the participants to introduce the notion of criteria:

- How would you recognise competent practice in this area?
- What standards should apply to work of this kind?
- What would distinguish good and bad practice?

We have used the following three main ways to establish criteria.

*Brainstorming:* each participant contributes by free association to a central list which is not evaluated until all contributions have been made. The quickest way of proceeding is to suggest that each person selects up to three criteria which attract their attention or with respect to which they may say they perform well, moderately well or less well.

*Individual reflection:* each participant considers the questions listed above and composes one criterion which is submitted to a pool. Having seen the range proposed, participants choose a combination of items which meet their needs.

*Consulting the literature:* participants collect criteria from the literature of the field. This takes longer than the other methods and is more appropriate to a third or later cycle of a self appraisal process.

Participants often have difficulty in thinking in terms of criteria. It can be helpful for alternative ways of expressing this idea to be suggested, for example: 'How would you recognise if someone was doing. . . very well?' Additionally, it can be useful to distinguish between minimal criteria and criteria of excellence. In the first instance it is easiest to focus on a restricted range of minimal criteria.

## 4. Devise methods to evaluate quality of practice (approx. 30 mins)

Once criteria have been established it is necessary to devise simple ways of checking to see if they have been met by individuals in their usual practice. Participants tend to be very creative in designing methods for gathering and recording data. Appropriate methods should be credible to participants and simple and easy to use without prior training. Examples of such methods have included: simple checklists plus reminders to use them, immediate retrospective analysis of samples of the chosen practice, the use of audio and video-recording with review by a trusted colleague, and observation of selected kinds of activity.

## 5. Informal/private self appraisal

Before the conclusion of the first session each person is asked to make a personal assessment of his or her performance with respect to the criteria chosen. The aim is to begin the process of self appraisal and to decide if the criteria and the methods can be used in practice. This assessment is not made on the basis of anything other than the individual's own recollection: it is an 'armchair' appraisal. One way we have introduced this is to ask participants to reflect for five to ten minutes on their chosen criteria and methods and imagine themselves applying these to their own work. If they have any difficulties in seeing how this might be done, there is further discussion of the previous stages and how the criteria and methods can be modified to suit the circumstances imagined.

Before departing, participants should have agreed on how to use the period between the two sessions and they should have made arrangements with each other about mutual assistance they can provide (eg, in observing classes or in discussing experiences).

### 6. Self monitoring in daily practice (undertaken between workshop sessions)

During the period between the formally scheduled meetings, each person applies the methods to aspects of the practice they have selected. They monitor their activities using the methods which they have defined and keep a record of their findings and their responses to using the methods. It is important to have arranged the meetings so there is ample opportunity to monitor practice during the intervening period.

### 7. Revise practice in the light of self appraisal

Monitoring of activities inevitably raises participants' awareness about their own practice and about the monitoring procedures they have used. They tend to want to make immediate improvements to either or both of these. As some participants have associated the process with a scientific experiment in which nothing should be changed until all the data has been collected, we have found it helpful to reassure them that it is appropriate for changes to be made as soon as the need for them is identified.

### 8. Report to peers on the application of the self monitoring process and the procedures adopted (approx. 30 mins total)

The group reconvenes for a second meeting to examine their experience of self monitoring in daily practice. We ask each person to report on their experience of monitoring as a way of starting the meeting.

### 9. Disclose self appraisal (approx. five mins per person)

Following a brief presentation of the next stages, each person is invited to choose which of stages 9–15 they wish to engage with. The group divides the time available to ensure that all participants are involved.

All participants who so wish, describe their self appraisal with illustrative examples from daily practice, including:

- the criteria they adopted;
- the methods they used to produce the evidence; and
- the effects of the self monitoring procedures on their performance.

Some of the following stages (10–13) may appear at first sight to be rather repetitious. Separate stages have been listed to emphasise the distinctions between different types of feedback and to draw attention to the need for participants to consider carefully the nature and import of the responses they make to their peers.

**123**

*10. Receive clarificatory questions (approx. five mins per person for stages 10 to 14)*

Following this statement of their self appraisal, clarificatory questions may be invited by the person making the appraisal. These are intended to clarify and elaborate on what was disclosed. We illustrate what constitutes a clarificatory question by giving examples of types of question: 'Can you explain what you did. . . when. . . ?', 'How did you manage to observe. . . ?', 'Could you expand on. . . ?', 'What do you mean by. . . ?' We distinguish these from undesirable questions such as, 'Don't you think you should have. . . ?', 'Why didn't you. . . ?', 'What would have happened if. . . ?' which participants may be tempted to make.

*11. Specified peer assessment*

The person presenting the self appraisal may then elect to hear the extent to which their peers agree with the appraisal of those matters presented regardless of whether there exist independent data to support these responses. Responses can be given by other members of the group in a set order, or at random.

*12. Receive critical, probing or challenging questions*

Individuals may elect to receive more penetrating questions to help them critically examine the validity of their appraisal, eg, to reveal blind spots, or disclose restricted criteria. It is essential that no one be pressured into revealing information about themselves which they do not wish to discuss.

*13. Negative feedback. . . amplified doubts. . . devil's advocacy*

The person presenting the self appraisal may then elect to receive comments from others to help them reappraise and refine their self appraisal. Feedback of any or all of the three kinds, which are progressively more challenging, can be received from the group members. We point out that it is helpful if the feedback from others at this stage is deliberately subjectified. That is, comments and observations are of the type, 'I felt. . . when you said. . . ', or 'My reaction to. . . was. . . ', rather than the spurious objectivity of: 'You are. . . ', or 'We can all see that. . .', or 'Obviously you. . .', which translates personal opinion into apparent matters of fact. Attention is also drawn to the manner in which feedback is given. Tone of voice, posture, etc. may inhibit the recipient from freely considering the comments offered.

*14. Receive positive impressions and appreciations*

This stage is necessary if the person making the appraisal receives critical or negative comments. When this occurs there must be an explicit opportunity given to receive positive and appreciative responses. Not only can a predominantly negative feedback session be unhelpful to the recipients but it can also hinder others who may then be more inhibited in their own presentations later. Positive feedback and an appreciation of areas of strength has the effect of helping individuals remain motivated to build on their strengths and improve practice in areas of weakness.

## 15. Review self appraisal (10 mins for stages 15 and 16)

It is helpful to arrange a time at the end of the previous stage when individuals can reflect on their self appraisal, either with the group, in pairs, or alone. This can be combined with the next stage.

## 16. Make action plans

Either during the group meeting or after it participants make detailed action plans with respect to changes in practice they wish to make, and strategies for achieving these changes. We have found it helpful to invite participants to clarify the support that they require to help maintain momentum to carry out the action plan, and solve problems encountered in implementing it.

## 17. Revise criteria and methods

Following the opportunities provided in stages 9 to 15 for each member of the group to make a self appraisal and get feedback on it, we return to the earlier stages of the process and focus on criteria for good work in the given area and methods for monitoring it. We pose the question, should the earlier criteria and methods of assessment be revised in the light of experience?

If the group wishes to continue meeting it may decide either to repeat the cycle from stages 2, 3 or 4 or else to extend their application of steps 9–15 and continue on a regular basis until the needs of the members are met. The group may also branch out from performing a strictly appraisal function to encompass activities designed to develop the skills and knowledge of the participants in areas of common interest.

## 18. Self and peer accreditation

In some circumstances it is appropriate for the group to end the self appraisal activities by having individuals accredit themselves in various areas of their performance. The aim here is for each person to formally indicate those areas in which they are and are not able to operate competently and to receive the comments of their peers. Self and peer accreditation is less likely to occur in formal educational institutions than elsewhere and it is included here for the sake of completeness. We have adopted it, for example, in the training of counsellors and group facilitators.

*19. Group debriefing (10 mins plus, as needed)*

Before the close of the workshop, we give participants the opportunity to raise any issues which have emerged for them from the preceding process and which they wish to consider in the group before parting. We invite each person to say whatever they wish, paying particular attention to those who appear to have been personally exercised by the self appraisal activity or the feedback received.

## Principles of practice

The elements involved in the workshop – self appraisal, disclosure of that appraisal, and giving and receiving reactions to it – provide an interesting challenge to the participants. To be effective, participants need to be open to themselves and to others. This quite naturally gives rise to apprehensions about the personal and interpersonal risks involved in sharing assessments. Underlying our approach is a deep appreciation of the vulnerability of each person to discoveries of personal frailty and fallibility, the effect this can have on self confidence and the need for acceptance, respect and support from others in attempting to confront the issues which arise.

## The role of the facilitator

We believe that it is necessary in most cases for one person to act as a facilitator for the process. This person may or may not be drawn from the group undertaking the appraisal, but if the person is a full participant in the group it is crucial that he or she aware of the importance of the balance between group process and task content in small group situations.

We recommend that facilitators, as far as possible, act as models and demonstrate each stage first. They should:

- enable participants to have confidence in themselves and each other
- help create a supportive climate especially in higher risk areas and parts of the process
- help participants understand and appreciate each stage of the workshop
- allow adequate time for the process to unfold
- be ready to defuse any tensions arising
- if necessary, interrupt irrelevant personal and interpersonal attacks and interventions, and offer appropriate ground rules for behaviour

- ensure that participants carry out only those stages that they voluntarily choose
- help individuals to achieve closure on each stage
- review the various processes.

The very act of making suggestions about actions and activities in some sense acts to apply pressure on participants to conform to the suggestions made. It is particularly important that the stress made on the voluntary principle is not used as a manipulative device to enforce conformity. It is desirable that facilitators provide a range of options at each significant part of the process and act in such a way that they are seen to respect and concur with the decision made by each individual on whether or not they participate in any activity.

For example, in the second meeting of the group, the level of disclosure of outcomes and findings depends on the level of trust and cooperation. We remind participants of the voluntary principle and that they have the right to choose the extent of their disclosure and the feedback which they require. We ensure that no one gives any feedback other than that requested by the person concerned. The presumption is that people may choose to modify their self assessments in the light of helpful comments from others, even if these are critical.

During disclosure of self appraisals, no comments are sought from the rest of the group, who are asked to listen in silence. There may be a tendency for others to comment or pose questions during or after the statements of self appraisal. We intervene to ensure that the contract is kept. It is generally best to present self appraisals in a voluntary, rather than a predetermined order. Individuals then elect to receive comments in one or more of the following forms: clarificatory questions; specified peer assessment on a chosen matter; critical, probing or challenging questions; negative feedback or amplified doubts; and positive impressions and appreciations.

Participants need to be encouraged to make sensitive and aware discriminations between these different kinds of feedback. Of particular importance are the discriminations between:

- personal reaction and projection
- the subjective, the objective and the pseudo-objective
- constructive (ie, supportive, even if negative) and destructive criticism.

This may merit a separate practice stage using provided examples.

Following the stage of disclosing one's self appraisal (9), the need is clearest for a facilitator to draw the attention of the person and the group to the options available and to guard against the person receiving feedback other than that which has been sought. The entire process is predicated on the notion of self assessment and this means that all are responsible individually for what they do and say. They do not have to be subjected to the unsolicited views of others.

## Conclusion

The example of the self appraisal workshop given here not only illustrates how a self assessment process may unfold over time, but also points to some of the interpersonal considerations which are important in facilitating such a process. While the context here is the university, the same sensitivities and need for clarity of process are required when working in any practice setting. Self assessment is closely related to how we see ourselves and feedback needs to be provided in a suitable context and in a manner which is conducive to the recipients acting appropriately in the light of it. The importance of establishing guidelines for peer feedback and some additional suggestions for its use are given in Chapter 16.

# Chapter 11

# Self Assessment in Different Domains

*Angela Brew*

The aim of this chapter is to demonstrate the range of uses to which self assessment is currently being put. In Chapters 6 to 10 a number of examples were examined in depth. Here the aim is to indicate the diversity of self assessment with a greater number of examples discussed in less detail.

The scope of self assessment in terms of knowledge, understanding, skills, capability, competences and learning outcomes was examined in Chapter 5. These were related to different knowledge interests. The framework discussed there provides the starting point and the structure for this chapter. In relating examples to this framework, however, what we find is a spectrum of use rather than mutually exclusive categories. This is particularly so in relation to the more innovative examples where knowledge, skills and competences all come together in an emancipatory way. The framework cuts across discipline boundaries. Indeed, we have included examples from a wide range of disciplines. The examples discussed in previous chapters are referred to where appropriate in order to locate them within the overall framework.

Examples in this chapter are drawn from a variety of sources. One of these is a survey of self assessment practice in the UK which we conducted in 1993–4. As the UK Enterprise in Higher Education (EHE) initiative was designed to encourage innovation towards more student responsibility and involvement in learning, we contacted all EHE directors and asked them to supply names of colleagues known to be engaged in self assessment practices. This generated 89 people each of whom was sent a questionnaire asking about their use of self assessment. Twenty-nine responses were obtained providing a pool of examples on which we have drawn for this chapter. Indeed many respondents sent us course materials, handouts, papers and reports. These, as well as additional published and unpublished articles, have been invaluable in preparing this chapter.

We have interpreted self assessment as applying to the assessment by individuals of their progress or work. However, it is clear from responses to the survey that the term self assessment is often used to apply to a group's assessment of its work. The 'self' in this case is the group! We have included two examples of this. Some examples given in the survey responses, however, were of peer assessment. We disregard these as they are outside the focus of this volume.

## Technical interest

Knowledge which expresses a technical interest, as we saw in Chapter 5, represents a knowledge of facts which are objectified. It is the view of knowledge expressed in the natural sciences but is not confined to them. The essential idea is the production of technically useful knowledge which is geared towards control of objectified processes. Understanding is a question of absorbing. Assessment of knowledge in the technical interest is, by and large, a question of checking what facts, ideas, etc. or how much information has been understood. Similarly, in this conception, skills are viewed as objectified skills. In many of the cases discussed here, they tend to be seen more or less independently of each other. The context in which they are developed is not considered particularly relevant in assessing them. Indeed, as we saw earlier, the notion of transferability includes the idea of being able to use a skill in a variety of contexts. Similarly, competences in the technical domain are viewed as separate objectified statements of expected performance. Assessment is again a question of checking whether they have each been achieved. Indeed, in all of these cases, the simplest form of self assessment is a set of statements, the students' task being to assess how far they have achieved them.

An example of self assessment of knowledge is provided in the electronics course discussed in Chapter 7. The task of the students there was to check their knowledge and understanding of various aspects of electronic circuits according to a 'model' answer sheet. We say this is in the technical conception because there are right and wrong answers.

A second example of self assessment of knowledge of course content in this conception has been developed by Miriam Solomon at the University of New South Wales, in a second-year medical biophysics course. Students check their knowledge and understanding according to pre-specified criteria through preparing concept maps. Concept maps are introduced through handouts and a presentation by the tutor. They are a way of portraying the key concepts in a given content area. They involve ordering the key concepts in a hierarchical sequence and describing the relationships between them (Novak and Gowin, 1984). There may be several parallel lines representing different aspects of a topic, and there may be extensive cross-linking between various parallel lines. The completion of a map is a means of encouraging a deeper understanding of a topic and is an effective way of demonstrating a student's grasp of the subject for the purposes of assessment. As concept maps are graphical devices, a single map on a sheet of paper can summarise and present a large amount of complex information.

Students complete a concept map on one of three defined topics within the general topic of 'excitable tissues', action potentials, sensory receptors, or central synapses and the neuro-muscular junction. They then make a self assessment according to the following specified criteria:

1. Choice of key concepts. Are they significant concepts which need to be understood?
2. Validity of relationships between concepts. Are they correctly described by the connecting lines and linking words?
3. Hierarchy. Does the map show hierarchy? Is each subordinate concept more specific and less general than the concepts drawn above it?
4. Cross links. Does the map show meaningful connections between one segment of the concept hierarchy and another segment? Is the relationship shown significant and valid?
5. Clarity of layout. Does it make sense and is it well set out?
6. Examples and/or experimental evidence. Are they relevant and important?

Students are provided with information on ways to prepare a concept map and detailed marking sheets with criteria and marks to be allocated to each map. Each student presents his or her concept map in a tutorial group and answers questions about it from their peers. They receive a mark from their peers for their map and their handling of responses to it. Students receive their own mark unless it differs by more than 10 per cent from that of the tutor.

Subsequently, in teams of about six, students complete and hand in a group map consolidating four related topics (those listed above plus 'the resting membrane potential' which is undertaken as a class exercise to introduce the idea of concept maps). This is assessed by the group and by the tutor. All members of the group receive their own group mark unless it varies by more than 10 per cent from that of the tutor.

Another example, devised by Mike Green and Sue Drew at Sheffield Hallam University, for the postgraduate diploma in Property Valuation and

Management uses a set of non-negotiable criteria which are first discussed with students. The criteria concern knowledge and professional competencies of the subject of valuation. These include:

Accuracy of floor area calculation.
Understanding of the client's, or employer's needs and clarity of recommendations.
Structure and organisation of the report and valuation.
Prose style and technical accuracy (spelling, grammar, etc.).
Quality of analysis of rental value evidence using zoning method.
Quality of analysis of investment yield evidence.
Interpretation of market evidence.
Collaboration with colleagues and ability to meet deadlines.
(Assessment Form: Valuation, Sheffield Hallam University)

All the criteria are treated as objectified statements of outcomes. Students rate themselves using a five-point scale on an assignment attachment form (eg, McDonald and Sansom, 1978) and state any problems they encountered. A similar assignment attachment form with a set of non-negotiable criteria is used in the Department of English Studies at Sheffield Hallam by Dave Hurry. The criteria on which students rate themselves include:

Assignment's relevance to title and nature and scope of the work as stated in your introduction.
Structure/organisation.
Understanding and use of relevant critical terms and concepts.
Originality of interpretation.
Persuasiveness of interpretation.
(BA English Studies Literature Assignment, Sheffield Hallam University)

This example moves us into the academic skills domain but still remains within the same broad technical conception of knowledge. Another example, devised by Blumhof and Broome at the University of Hertfordshire, takes us further. The purpose of their self assessment process is to raise students' awareness of the importance of transferable skills, enable them to 'reflect on the importance of different skills and help them to identify skills areas to be worked on' (Blumhof and Broom, 1991). The procedure has been designed in the Division of Environmental Sciences but could equally be applied in any discipline area. It enables students to identify the skills that will need their special attention and to map their improvements. The list of skills is as follows:

1. *Communication and study skills*
   effective reading
   writing
   verbal
   listening
   visual/presentation
   foreign language
   numeracy
   computer literacy
   information skills
2. *Social skills*
   teamwork
   assertiveness
   leadership
3. *Intellectual skills*
   problem solving
   analytical thinking
   creativity
   (Blumhof and Broom, 1991)

Personal skills, management and career development skills and technical skills are also so defined. In each of three terms, students assess whether they are weak, average or strong and identify areas to be worked on.

An example of transferable skills being developed alongside subject-specific skills, but considered and assessed quite separately, is provided by Pandy Brodie from Chester College, Department of Physical Education and Sports Science. Students assess themselves and each other on a five-point scale (poor, acceptable, fair, good and very good) on a range of personal skills:

A willingness to take personal initiatives.
Innovation in problem solving.
A willingness to take risks.
A concern to gain maximum effect from your effort.
A capacity to sustain self-directed effort.
A concern to gain maximum effect from materials, resources, etc.
An ability to communicate values, ideas, and instructions effectively.
An ability to gain the co-operation of others.
A capacity to deliver to deadlines.
An ability to develop a critique of those aspects of enterprise which are contentious or controversial as values.
(Chester College, 1993a)

Questions are provided to prompt students' responses. For example the prompt for the last skill is:

> Do I (am I prepared to) recognise and understand reasons for actions and opinions which contradict my own values? eg. within Enterprise. Do I stand up for my own values? Am I prepared to see the world from somebody else's point of view? Am I prepared to accept that people have a right to actions/opinions which contradict my own views? (ibid, 1993a)

These skills, as in the previous example, are objectified. They are separated from the course content and assessed separately. This is therefore an example of the self assessment of transferable skills with a technical interest. Students on this course also assess themselves, again on a five-point scale, on a range of course-specific skills which include:

*Climbing:*
1. Fitting harness and helmet.
2. Rope handling.
3. Climbing rock face.
4. Belay.
5. Abseil.

*Canoeing:*
1. Paddle action.
2. Kayak control forward.
3. Kayak control backward.
4. Kayak control basic turning.
5. Capsize drill.

*Sailing:*
1. Rigging.
2. Sailing from shore.
3. Turning – going about.
4. Sailing to a mark.
5. Gybing.
6. Capsize drill.

(ibid, 1993a)

Again we see a separate objectively assessed set of skills. In these examples the checklists prompt discussion prior to students' final assessment. Students provide examples demonstrating appropriate behaviours to support their assessment decisions.

As far as competences in the technical conception are concerned, lists of objectified competency statements or learning outcomes are provided by a tutor or perhaps professional body. The student assesses his or her competency against the given standard. An example in the domain of practical teaching (teaching practicum) is provided by Sally Heaney also at Chester College. In her response to the survey she described how the current approach evolved:

> At the outset, students decided the criteria for assessment, as part of the appraisal process. This has had to change to accommodate various governmental directives. There is now a specification of criteria for each phase of school experience which sets the agenda for the appraisal processes.

Broadly the competences of primary school teaching which are reviewed and assessed concern:

- content, planning and preparation.
- teaching skills.
- observation, assessment and evaluation.
- classroom management.
- professional development.
  (ibid, 1993b)

For each of these categories of competence an assessment level is recorded. This is based on the criteria adopted for each of the three appraisals. The competence descriptors are:

5  developed to a high level
4  well developed
3  competent
2  needs further development of practice/shows some inadequacies
1  limited response
0  not evident.
(ibid, 1993b)

Students are advised to prepare for appraisal by making a self assessment using the competences listed for attention during the term. They then ask a student colleague, one who has made an observation of children's learning for them, to discuss the agenda with them and record their shared view of achievements. They then repeat this procedure with their placement class teacher. They discuss the agenda with their college tutor, draft the summary of achievements and points for development in the light of these discussions and submit a copy of the completed appraisal for practical teaching to their tutor.

Each practical teaching appraisal has to contain a report from their supervising schoolteacher and the summary of strengths and points for development, which has been assessed, graded and completed by their tutor for school experience. All three appraisals of practical teaching must be complete and a copy of each submitted to achieve a pass for practical teaching. Some of the competences used in the Summer term are as follows:

*Preparation and planning skills*
Demonstrates knowledge of the subject.
Demonstrates knowledge of National Curriculum requirements.
Is able to promote the development of children's literacy and numeracy.
Is able to promote the development of children's social and problem-solving skills.
Etc.

*Teaching skills*
Is able to sustain children's attention.
Uses children's contributions productively.
Incorporates the use of information technology effectively.
Uses questioning and explaining strategies, and is able to give of instructions, effectively.
Etc.

*Observation assessment and evaluation skills*
Observations are used to record children's achievements.
Is able to present reports to parents on children's progress.
Etc.

*Classroom management*
Is able to manage teaching the whole class.
Uses technology equipment and materials effectively.
Maintains an aesthetically pleasing, orderly and stimulating learning environment.

*Professional development*
Contributes positively within the school context.
Engages in professional dialogue with colleagues regarding the specialist teaching subject.
Identifies personal professional development needs.
Identifies strategies for meeting these needs.
Etc.

*Subject knowledge and application*
Demonstrates an adequate command of the teaching of:
Science.
Art.

Music.

A selected cross-curricular theme from the National Curriculum.

The specialist teaching subject in school.

*Final criteria*

Is able to teach effectively and to secure effective learning.

Is able to maintain discipline and manage pupil behaviour.

Is ready to take a class of his or her own as a newly qualified primary teacher next September.

(Chester College, 1993b)

## Communicative Interest

In the second group of examples, knowledge is, broadly speaking, viewed as a construction. It is negotiated in communication with others. In this domain, a number of different and sometimes competing conceptions of reality may come together. In the process of understanding, students develop their personal meaning. They make socially constructed knowledge their own. From a communicative perspective, skills are viewed as part of a process of negotiation; the outcomes of some kind of dialogue or conversation. Transferable skills are likely to be integrated into academic study. They are viewed as part of a composite of skills within a broad capability in each person. Indeed, skills are more likely to be seen as integral to the process of acquiring knowledge. In this domain, competency is viewed as a professionally defined construct. Indeed, we see the holistic notion of competences as described by Hager *et al.*, (1994, p.5):

> They are holistic in that competence is a construct that is inferred from performance of relatively complex and demanding professional activities (or elements). The relative complexity of the elements can be gauged from the fact that a typical profession involves no more than 30–40 such key professional activities.

In the engineering design example discussed in Chapter 7, the self assessment procedure recognised that there are different ways of approaching a design task but that decisions have to be taken at a number of clearly recognisable stages. Students were asked to make qualitative judgements about the ways in which they tackled each of these.

Another example of self assessment being used to test knowledge and understanding and which has a communicative orientation has been devised by Peter Lindler for third-year botany students at the University of Cape Town. The aim was to bring to a test situation a measure of discussion and self marking so that students would improve their ability to assess their own knowledge. Through discussion and negotiation, students progressively come to understand what constitutes a good answer and the extent to which they have achieved it. How the test was conducted is described by Greg Pastol from the Teaching Methods Unit:

> The students were told about the test in advance, and had to prepare as for a conventional test. At the test, the students were seated in a U-shaped arrangement facing the board. In front of the board sat the two academics who administered the test, Peter Linder and John Bolton and myself, as an observer. The testers began by distributing a test question-paper to which they had both contributed questions.

> They then selected one particular question from the paper and gave the students five minutes to tackle the question individually. The students were instructed *not* to provide a full written answer, but to sketch an *outline* of the way they would have answered the test question in an examination situation.

> When the time was up, Peter asked them to stop writing, and called upon one student to describe her answer to the class. Peter then brought other students into the discussion, inviting them to add to the content already aired or to challenge aspects of the first student's answer.

> After getting as much out of the class as was reasonably possible in the given time, Peter summarised verbally the ingredients expected of a 'good' answer to the test question. He then asked the students to write underneath their own answer-outlines a mark out of 10 for how much they had known in relation to the criteria for a 'good' answer.

> They handed in their slips of paper, and proceeded to tackle the next question while the two testers read over the answer-outlines and made some comparisons. During this stage the testers moderated the students' self assessments by allocating a mark of their own. They recorded for each student and each question answered, the student's own mark, the tester's mark and the difference between the two. Such records reveal whether a given student was likely to over- or underestimate his or her own performance consistently.

> On this particular occasion the testers found that they tended to concur with the self-ratings of one third of the class, pushed up the marks of roughly one third and reduced the marks of one third. Over a number of questions, a given student's self-ratings were sometimes accurate and sometimes not.

> A number of test questions were dealt with in this way. Discussion became livelier as the test progressed. At the end of the test each student was asked to state openly what percentage he or she deserved for the whole test, and what had been gained by the experience.

Student comments indicated a widespread recognition that there are distinct advantages in this method of testing. Although a minority of students had felt uncomfortable by being made to speak in front of a group, the predominant feeling was that this kind of test:

1. Obliges one to know one's work thoroughly in the first place, since one can no longer rely on the usual test-taking strategy of dropping key words and hoping the examiner won't pay too much attention to the weak links between them,
2. Gives one a sobering perspective on the extent of one's knowledge relative to the knowledge of other class members, and
3. Should be used more often, and introduced as early as possible in one's course of study, in order to wean one off habits of straight-forward regurgitation.

(Pastol, 1993, p.3)

In this instance, performance on one of the test questions provides a trigger for the discussion of assessment criteria.

At the University of Lancaster in 'Sociological Methods and Analysis', each student is given a project report written by a student in a previous year of the course. Students then divide into groups of three. They read and discuss their reports and attempt to allocate a mark to each. They then develop a short list of the criteria they have used. In the second part of the workshop, group rapporteurs bring back to the whole class their ideas and questions, and with the help of the class tutor a list of agreed criteria is drawn up on the overhead projector. Students assess themselves according to these criteria (Knight, 1993).

Another example of students progressively coming to understand criteria is provided by Maggie Huscroft for second-year design students at the University of Westminster:

> . . . we began the project with an assessment of professional information graphic design.

> Step one: The entire year group visited The Natural History Museum to see how other designers tackled the problem of giving the general public information about a variety of subjects. Each student was asked to choose a specific exhibit and write an analysis of it. They were asked to state how it succeeded in its communication and why they thought it successful.

> Step two: Back in the studio, a couple of days later, I met the students in two seminar groups, and we drew out a list of attributes for a successful piece of graphic information design. This list was to form the criteria for evaluation of the students' own work.

> Step three: A mid way evaluation of design proposals, sitting around the

'board room table' and using staff and peers for feedback. An informal discussion with no script.

Step four: I led an end of project seminar, using notes that I had made from the students' written analysis of the museum exhibits. We checked out the work displayed, against the students' statements of what constituted good graphic information design practice.

Step five: At the end of the seminar I distributed a project evaluation script for the students to complete over the following two days. Their evaluation of their progress on the project determined how they would proceed with the project, whether they would continue with it or shelve it and begin a new problem, based on a design for print.

Step six: The assessment of the project was concluded through a series of small group tutorials where students can compare their evaluation with that of peers and staff who have access to the evaluation scripts. (Huscroft, 1993)

Another example where students are involved in negotiation with each other and with the tutor is presented by Jill Spencer from the University of Plymouth. This example moves us into the self assessment of skills viewed from a communicative perspective. Students negotiate criteria by which their performance will be judged, demonstrate their skills, examine critically their own and others' performance using the agreed criteria, review and reflect on their performance and identify areas of strength and areas for improvement. The module focuses on the interpersonal skills needed by lawyers. The aim of it is to develop students' confidence and competence in the skills of drafting (letters and documents), client interviewing, negotiation and advocacy. Spencer describes how one of the skills is learnt and assessed:

### Generating Criteria for Drafting Skills

All students on the course have at some time written a letter. They may not all have created a document, although most have probably seen one. All are likely to have views on what the characteristics of a well-written letter or document are. The first lecture/discussion period on drafting involves students generating criteria by which they feel a letter should be judged. These are noted by the tutor on the overhead projector.

Typically the 'easy' criteria are picked out first, correct spelling, grammar and punctuation, then other features are addressed: whether the language used is appropriate to the recipient of the letter. The most difficult, also the most important, issue is likely to be addressed last: does the letter achieve the writer's objectives? Students are driven ultimately, if perhaps reluctantly, to the conclusion that even though a letter is beautifully set out, with no spelling or grammatical mistakes, it is of no use if it appears that it will not achieve what the writer wants and intends it to achieve.

In the initial workshop students are given a badly written (fictitious) letter from a solicitor to his/her client and are asked to use the jointly agreed criteria to pick out the letter's faults and to compare their observations with others in the class. They are asked to redraft the letter eliminating the faults as a homework exercise. They bring their efforts to the next workshop and share and compare their work. In this way they appraise each other's performance, are supplied with models of alternative solutions, and obtain tutor feedback. The same sequence is then followed in respect of document drafting.

The complexity of the tasks given to students increases each week. They are asked, in role-play situations, to write letters and draft documents to secure specific, given objectives. They are introduced to the use of a 'precedent' document for drafting purposes and learn that it requires an intelligent and holistic adaptation to be appropriate for use in a novel situation. In the light of their experience and the expertise they have gained students are given the opportunity to add to, or amend, the initially agreed criteria. The result is that at the end of the six week block the students have themselves, in negotiation with their tutor, created the criteria by which their summative assessment will be judged.

### Peer Appraisal

Peer appraisal is one of the essential features of the module. Students require guidelines on the giving and receiving of feedback in order to be able to gain maximum advantage from the process. In the early stages they are apt to make only positive, non-specific comments. It may be nice to hear that someone thinks your work 'good' but it is not of much use if you are not told why . . . Guidelines were introduced to the students who became skilled in their use as the module progressed.

While students may be reluctant . . . to engage in a peer assessment exercise which involves quantitative judgements, ie, the awarding of marks or grades, they more readily adopt a supportive and constructive approach to a detailed qualitative assessment of each other's perfor-mance once they are familiar with the guidelines.

### Summative Assessment

At the end of each six week block students are assessed on progress made with the skill on which they have been working. The mechanics of the assessment are:

- Students and tutor agree the criteria on which performance is to be assessed.
- Students are briefed, verbally and with written instructions, on the

task to be undertaken. The task will test their ability to perform the skill in question.

- Students carry out the task and demonstrate their level of attainment in the skill.
- Students obtain verbal and written feedback on their performance, based on the criteria agreed, from at least two peers of their choosing.
- Students self assess in the light of peer feedback received.
- Students make an appointment with the tutor to discuss their performance and to negotiate their final mark.

For the summative assessment in drafting, each student is allocated a minimum of twenty minutes of the tutor's time to negotiate his/her final mark. (In the case of the remaining skills, where students are assessed in pairs, a minimum of half an hour per pair is allocated.)

Prior to this assessment tutorial the tutor will have reviewed the student's work and evaluated it against the jointly agreed criteria. The work for the drafting assessment consists of a letter and a document. For the other skills it is a video of the students' performance in a role-play exercise lasting approximately twenty-five minutes. (The students themselves have a copy of the video to study and to show to the peers they have chosen to give them feedback.)

(Spencer, 1993)

In this example the assessment reflects the fact that the development of legal skills goes hand-in-hand with the development of knowledge. All are part of a process of negotiation. This example focuses on a similar issue to the one presented in Chapter 8, namely, how to assess law skills. There the students developed criteria and assessed themselves in the skills of group participation.

The negotiation of criteria for assessment is one way in which self assessment reflects a communicative interest. Yet such negotiation is not always needed. An interesting example where a set of criteria is given for student self assessment and for negotiated group self assessment has been developed by Allan Davies at Worcester College of Higher Education. His approach had the intention to develop a deep approach to learning. Criteria were developed in four domains of art and design practice:

A. the conceptual
  1. ideas
  2. information
B. the productive
  1. design
  2. materials
  3. media

142

C.  the contextual/critical
D.  lifeskills
    1.  personal skills
    2.  interpersonal skills
    (Davies, 1994)

The carefully developed criteria were based on the four categories in the SOLO taxonomy (Biggs, 1987) which describe learning outcomes in terms of the levels of understanding students have. For example the 'ideas' domain included the following:

1.  Generated only one or two ideas for selection.
    Demonstrated limited judgement in selection.
    Developed the ideas to an obvious conclusion.
2.  Deliberately generated several ideas for selection.
    Some of the ideas were of good quality.
    Demonstrated judgement in selection.
    Developed the ideas beyond the obvious.
3.  Generated a substantial number of ideas.
    Many of the ideas were imaginative.
    Demonstrated a clear understanding of appropriateness of ideas in selection.
    Developed the ideas to a sound and imaginative conclusion within the set deadline.
4.  Demonstrated a broad range of mature ideas.
    Most of the ideas demonstrated a developed imagination.
    Demonstrated sound understanding in selecting ideas to progress.
    Demonstrated imagination and innovation in the development of the ideas and concluded the task within the time set.
    (Davies, 1994)

Students worked in learning teams of five or six. At the end of the project they discussed their own and each others' projects according to these criteria.

> By focusing on learning each member of the group was able to explain and test out their ideas and modify them in the light of supportive comments. (Davies, 1994)

Another example of self assessment where a group of students assesses their performance on a project is provided by Peter Hedges from the Department of Civil Engineering at Aston University. The project's objectives are:

1.  knowledge acquisition: eg, water resource development projects, the UK planning process;

2. teamwork and communication skills development;
3. development of decision-making skills (the project is open-ended);
4. introduction to the environmental and social implications of a major civil engineering scheme.
   (Hedges, 1993)

Students work on a simulated public inquiry project in small groups. Their ability to work in a team and how they explore the various aspects and the implications of a major water resource development dictate how they perform. Peter Hedges describes the process:

> For the past two years the subject of the project has been the Broad Oak Reservoir scheme in Kent. Documentation relating to an actual inquiry into this scheme is available, and the information forming the core of the project has been distilled from this. For the scheme under consideration outline data relating to demand forecasts, engineering works, and costs have been gathered together in a single 'Engineering Report'. Information on possible alternative developments and the less tangible aspects (eg, visual intrusion, effects on water quality, natural habitats, employment, etc.) has also been extracted, and forms a pool of additional data made up into some twenty separate reports.
>
> In the initial stages students assume the role of the water companies with the object of deciding whether or not they wish to promote the scheme. Their decision has to be made on the basis of the facts provided in the Engineering Report, the company's statutory duties and the additional information which they acquire. This information, usually in the form of the supplementary reports referred to above, is supplied the week after a formal request has been submitted.
>
> Mid-way through the project each group informs the supervisor which scheme it favours and is allocated their role for the Public Inquiry. Proofs of Evidence and QCs' speeches are prepared, and distributed to the other groups prior to the Inquiry.
>
> The Inquiry is conducted strictly in accordance with the procedures adopted in real life. Groups which have concentrated on the technical and financial aspects of the scheme invariably fail to be convincing, whereas those who have taken the environmental and social implications into consideration are much more successful.
>
> The final activity is a debriefing session and the self/peer assessment exercise. The first attempt at introducing self/peer assessment was on an ad hoc basis. Each group of students was asked to award a mark out of twenty to each of its members – a maximum of five marks for each of: contribution to group dynamics; teamwork; understanding; and initiative.
>
> No formal feedback was attempted following this experiment, but observations of student behaviour proved very enlightening. Of the six

groups taking part, three worked openly and discussed each individual's contribution in turn. One group worked in total silence, each individual assessing all group members. The marks awarded by each individual were subsequently averaged to produce a final mark.

At the extremes, one group sent each individual out of the room in turn whilst their contribution was discussed and a mark arrived at. The individual was then invited back, told of the decision and given the opportunity to negotiate a revision if they felt the mark was unfair. The final group clearly found the process extremely threatening. All members of the group were given the same mark, the magnitude being determined by averaging the score given by each member. Within this group, one individual abrogated responsibility totally and awarded everyone maximum marks.

The following is the sequence of steps which, based upon this experience, have subsequently been employed in the self/peer assessment process:

1. Working together each group assigns weightings to the six criteria to be used in the assessment (see Table 11.1) – weightings should be made on the basis of how important each criteria is felt to be relative to the other five. 30 points are available for distribution between the criteria. A group could choose to give all the criteria equal weight (ie, assign them each 5 points). Alternatively they may decide, for example, that 'Application/taking fair share of work' is of more importance than 'Attendance and timekeeping' – they then might assign 6 points to criteria 4, and only 4 points to criteria 3. A record of the agreed weightings is maintained and values are inserted into the appropriate spaces on each of the forms used.

**Table 11.1** Table used in assigning weightings to the six assessment criteria

| Skill | Criteria for self/peer assessment | Weighting |
|---|---|---|
| Ability to work as part of a group | 1. Ability to arrive consensus/overcome difficulties<br>2. Giving & accepting support/facilitating group effort | |
| Contribution to group | 3. Attendance and timekeeping<br>4. Application: taking fair share of work | |
| Initiative | 5. Ability to generate good ideas/solve problems<br>6. Gathering/researching additional/new information | |

2. Each individual takes one of the appropriate forms and assigns him/herself a mark between 1 and 5 for each of the criteria listed (1 = poor ... 5 = excellent). This is followed by a brief comment, in the space provided, justifying the mark selected. This activity should enable the individual to compare his/her own perception of their contribution, with that of the group as a whole. This sheet remains

the property of the individual and is not discussed with the other members of the group, unless *all* members of the group agree to do so.

3. The group is split into two or three sub-groups. The sub-groups then give each individual within the full group a mark for each of the six criteria. Again the mark is on a scale of 1 to 5 (where 1 = poor ... 5 = excellent), and each mark should be followed by a brief comment justifying the decision.

4. The full group reassembles, and using the results from the deliberations in the subgroups, a final mark between 1 and 5 is negotiated for each criteria for each individual. The final marks, recorded on another form, must be followed by a comment justifying the group decision.

5. The Summary Sheet is completed to determine individual overall marks out of 30.

Students are provided with a set of guidelines for the self/peer assessment exercise, which explain and set out the above sequence. In addition, the following observations (quoted from the guidelines) are made to indicate to the students that the problems they may experience during the exercise are recognised:

> This may well prove to be a very difficult, even threatening, exercise for everyone concerned. It is therefore essential that you are totally honest with each other *and* with yourselves. (Hedges, 1993, p.6)

An example of self assessment used in relation to competences and with a communicative knowledge interest is given by Sally Heaney from Chester College. The Teaching Competence Profile is a development of the Appraisal of Practical Teaching discussed previously. A portfolio has been described as:

> a means of supporting development and assessing achievement in areas of technical, professional and personal competence not necessarily covered by more traditional forms of teaching and assessment. (Payne *et al.*, 1993, p.87)

At Chester College, students support their claims to competency with evidence compiled in a portfolio. The evidence may include their academic and professional qualifications, in-service courses attended, lesson notes, notes on lessons observed by colleagues, children's work and self-evaluation notes. The competences are arranged under the following headings:

Curriculum content, planning and assessment.
Subject knowledge and application.
Assessment and recording of pupils' progress.

Teaching strategies and pupils' learning.
Teaching strategies and techniques.
Further professional development.

The competences are more holistic than in the Appraisal of Practical Teaching. For example some of the competences under 'Teaching Strategies and Techniques' are:

Newly qualified teachers should be able to:

- establish clear expectations of pupil behaviour in the classroom and secure appropriate standards of discipline.
- create and maintain a purposeful, orderly and supportive environment for their pupils' learning.
- present learning tasks and curriculum content in a clear and stimulating manner.
- teach whole classes, groups and individuals and determine the most appropriate goals and classroom contexts for using these and other teaching strategies.
- use a range of teaching techniques, and judge when and how to deploy them.

The students do not negotiate and critically evaluate the criteria as in the emancipatory examples discussed later. However, neither are they as cut and dried as in the Appraisal of Practical Teaching. This is an example of self assessment of competences in the communicative interest because of the negotiation regarding achievement of these broad areas of competency based on a portfolio of evidence. This is similar to the use of self assessment for the recognition of prior learning. Here the profile emphasises the need for the student teacher to remain reflective about his or her own teaching for the future.

Another example of self assessment of competency in the communicative interest is the use of portfolios for the assessment of nursing practice at the University of Portsmouth. The portfolio here is a continuous piece of work, so assessment is both formative and summative. It is done by students assessing themselves in discussion and negotiation with their peers and with the academic and clinical placement tutors. Melanie Jasper describes how it works:

The starting point for the portfolio is a clear identification of the outcomes expected by the student. These relate to the professional competencies required by the regulating body, but are transformed into 'student-friendly' language so that the student can see exactly what they have to achieve within the specified timescale. They relate to theory, skills, and practical competence. In order for the student to negotiate a way through the course, the learning outcomes are broken down into a manageable series of themes, which continually build upon each other. The student builds upon this framework by adding their own material in the form of reading, care plans, notes, etc. Thus the portfolio becomes a comprehensive record of their training, individualised to their particular needs.

The individual work by the student is supplemented by a regular planned tutorial with the academic tutor, group work, and clinical supervision in the workplace.

Essential reading, clinical and theoretical objectives are identified for the student by the teacher leading the theme. Students are guided to key texts and expected to read these prior to the start of the week's theme. The theoretical objectives provide the level of the knowledge to be achieved, and thus enable the student to gauge their own workload needs. The clinical objectives relate to competencies expected by the end of the course. (To enable the student to gain an overview of the clinical competencies they are given all of these in a separate document.) By attaching these objectives to the weekly theme they become manageable for the student and practice supervisor, and assist the bridging of the theory-practice gap.

The first task for the student, in using the portfolio, is to evaluate their previous learning and accomplishments relating to that theme (Lyte and Thompson, 1990; Lambeth and Volden, 1989). This enables the student to assess their own levels of knowledge and plan to remedy any deficits identified. The students write their own objectives for meeting these, both theoretical and practical. . . .

The student turns the objectives into a learning plan, which is reviewed with the academic tutor. The individual components of this are entered into a grid which documents their acquisition on an incremental basis.

Each week the student analyses a critical incident relating to the week's theme. This is subsequently used at the weekly portfolio workshop. The emphasis for this component is placed on an incident that is significant for the student in terms of their learning, and that provides the material for examining the relationship between theory and practice. It also serves the important purpose of identifying the areas that the student finds stressful, providing an indication for extra work related to the theme, or increased tutorial support.

The Reflective Journal is the culmination of the week's work and focuses the students on the learning outcomes of the course in general. The students are asked to review their week and identify the objectives that have been achieved, and those that are yet to be acquired. By reviewing their progress on a regular basis the students gain the satisfaction of monitoring and controlling their own learning. (Jasper, 1994)

Formative assessment takes place first in a monthly tutorial. In this the student is helped with their self assessment in relation to their professional development and the acquisition of competences. Secondly, there is a portfolio workshop where students work in small groups with their academic tutor. Thirdly, formative assessment takes place in clinical supervision. Summative assessment is criterion-referenced according to student guidelines for the portfolio and portfolio marking criteria. The strategy of providing students with clear guidelines for the assessment at the beginning of the course enables them to plan their work to meet these criteria. The idea is that the marking criteria are sufficiently broad to encompass the individuality of each student whilst ensuring a uniform standard is met.

## Emancipatory interest

A key component of the emancipatory domain of knowledge interests is a meta-critique of the very determinants of constructed knowledge. Students not only construct meaning for themselves, they also come to a critical understanding of the way in which that is done. In the emancipatory perspective, meta-level skills including critical reflection may be developed through a change in teaching towards an emphasis on student autonomy and responsibility or through other strategies where there is a questioning of assumptions. Where competences are concerned, criticism of the competences themselves is a characteristic of this mode. Competency statements are viewed as attempts to make relatively stable statements of learning outcomes which are to be questioned through the practice of self assessment. In the emancipatory conception, skills, knowledge and understanding, competences and learning outcomes are often difficult to separate. However, as mentioned above, we are concerned here not to set up reified categories, but rather to illustrate different domains of the usage of self assessment.

In the emancipatory interest, self assessment often merges into critical self-reflection and vice versa:

> We believe that student self-evaluation represents this kind of transformative assessment at its best. It represents two crucial views of assessment: as a dialogue, something done with, not to, students; and as a reflection of individual meaning-making, a way of constructing meaning that in turn profoundly influences behaviour. Incorporating student self-evaluations into an institution's array of assessment efforts thus suggests a deeper understanding of assessment than the way it is typically understood. More importantly, the use of student self-evaluation signifies a richer understanding of learning and the purposes of

higher education. Recognition of the significance of student self-evaluation calls educators to 'revision' learning as transformation and to reposition students and their relationship to the subject matter as the core of the educational enterprise. (Moore and Hunter, 1993, p.79)

John Cowan (1988) describes how he and his students came to see assessment as a process where course objectives, criteria and performance were identified and compared 'as objectively as possible by the learner'. In his example of self assessment in Civil Engineering Design at Heriot-Watt University, he demonstrates the interrelationship between course content, development of student understanding and the way in which teaching has to change if students are to develop control over the self assessment process. He describes what he agreed with the students:

1. Each student would have complete control over the weekly choice of objectives and over criteria and assessment. Even if requested, I would not do anything which could influence the decisions taken – although I should facilitate the processes involved if I were invited to do so. Other students would comment on objectives and outputs, but they too would have no other influence on the assessment.
2. Each student would give and receive comments on the objectives and activities of others when asked to do so.
3. Each student would carry out a formal self-appraisal (in a manner which we did not specify) twice during the academic year, exposing the same to comments and questions and making reasonable response to these – even if only to explain the grounds for rejection or disagreement.
4. The students would make their learning available to other members of the group on request.

(Cowan, 1988, p.193)

In commenting on this process Cowan noted:

Introducing and consolidating a self assessed course in my department called for a complete change in my role as a university teacher. The old authoritarian strategies which had served me well when I controlled assessment (and hence the hidden curriculum), were rendered totally inappropriate. I now took authority only for the decision to pass authority to the learners, and then I had to devote time and effort to learning my role in this entirely new situation. For I still had a responsibility to facilitate learning and development; although I had deliberately passed over to the learners the authority for the direction of their learning and for the appraisal of it, I could not regard this as an abdication of my responsibility as a teacher – which I now had to work out and define in these strange new circumstances. (Cowan, 1988, pp.193–4)

Another example is provided by Robert Edwards at the University of Glamorgan in a Computer Science course on data processing. His students perform defined tasks and then set up their own competency standards and assess themselves according to these. This example falls in the emancipatory domain because the discussions which take place are not about whether the student has met a set of pre-negotiated criteria, as in the examples in the communicative domain discussed above. The criteria and students' understanding of them develop as they proceed. Like John Cowan, whose work, he acknowledges, influenced him, Edwards had to change his teaching as the students' self assessment developed. He describes the procedure like this:

> In order to exercise and test their understanding of the subject, students were asked to use a computer to create files and then to process them. Three separate but related tasks were set. Each one was open-ended to a certain extent, and there were several valid ways in which each one could be tackled.
>
> . . . there was freedom for the student to decide not only how to do the task, but also what to do, and that she is prompted to decide why she is doing each task, and *what* she is learning. The student has to decide not only her own criteria for marking but also her own marks.
>
> Throughout the time that the tasks were being worked on, I constantly encouraged students to ask me questions and to see me individually or in groups, in tutorial time or outside it about any difficulties they had. Whether or not such persuasions are successful must depend a great deal on the lecturer's style and personality. Although many comments from students indicated that I had succeeded in this area, there were still several students who never asked for help but who appeared to me to have needed it.
>
> In order to have her marks recorded in my register of marks, a student had to spend at least 10 minutes discussing with me what she had actually *done* to deserve her marks. This discussion allowed me to point out where the responses to the tasks were not fulfilling my expectations, and where the student seemed to have missed the point of them. It also allowed me to suggest points or ideas the student might have missed: to clear up misunderstandings; and, perhaps most importantly, to monitor the results of my lectures.
>
> I had adopted the obvious rule that self assessment must mean what it said, and committed myself in advance to accepting the students' mark. I was apprehensive of the consequences of that self-imposed rule, but I need not have worried. When a student gave herself a very high mark for what seemed to me to be poor understanding of the ideas involved, I simply asked appropriate questions, ending with 'Do you really deserve the mark you have given yourself?' Every student seemed content to

reduce her mark herself. Equally frequently, students gave themselves below-average marks for very good understanding. Here I tried to help the student to compare her work with that of others, and so to accept that she deserved a higher mark. Despite the occasional need for me to intervene in this way, more than three-quarters of the students' marks needed no such discussion.

I tried hard to impress on students that there are many ways of learning: from books, from fellow students, from trial and error, from thinking while walking or sitting on buses, from lectures, from lecturers and from tutorials. I encouraged students to help each other by sharing data files (thus learning how to transfer files), by pooling ideas (thus benefiting from each other), by sharing programs (later having to explain to me what their programs actually did) and by teaching each other.

One or two students told me that they found the tasks so easy (due to their prior experience) that they felt they would not be making enough effort to deserve high marks, I suggested that they should find other students who were having difficulties, teach them, and then accept the same marks that their 'pupils' awarded themselves for what they had learned. (Edwards, 1989, pp.7–8)

A number of the more emancipatory examples of self assessment focus on the use of writing to reflect on a learning process or event. Taylor (1995) for example describes self assessment as an act of self reflection followed by a written exercise which helps the learner focus on her learning. The essential point, she says, is to invite the learner to examine how she learns. In writing about their experiences of returning to study, for example, women develop understanding of themselves; a process which, Taylor argues, can be transformative.

Kramp and Humphreys (1993, p.83) also make use of narrative as a tool for self assessment. Narrative, they argue: 'centres on change, development, growth. Narrative re-presents, revives and makes present the past, in ways that shape future experience'. One of the courses they describe involves students reading and interpreting sections of the Hebrew Bible/Christian Old Testament: 'The goal was to empower students to connect learning in our courses with experiences prior to and outside of these courses, and especially to shape future directions for their learning' (ibid, p.84).

Students were asked to write about a learning experience which they had either during the course or earlier, to provide vignettes of what stood out or was significant for them when preparing assessments or exercises in the course throughout the term, to tell their story as a learner based on these materials and other significant experiences during the year, and to compare their story as a learner with a novel chosen by the course tutor.

We found time and again that the students' own words were highly compelling. For example, the chance to tell the story of themselves as learners over the course of the term led sometimes to striking integrative observations. As one student said: 'I didn't really notice it happening to me, until I kinda stepped back away from it, like the painting, you know, where you stand too close you just see the little dots, and once you back up, you go '"Wow!" and you see the whole thing'. . . . We also found that student narrative enriched our understanding and appreciation for the many aspects of self assessment. Our primary focus was on our students and on the insights they gained in telling the stories of their learning experiences. Making space for stories in our courses showed that we respected these experiences. Many students became aware of themselves as learners and of their particular modes and strategies of learning in ways that empowered them to make judgements about their effectiveness, change what they deemed appropriate and set directions for the future. Our students' stories also challenged us to re-think our understandings of ourselves as teachers, to examine particular instructional strategies and to pay more attention to the individuality of each student. (Kramp and Humphreys, 1993, pp.85–7)

In the foregoing examples the development of the skills of learning go hand-in-hand with the development of knowledge of the subject matter. There is also a merging of the boundaries between self assessment and critical reflection; an issue that was discussed in Chapter 3.

This merging of self assessment and critical reflection is also true of the example discussed in Chapter 9: the use of negotiated self assessment schedules. This is another example of self assessment in the emancipatory mode because learners are encouraged to set up and to critique their own standards. Students have the freedom to use the schedules as they wish. The educational experience is again viewed as a whole. Skills and knowledge are integrated.

Moving beyond the holistic notion of competency as outlined by Gonczi and colleagues, is the emancipatory mode where competency standards become subject to critical scrutiny. In the example of self appraisal for university teachers given in Chapter 10, the teachers set standards of their own competence in conversation, apply them to their own competence and review practice in the light of this. Critique of the standards, which makes this an example in the emancipatory domain, is then encouraged at a later stage.

## Conclusion

This chapter has demonstrated the way in which self assessment is being used in a large number of disciplines and organisations. It has illustrated an enormous variety and ingenuity in approaches. Hopefully these can provide a stimulus to the development of self assessment practices.

In the chapters that follow the factors which need to be taken into account in implementing self assessment are addressed. These assist the development of self assessment practice by building on the experiences of others, facilitate the critical evaluation of self assessment and hopefully move forward our understanding of what we are trying to achieve when we ask our students to engage in the often challenging task of assessing their own learning.

PART III

# SELF ASSESSMENT AND MARKING

## Chapter 12

# What does Research Tell us about Self Assessment?

*David Boud and Nancy Falchikov*

This chapter reviews the literature on self assessment and focuses on the comparison of student-generated marks with those generated by teachers. Studies which include such comparisons in the context of higher education courses are reviewed. The chapter is concerned to address the following questions: do students tend to over- or under-rate themselves *vis-à-vis* teachers? Do students of different abilities have the same rating tendencies? Do students in different kinds or levels of course tend to under- or over-rate themselves? Do students improve their ability to rate themselves over time or with practice? Are the same tendencies evident when self-marks are used for formal assessment purposes? And, are there gender differences in self-rating?

Many studies which describe themselves as studies of self assessment do not involve students in the selection of criteria. They simply ask students to rate themselves according to some pre-established scale. Unfortunately, most of the empirical papers discussed here are of this type and caution must be exercised in generalising their findings to wider realms of self assessment.

## Types of studies

The literature on student self assessment can be broadly classified under three headings: conceptual, practical qualitative, and quantitative.

## Conceptual

The conceptual group of studies includes such related work as that by Argyris and Schön (1974) examining professional competence and the role of self and peer assessment in developing 'theories-in-use', and Schön (1983, 1987) on the 'reflective practitioner'; Elliott (1978) on teacher self-monitoring; and the burgeoning literature on meta-cognition and learning-how-to-learn (eg, Baird and White, 1982; Biggs and Moore, 1993; Flavell, 1979). There has been little directly connecting this work with student self assessment in higher education, so that Heron's (1988) important clarificatory analysis of the nature and politics of the assessment process (originally published in 1981) and Rogers' (1983) discussion of the role of self assessment in promoting student responsibility for learning, stand as major contributions to thinking on student self assessment.

## Practical qualitative

The practical qualitative group deals mainly with the processes involved in introducing and using self assessment in different situations. It includes discussion in the context of foreign language learning (Oskarsson, 1980), health personnel education (Barrows and Tamblyn, 1976; Heron, 1981; Perkins and Anderson, 1981; Rotem and Abbatt, 1982), student writing (Butler, 1982) and engineering education (Cowan, 1975, 1988). There are also discussions about the role of teachers in facilitating self assessment (Bailey, 1979; Van Riper, 1982), and the use of repertory grid techniques in monitoring one's learning (Candy *et al.*, 1985; Thomas and Harri-Augstein, 1977).

## Quantitative

The quantitative group focuses on comparing student self-ratings with the ratings of students by teachers. Measures of agreement between teachers and students are often calculated and analyses of over- or under-rating conducted.

This chapter focuses on the quantitative group of studies. It identifies the methodological and conceptual limitations of such studies, and elucidates what can reasonably be said about their outcomes. It addresses whether students tend to over- or under-rate themselves compared with teacher ratings, and whether this varies depending on factors such as the ability of students, the level of study and the use of student ratings for formal assessment purposes. It addresses three general questions: are the studies themselves sufficiently sound for us to be able to draw conclusions from them with confidence? What does the evidence tell us about the quantitative aspects of self assessment? And, what needs to be done to obtain better quality information?

It is important to acknowledge that although the making of quantitative measurements to judge the reliability of student self marking is a significant practical issue, it is certainly not the most important aspect of self assessment. However, the 'accuracy' of student ratings has been the single most discussed topic in the literature on self assessment and this fact alone warrants attention.

Individual students will for a variety of reasons not rate themselves in exactly the same way as they would be rated by teachers. The policy question is: are there any consistent patterns for classes, groups or types of student as a whole and if so, what are they? The answers to these questions have important implications for whether self assessment *can* be used as part of formal assessment procedures (whether it *should* be used is another matter); for whether students are sufficiently accurate in their self assessments not to need to develop their skills further in this area; and for whether students are perceptive about their achievements in ways which teachers would judge appropriate.

## Methodology of this review

The studies selected for review were obtained from searches of computerised databases in education and the social sciences, from studies quoted by authors of the papers located and from other published studies obtained by conventional literature searching which were not uncovered otherwise. The scope includes reports of data relating to student self assessment and teacher marks. Studies dealing with comparisons of self and peer marks were not included unless they also included self and teacher comparisons.

Having located the corpus of quantitative self assessment literature it was possible to address our research questions. For example, is it possible to discern any overall pattern in the results reported? Do the studies as a whole suggest anything over and above individually reported results? The first step in the development of understanding of the relationships between self and teacher marks was to identify and analyse the variables available and which are thought to affect this relationship.

## Limitations

Among the studies examined there were examples of a wide variety of elementary methodological weaknesses. Very few, indeed, were free of technical flaws. For example, the scales used were not specified, or teachers used different criteria to students. There is a noticeable improvement in quality over time, but unfortunately there is no agreement on the form in which comparisons should be reported. It was striking that there was relatively little cross-referencing of publications: it appears that the errors of one were not spotted and corrected in subsequent studies.

Although it is difficult to make comparisons between different studies when different rating scales are used, it is not necessarily desirable to try to standardise on these as it is likely that ratings will only be valid when students use scales with which they are familiar. Student over- or underrating is with respect to something with which they are familiar. Unfortunately the 'natural' scale in a given situation is not necessarily one which leads to easy comparison across studies.

In general, insufficient description of the context was reported. In particular, there was little or no reporting of the circumstances in which students were asked to rate their performance and in the majority of cases it is not clear whether or not the student-generated marks were formally used for assessment purposes. A detailed discussion of methodological weaknesses in the studies examined and recommendations on criteria to be used in judging the technical adequacy of research on self assessment is discussed in Boud and Falchikov (1989).

One of the assumptions behind the perspective taken here is that teacher marks should be the independent variable against which student self assessments should be judged; that is to say, teachers define the accuracy of self-ratings. At the simplest level of performance where we can assume teachers to be experts and students to be novices there is little difficulty in adopting this as a valid working assumption. However, as students progress to higher levels of sophistication and begin to apply their knowledge and understanding to increasingly complex professional questions which begin to fall outside their teachers' immediate area of competence, then the assumption begins to be less valid.

In addition we need to recognise that teachers have limited access to the knowledge of their students and in many ways students have greater insights into their own achievements. Thus, we can only discuss one aspect of students' self assessment in studies of the kind we are examining: that which deals with information known to teachers. There is much information known to students which is not known to teachers and, of course, there is information not readily accessible to either party which may need to be taken account of in some circumstances.

Also, a major difficulty arises with the unreliability of teacher marks. Many studies, from Hartog and Rhodes' (1935) classic on, have demonstrated that there are discrepancies between markers and with the same marker over time even when there is apparent agreement on what is being assessed (see, for example, Rowntree, 1987).

Furthermore, teachers and students may have different perspectives and differing ideas about what is important. This is, perhaps, most evident where students are rating effort, and teachers the product of this effort. Even when individuals, their supervisors and their peers are rating performance on the same dimensions, differences of perspective can give rise to differing interpretations (eg, Holzbach, 1978; Kegel-Flom, 1975).

Examining the rationales given by authors for their investigations we find that a simple 'look and see' motivation is the most prevalent in quantitative self assessment studies (eg, Gaier, 1961; Wheeler and Knoop, 1981). A desire to enhance educational benefits is the next most frequently cited motivator (eg, Denscombe and Robins, 1980), with dissatisfaction with the traditional assessment system closely following (eg, Burke, 1969; Filene, 1969). Some more recent studies are beginning to focus on investigation and evaluation of the assessment process (eg, Arnold *et al.*, 1985).

## Evidence about self-marking

### 1. Do students tend to overrate or underrate themselves compared to staff?

In most studies greater numbers of student marks agree than disagree with staff marks. It is often difficult to quantify this as both the grading categories and the definitions of 'agreement' varied widely in different studies. Not surprisingly, there is a much greater chance of agreement between staff and students when a five-point scale is used rather than percentages. However, in most studies there was a clear tendency towards some degree of over- or underrating. Some studies reported the numbers of students who over- or underrated themselves; a few discussed the magnitude of the differences for individual students. There was a small tendency for earlier studies to report overrating and later studies to report underrating. The studies can be summarised as follows.

*Those reporting overrating*

Sumner (1932): the averaged marks of undergraduate psychology students exceeded teachers by 9.3 per cent.

Doleys and Renzaglia (1963): the overall average of freshmen English students exceeded teachers by a difference of 0.37 on a five-point scale. Students were reluctant to use the extremes of the scale.

Murstein (1965): overall general overestimation by undergraduate educational psychology students.

Burke (1969): students in a MBA subject produced many more As than Bs compared to teachers.

Filene (1969): 40 per cent of history students graded themselves higher than they were graded by teachers, 3 per cent lower. However, effort was included as a criterion.

Chiu (1975): senior student teachers rated their performance on their first teaching practice higher than did experienced teachers.

Borman and Ramirez (1975): in a graduate counselling practicum, students' higher ratings contributed to significant differences on two of the three sub-scales on the measuring instrument.

Stover (1976): in an undergraduate law course the average difference between teacher and student was 2.68 to 3.32.

Larson (1978): in undergraduate thermodynamics and fluid mechanics 19.8 per cent of student grades reduced, 9.8 per cent of student grades increased.

McGeever (1978): in an undergraduate politics course student grades exceeded those given by teachers, with the differences on a five-point scale ranging from 0.69 to 1.45.

Stanton (1978): in a class of educational psychology undergraduates, 33 per cent of the class rated themselves higher, 6 per cent lower than the teacher's mark.

Greenfield (1978): students gave themselves marks higher than those of teachers on eight out of ten competences in a music therapy clinical practicum.

Davis and Rand (1980): on the final paper in an undergraduate educational psychology course the mean of self-scores was 77.03 compared to teacher scores of 73.28, but the student rating included an element of effort.

Wheeler and Knoop (1981): in an undergraduate teacher education course there was an overrating by students of their teaching performance.

Israelite (1983): graduate students in an education course overrated themselves on three out of four assignments.

Fuqua *et al.* (1984): before training, the mean self rating of pre- practicum counsellor trainees was 18.61 (sd=2.14) compared with a mean of 17.25 (sd=4.06) for supervisors. After training, mean self rating was 21.33 (sd=2.43) and mean supervisor rating was 19.84 (sd=3.62).

Gray (1987): in an undergraduate engineering materials course there was some grade inflation.

*Those reporting underrating*

Mueller (1970): in an undergraduate psychology final exam 'four times as many students assigned themselves a lower grade than a higher grade'.

Morton and Macbeth (1977): in fourth year surgery performance, four-fifths of the self assessments were equal to or lower than staff assessments – five out of six students who recorded a fail for themselves were passed by staff.

Stanton (1978): in a graduate class in educational psychology 4 per cent of students rated themselves higher than their teacher's rating of them, 16 per cent lower.

Denscombe and Robins (1980): self marks for undergraduate sociology essays were usually below tutor marks by 5 per cent.

Stuart *et al.* (1980): in eight clinical skill areas in family medicine, mean self-scores were lower than mean faculty scores.

Pitishkin-Potanich (1983): 14 per cent of fourth year students on an education course underrated their performance, compared with 8.4 per cent who overrated.

Sclabassi and Woelfel (1984): in third year anaesthesia clinical skills, 53.1 per cent of students rated themselves lower than their teachers' score by an average of 6.1 points, 42.3 per cent rated themselves higher by an average of 4.8 points.

Arnold *et al.* (1985): there was a small underrating by medical students on performance and other desirable attributes from 4th to 6th year.

Falchikov (1986): in the assessment of an undergraduate psychology essay 57.1 per cent of students rated themselves lower than the teacher, 42.9 per cent higher. However, 73.8 per cent fell within the agreed range of tolerance.

Jackson (1988): in a second year course in political analysis, 36 per cent of students overestimated their performance on an essay assignment compared to 55 per cent who underestimated their marks.

Wilcox (1988): in an introductory Australian politics class, the mean self-mark on an essay assignment (58.1 per cent) was lower than the mean teacher mark (60.6 per cent).

*Reporting variation from year to year*

Boud, *et al.* (1986): in an undergraduate engineering design subject, students on average overrated themselves in two out of the three years studied and underrated themselves in the other.

**161**

*Reporting variation depending on type of scale used*

> Boud and Tyree, (1980): in assessing class participation in an undergraduate law class, found that overrating or underrating depended on the type of rating scale used by students.

Seventeen studies report overrating, twelve underrating. However, there are on balance more studies with methodological flaws in the former group and so there is no clear overall tendency to be identified. The only four studies of medical students were all in the underrating group. All that can be concluded is that under different circumstances there are different trends towards over and underrating.

## 2. Do students of differing abilities tend to overrate or underrate themselves compared to teachers?

One of the factors which can be tested in the data is that of student ability as indicated by their overall position in the group as judged by teachers. The earliest finding was that 'good' students tended to underrate themselves compared to staff marks, whereas 'weak' students tended to overrate themselves.

> Sumner (1932): found that when dividing the class into quartiles the top quartile rated themselves on average 4.1per cent below the teacher, the next 3.4 per cent above the teacher, the next 9.8 per cent above and the bottom quartile 27.9 per cent above the teacher's mark.

> Doleys and Renzaglia (1963): 'Intellectually more able students tend to underestimate or accurately estimate their college performance, while less able students tend to overestimate their future grades'.

> Murstein (1965): those receiving A and B grades ('high students') were generally realistic, lower performing students generally overestimate their performance. 'High' students are highly accurate in their expectation of the grade ultimately received, 'low' students have unrealistically high expectations.

> Keefer (1971): students who are in the upper quartile are more accurate predictors of achievement than those in lower quartiles.

> Daines (1978): low achievers in undergraduate educational psychology overestimate themselves, high achievers are quite realistic.

> Cochran and Spears (1980): in undergraduate clinical nutrition there is closer agreement between teachers and students for those students with grade point averages above the mean.

> Moreland *et al.* (1981): in an undergraduate introductory psychology course, 'poor' students were less accurate than 'good' when judging their own work.

Forehand *et al.* (1982): in a pre-clinical restorative dentistry class, students who received high grades (A or B) tended to underestimate their performance compared to teachers, while those with lower grades (C, D or F) tended to overestimate their performance. There was a direct relationship between decreasing grade and increasing over-estimation.

Falchikov (1986): the majority of overmarking occurs amongst those students of average ability.

Jackson (1988): in a political analysis course, the mean undermarking of the top quartile of students was 12.9 per cent compared with a mean overmarking of the bottom quartile of 3.4 per cent.

Magin and Churches (1988): students in the highest quartile underrate by 8.9 marks while those in the lowest quartile overrate by 5.7 marks.

The general trend in these studies suggests that high achieving students tend to be realistic and perhaps underestimate their performance while low achieving students tend to overestimate their achievements probably to a greater extent than the underestimation.

## 3. Do students in different kinds or levels of class tend to over- or underrate?

Some studies have included more than one level or group of students. For these it is possible to examine whether, for example, there is any difference in the trends for introductory compared with advanced classes, or for junior compared with senior students.

Filene (1969): senior year students and graduates conformed most to instructors grades, followed by sophomores, with least conformity by juniors.

Bishop (1971): ratings of graduate student counsellors did not differ significantly from those of supervisors.

Keefer (1971): upper class members (juniors and seniors) were more accurate than freshmen.

Pease (1975): there was significant agreement between self-rating third and fourth year student teachers and their instructors.

Stanton (1978): found that undergraduates tend to overestimate whereas postgraduates in a similar subject tend to underestimate themselves.

Arnold *et al.* (1985): from years 3 to 6 in a medical course there is a tendency for increasing underestimation of performance.

Henbest and Fehrsen (1985): mean scores of final year undergraduates were found to be lower but not significantly different from those of faculty members (6.5 vs. 6.7).

Falchikov (1986): there was some over-marking by the youngest students in the group (age less than 18 years 9 months).

The trend in these studies is that students in later years of courses and graduates have a tendency to either become more 'accurate' in their ratings, or to tend towards increasing underestimation of their performance.

## 4. Do students improve their ability to rate themselves over time or with practice?

While most studies examined one group of students, some allowed consideration of improvement in the light of feedback or development over time.

Murstein (1965): as the final examination neared there were no significant changes in the grades students believed they deserved.

Larson (1978): apart from an improvement on the final (ninth) rating, undergraduates in a thermodynamics and fluid mechanics course seemed to become less accurate with practice.

McGeever (1978): undergraduates in a politics course became less accurate with practice (first self-rating: self-awarded grade 3.73, cf. 'hypothetical' instructor grade 3.04; second self-rating: self-awarded grade 3.71, cf. 'hypothetical' instructor grade 2.44; third self-rating: self- awarded grade 3.68, cf. 'hypothetical' instructor grade 2.23).

Peterson (1979): senior undergraduate architecture students improved the accuracy of their self-estimation after hearing detailed criticism of their work.

Cochran and Spears (1980): students improved their self-rating over time.

Everett (1983): the correlation between teacher and student marks in an introductory dental hygiene course increased from 0.33 (mid-term) to 0.58 (final).

Arnold et al. (1985): over four years students increased their own self-ratings, but to a lesser extent than staff ratings of them increased.

Cowan (1988): undergraduate civil engineering students improved the accuracy of their ratings during the year.

There are insufficient studies of improvement over time in general to draw any firm conclusions and there is particularly a lack of studies on the influence of practice on self marking. The connection between self assessment and developmental change is becoming of greater interest, however (Haswell, 1993, Taylor, 1995).

## 5. Do students overrate or underrate when self-marks are used for assessment purposes?

In general, it is difficult to determine an answer to this question as studies do not consistently specify whether the marks of students are formally recognised. However, in those cases where student marks appear to count (Burke, 1969; Cowan, 1988; Davis and Rand, 1980; Filene, 1969; McGeever, 1978; Stanton, 1978; Stover, 1976), students tend to overrate themselves, except for Stanton's 1978 graduates and Cowan's 1988 undergraduate civil engineers.

## 6. Are there any gender differences in self-rating?

Studies of gender differences remain inconclusive. Six studies examined sex differences (Arnold *et al.*, 1985; Filene, 1969; Hoffman and Geller 1981; Jackson, 1988; Keefer, 1971 and O'Neill, 1985) and only three of these found any differences between the ratings of men and women. Although, overall O'Neill (1985) found little agreement between student teachers' ratings and those of their supervisors, agreement for women students was greater than for men. Hoffman and Geller (1981) found opposite results in their two studies: male teacher trainees in elementary classrooms overrated them-selves relative to the teacher supervisor, and females underrated themselves, but this finding was reversed in non-elementary classrooms. Jackson (1988) found in his politics class that while both males and females underrated themselves compared to the teacher, the tendency for men was less marked. Finally, Stefani (1994) reports no significant differences between males and females as assessors or assessees. Some practical guidelines for dealing with potential gender effects are provided in Chapter 15 and there is further consideration of issues in this area in Chapter 17.

## Conclusions

The present overview has gone some way towards providing answers to our questions about student self assessment. Certain trends have emerged, but others have failed to do so. Only by comparing the results of many studies can we see that there is no consistent tendency to over- or underestimate performance. Some students in some circumstances tend towards one direction, others in the same or different situations towards the other. The literature reviewed also highlights the variety of self assessment perfor-mances across studies. Some students appear to assess themselves in very similar ways to those in which they are rated by teachers, while others are less reliable in this respect. Several studies tentatively explore these differences by comparing the self assessments of groups of students; undergraduates and graduates, for example. Here, common sense predictions favouring the more experienced students are supported. The review also points to the ability of self assessors as a salient variable, with the more able students making more accurate self assessments than their less able peers.

When students are asked to rate themselves on a marking scale, relatively able and mature students are able to do so in a way which is identical to the way in which they would be rated by teachers and some are quite critical in their assessments. Able students working in a new subject are likely to be aware of their own deficiencies and thus the results of underrating which we see are also not unexpected. Also unsurprising is the fact that weaker and less mature students tend to overrate themselves and the weaker they are, in terms of teacher ratings, the greater the degree of overrating. Not being aware of, or choosing not to subscribe to, the standards set by teachers, they err on the side of optimism.

A meta-analysis of research studies was conducted following the publication of the paper from which most of the data reported in this chapter are taken. This focused on the magnitude of differences between self and teacher ratings and involved statistically converting these differences to a common scale which enabled direct comparisons between studies. Using a very similar set of studies to the ones reported here, the following was concluded:

> Factors ... important with regard to the degree of correspondence between self and teacher marks were found to include the following: the quality of design of the study (with better designed studies having closer correspondence between student and teacher than poorly designed ones); the level of the course of which the assessment was a part (with students in advanced courses appearing to be more accurate assessors than those in intoductory courses); and the broad area of study (with studies within the area of science appearing to produce more accurate self assessment generally than did those from other areas of study). (Falchikov and Boud, 1989, p.395)

There is rather more research on student self assessment than is apparent to the casual reader. However, too much of it is both conceptually and methodologically unsound. Perhaps the greatest needs for further development are for well-formulated studies to investigate the issues which we have begun to address above and for research to be conducted on self assessment schemes which aim to maximise the benefit to student learning.

# Chapter 13

# The Role of Self Assessment in Student Grading

While the educational benefits of student self assessment are being increasingly recognised, the use of self assessment for grading purposes is a more controversial matter. Is there a role for student self assessment in formal assessment proceedings? If so, what should it be? This chapter focuses on these questions and examines why a marking role for self assessment should be considered. Strategies are proposed to improve student markers' reliability and to incorporate self assessment indirectly into the formal assessment process.

If self-generated student marks are to be used as an element of officially recorded assessments, it is necessary *inter alia* to demonstrate that students can produce marks which are acceptable to teachers – this has usually meant ones where there is a very high probability that student marks are the same as staff marks for a given assignment. It is also necessary to demonstrate that, if students can produce marks which are acceptably similar when they are not formally recorded, the context of formal assessment proceedings does not distort their ratings so that students produce unrealistic assessments of their performance under these conditions. If these points cannot be demonstrated, then student self assessment should either be restricted to a purely learning role and as a skill to be developed, or it should be used in a way which recognises the potential for bias and distortion, and controls for this through some form of moderating device or other strategy which does not feed raw scores from students directly into formal records.

This chapter commences with consideration of why students should be involved in assessment for grading purposes. It goes on to draw on two sources: first, a critical analysis of the literature on the comparison of teacher marks with student self-ratings; second, my experience in using self assessment in grading situations where student marks are not accepted uncritically or used directly. General issues of reliability of marking are also noted in passing. The poor quality of quantitative research on self assessment which was discussed in the previous chapter is acknowledged and questions are raised about the kinds of strategies which teachers can adopt to involve students in the formal assessment process. It ends with a brief discussion of the kinds of research which are needed to illuminate the issues in this area.

## Why should we be concerned about a marking function for self assessment?

If self assessment is a worthwhile activity in its own right, why consider using it for marking purposes? The almost universal move towards a greater component of 'continuous' assessment in higher education courses has encouraged students to seek all work to be marked and counted towards their final grading. Assignments set by teachers which are not marked appear to be treated less seriously than those that are. Students are less willing to engage in work which does not have an extrinsic reward. In these circumstances, some students are unwilling to take part in self assessment exercises if they are not weighted for formal assessment purposes, even when they see value in a self assessment exercise, for example as discussed in Chapters 6 and 7.

Also, if there is a high correlation between marks generated by students and those generated by staff, why bother involving students if their contribution makes no difference to the final grades? There are at least two arguments for students to be involved in generating marks over and above any qualitative form of self assessment. The first is what might be called the *reality* argument. This recognises that self assessment never exists in a vacuum, it always occurs in a context. Sometimes the setting is quite benign and the individual's standards are quite sufficient; on other occasions, the context constrains and may distort the individual's sense of what is an appropriate self assessment. Self marking provides practice in the interpretation of the often arbitrary requirements which most public work needs to satisfy. Students need to be able to assess themselves in situations where they have only partial knowledge of the criteria to be used by others and when they may not fully accept the criteria which others will apply to them.

The second argument is one based upon *expediency*. If students can take a greater role in assessment, there is potential for saving staff time on the often tedious task of marking. Staff time is valuable and that devoted to marking which does not result in feedback to students, such as for final projects or examinations, is time which is not devoted to facilitating learning. If students mark their own work, either with respect to specified standards (for example, model answers) or their self-established criteria, they not only release staff for more educationally worthwhile activities, but they are encouraged to reflect on their own work and the standards which can be applied to it.

However, if students are not able to mark their work reliably as judged by teachers, then these arguments may not be enough for student marking to be used formally. There is some evidence, discussed below, that student self marks are in many cases not sufficiently consistent with teacher marks for them to be used straightforwardly. This leads some teachers to drop all notions of self assessment despite other educational benefits. At the other extreme, others believe the benefits of self assessment are so great that they should trust their students to act appropriately even when there is a risk that they might not award themselves the same marks as would be given by a staff member (Cowan, 1988).

## The quantitative evidence

Empirical research studies can throw light upon two aspects of this concern about inconsistency. First, is there any systematic bias among students as a whole which leads them to give themselves higher or lower marks than those awarded by staff? Second, is there a tendency for individual students to over- or underrate themselves? If there is, is it a conscious act or not? As we saw in Chapter 12, evidence from the literature is available on the first, but the second question is difficult to disentangle from the general question of marker reliability. There already exists well-documented variations between staff markers and with the same marker over time (Heywood, 1989). One might expect at least a similar variation among students, perhaps more so as they are relatively inexperienced in these matters.

## Implications of the findings

If there are problems with consistency when using student-generated marks, does this suggest that the use of student self assessment for marking purposes should be abandoned? Not necessarily. Studies which have identified the unreliability of teacher marks have not led to calls for teacher grading to be abandoned, rather they lead to considerations of how the marking process can be made more reliable. The problem may not be the inadequacy of students as markers *per se*, but the difficulty of their giving a sufficiently unbiased opinion about their own work. For example, Orpen (1982), in studies of two courses in which papers were marked by five students and five lecturers, found that marks given by student's peers correlated highly with those given by the lecturers.

Two approaches to the improvement of performance of student markers suggest themselves: those associated with improving marker reliability generally and those which involve ways of indirectly incorporating student self marking in formal assessments.

## Improving marker reliability

Most of the strategies for improving marker reliability can be applied to student markers as well as staff markers. So, for example, improvements may be made by:

- establishing explicit criteria for satisfactory and unsatisfactory performance;
- using scales in which the categories are unambiguously defined;
- not using scales which are more sensitive than the fineness of discrimination allows;
- training markers through practising the application of accepted criteria to typical examples of work to be marked and the resolution of differences through discussion between markers to reach consensus on the interpretation of the criteria.

Further strategies may be found, for example, in White (1985).

These principles are rarely applied by staff to their own marking tasks so it may be unduly optimistic to expect to see them used extensively with student markers. There are additional educational reasons why they should be used with students, however. For example, Gibbs (1981) and Ballard and Clanchy (1988) argue that it is very important for students to be involved in considering and using criteria which will be applied to their work if they are to learn effectively, whether or not they are involved in formal self assessment exercises. Unless students can appreciate what requirements good work in their chosen field should satisfy it is unlikely that they will be able to contribute effectively to it themselves. There are alternatives to the direct use of student marks which have been used, some of which have the benefits identified by Gibbs and by Ballard and Clanchy.

## Strategies for incorporating student self marking

If the potential for improving marker reliability is limited, it is necessary to explore some of the indirect strategies for using self marking in formal assessment. The main part of this chapter is therefore devoted to discussing a selection of strategies which have been used for this purpose. Each strategy is described briefly and its advantages and disadvantages noted. Where there is potential for the saving of staff time this is also noted. Some of these approaches draw on discussions in previous chapters but the main points relating to student marking are considered together here.

- *Self assessment schedules with marks justified and moderated by staff*

Students prepare a statement of what they have achieved in the form of a self assessment schedule and assign a total mark (and a justification for it) to these documented achievements according to their interpretation of the grading policy of the course. The performance of each student in agreed areas is independently assessed by staff following a reading of the self assessment schedule, but without knowledge of the specific mark awarded by the student, and a staff mark recorded. If the marks from the two sources are within, say, 5 or 10 per cent of each other, students are formally awarded their own mark. If there is a greater discrepancy than this, discussions take place in which the justifications for the marks are explained. If there is no agreement following this meeting, a totally independent assessment based on the documented evidence is made by a third party. This approach was discussed in detail in Chapter 9.

An advantage of this approach is that students can present all their achievements for consideration by staff and, if there are disagreements, the rationale for marking can be explained. However, students can find it difficult to arrive at a mark in a norm-referenced grading context when they do not have access to the work of more than one or two others.

- *Self marks moderated by peers*

Another approach is to have one or more student peers also mark the individual and have work with discrepancies between self and peer scores re-marked by staff. For example, in the study of examination marking presented in Chapter 6, students used detailed model answers to mark anonymously one other student's paper and, the following week, their own. It was argued that the gap between sitting for the examination and marking their own helped students to gain distance from their work and the experience of marking another's paper enabled them to appreciate the model answers more fully than if they had to use them immediately to assess their own paper. The self mark and the peer mark were then compared and staff only re-marked those where there was a discrepancy greater than that expected from the normal error. Random checking of other papers was used to encourage students to take the exercise seriously and to check for marking consistency. Even allowing for the extra time spent in preparing model answers, administration of examination scripts and re-marking, it was estimated that staff time could be saved and an acceptable mark produced in classes with more than 20–60 students.

A disadvantage for some in this approach is the pressure on staff – although they spend less time, the time they do spend is on more challenging matters than marking – and there is also the danger that if the scheme is not administered carefully, students will collude with each other and undermine its intentions.

- *Criteria generated by peers*

One of the factors which contributes to the lack of reliability of student marking is that, relative to staff, students have a less well developed sense of the criteria which should be used to judge their work and they may find it difficult to interpret effectively criteria with which they are provided. A strategy to be discussed in detail in Chapter 15 involves a group exercise in which students establish a common set of criteria for an assignment and use the specific criteria which are generated by this process as the yardsticks for judging individual performance. A nominal group process is used to identify and refine criteria suggested by students. These criteria provide a checklist which students use to assess their own work. They hand in the completed checklist with their assignment.

This approach is particularly effective if students generate criteria which are endorsed by staff. Indeed, at the end of the criteria-generating phase students commonly ask staff whether the list they have produced is acceptable. In the cases where such an approach has been used, staff have been impressed with the range of thoroughness of the criteria generated. If it is used in conjunction with staff marking, it is necessary for staff and students to adopt the same marking strategy with the given criteria.

- *Weighting for the quality of self assessment only*

If self assessment is to be encouraged, it is not necessary for students marks to be weighted at all. In the context of self assessment in a mechanical engineering design course discussed in Chapter 7, students were marked by staff on the quality of their self assessment as if this were one of the assignments for the course (contributing 4 per cent of total marks). Students who had not performed well on other assessment measures could score highly if they were perceptive in their self assessment and could pinpoint their weaknesses. Otherwise higher scoring students could perform poorly on their self assessment if they had little awareness of their strengths and weaknesses.

This approach turns self assessment into another course assignment and may lead to it being regarded simply as a barrier to be overcome in the quest for good marks. It colludes with the attitude that students should not expect to do anything unless it is marked. However, it may encourage critical self assessment.

- *Marks count after practice and demonstration of student competence in self assessment*

One of the main difficulties in using student marks in most contexts is that students have had very little opportunity to develop their self assessment skills. It is therefore not surprising that they are not as effective as they might be. Another strategy for counting self marking is that students' marks only be used after the students have demonstrated that they can be reliable appraisers of their own work through doing so on a number of occasions of the type discussed above or simply as part of formative assessment activities. Of course, knowledge that students can mark themselves reliably is no guarantee that they will indeed do so.

A variation on this strategy in which a lecturer persevered with students producing manifestly inappropriate mid-course marks, but trusting them to be realistic in the end is discussed by Cowan (1988) and mentioned in Chapter 11. His thoughtful reflections on the process of facilitating student self assessment are helpful for anyone embarking on this approach to assessment. He particularly draws attention to the importance of making a commitment to the process from the start and maintaining trust in students even when for considerable periods they may be producing results which would in other circumstances be unacceptable. Through establishing and fostering a climate in which students can be self critical without the continual imposition of teacher's standards, he demonstrates that formal self assessment can have an extraordinarily positive influence on the quality of learning.

Two other examples which take quite a different approach to self assessment have been widely used; these are discussed below.

- *Use of learning contracts*

Learning contracts are being increasingly used in tertiary institutions as a means of managing self-directed learning (Anderson *et al.*, 1994, forthcoming; Knowles, 1975; Knowles and Associates, 1986). In a course which uses learning contracts, each student prepares a plan which specifies goals and objectives for a particular task, the approach to learning which will be adopted, the criteria which will be used to judge success and the mechanism for making judgements (by specified others who may be neither staff nor students). This contract is discussed with a staff member and, after negotiation and modification if necessary, it forms the basis for work for a given course. Contracts can include criteria for specific grades.

Procedures for determining the role of self assessment may vary from one contract to another and there can be difficulties with consistency over all students.

- *Grade contracting*

Contracting for grades is a variation on the theme of learning contracts (Beeler, 1976; Hassencahl, 1979; O'Kane, 1971; Parks and Zurhellen, 1978; Polczynski and Shirland, 1977; Poppen and Thompson, 1971; Shirts, 1968; Taylor, 1971; Warner and Akamine, 1972). In grade contracting, students set their own goals and specify which grade they intend to aim for and the criteria which would indicate success. After negotiation and approval, students automatically get their chosen grade if they satisfy the contracted requirements.

The disadvantage of grade contracting is that it locks students into a particular grade in advance. They can end up with no grade at all if they aim high and just miss, or they can obtain a lower grade than they would normally be awarded if their work is clearly superior to the grade level which they have set in advance. Grade contracting is only appropriate if there are opportunities for renegotiation of the contract at reasonably late stages in the process – this is often difficult to arrange.

## When is self assessment for grading purposes appropriate?

In reflecting on the range of examples given above it is possible to identify situations in which the use of student marks may be legitimate. These are when:

(a) there is a high-trust, high-integrity learning environment;
(b) students are rewarded for high-integrity marking;
(c) marks are moderated by staff so that deviations from staff marks need to be justified;
(d) blind peer marking is used as a check;
(e) random staff marking is used as a check;
(f) a major goal is the achievement of effective self assessment and students have had ample opportunity to practise and develop their skills;
(g) the criteria against which achievement is to be judged have been sufficiently unambiguously defined for there to be little scope for misinterpretation of grade boundaries;
(h) effort is explicitly excluded as a criterion.

Some of these are mutually exclusive. Different approaches may be required for large classes and those with multiple staff members. What can be done when there is a close relationship between teacher and students is very different from when there are mass enrolments.

The weighting given to self assessment can vary greatly: in the examples given above, from 4 to 100 per cent. Clearly, the risks involved in having a somewhat unreliable form of marking are much greater when the entire formal assessment is based upon one measure.

## Conclusions

Experience to date suggests that there needs to be a balance between a system which is so restrictive that student involvement is eliminated and self assessment effectively discouraged, and a completely trusting system which is open to abuse, particularly in highly competitive, low-trust, professional courses. How this balance is to be achieved in a given context is a challenge to the professional judgement of staff.

Consideration of the issues raised in this chapter suggest the need for particular research on the following:

- Studies on the psychodynamics of assessment and the influence of contextual factors: what leads to 'cheating'? What are the circumstances in which students will make fair and reasonable self appraisals? What features of a self assessment process encourage a self-critical approach?
- Further monitoring of innovations in self assessment to determine which can be used more widely and in which circumstances they can be adopted. This can involve both replication studies of the strategies discussed above in different contexts and also the development of other innovative approaches. There is great potential for various forms of peer involvement in this area.
- The use of collaborative approaches to research to take account of student perspectives as well as those of staff (see Reason and Rowan, 1981). Students have access to their own knowledge in a way that staff can never have. Research needs to be undertaken which respects this feature and enables the student perspective to be properly incorporated into our understanding.

# PART IV

# DESIGN, IMPLEMENTATION AND EVALUATION

## Chapter 14

# How can Self Assessment be Implemented?

In many respects the introduction of self assessment is no different from the introduction of any innovation in teaching and learning and similar considerations apply to it. Even when it is implemented well, there is likely to be initial scepticism and resistance followed by cautious acceptance and, hopefully, enthusiasm. Again, like any teaching innovation, staff who promote it may be seen as slightly odd by their colleagues and questions will be raised about whether the idea is a sound one. The individual innovator is likely to be questioned about whether they are doing the right thing and whether they are doing it in the best way.

This chapter discusses the process of introduction, implementation and evaluation of self assessment practices. Much of what is included applies equally to other innovations, but some issues are especially significant in self assessment and particular attention will be given to them. Matters linked with assessment have an emotional charge to them. Assessment is associated, perhaps subtly, with control and advancement. The impact of assessment on individuals and their aspirations is likely to be greater than for other teaching and learning matters. For this reason, particular attention needs to be given to implementation issues in this area. The following two chapters concentrate on specific issues in implementation: the design of self assessment strategies and the use of peers in self assessment processes.

## Getting started

The starting point for most plans for self assessment is the question: why use self assessment at all? As has been discussed earlier, there are many motives for doing so, ranging from the purely educational – to enhance student learning – to the grossly pragmatic – to reduce time spent by teaching staff. These are not necessarily incompatible objectives, but too great an emphasis on the cost-cutting side is likely to lead to suspicion by students of the motives of the exercise and to an activity which does not realise as much of the educational potential as is possible. A useful working principle is that the introduction of self assessment should not normally place an additional burden on staff. Scope for reductions in repetitive tasks which have little educational impact (eg, marking which leads to grades but no feedback) should be sought assiduously. It is important also that the impact on students be similarly considered. The equivalent principle for them is that their overall workload should not increase above the norm for similar subjects and that, where at all possible, their effort be redirected into activities which engage them in tasks which have a direct benefit to the kind of learning that engages them with the central goals of the course. In the case of both staff and students, perceived workload is often more important than actual workload at the point of introduction.

It is not prudent to introduce self assessment practices without involving students. Students are unlikely to view sympathetically an argument for self assessment which involves taking greater responsibility if they feel the idea has been foisted on them. As many students will be unfamiliar with self assessment and have no direct experience of its formal use within a course, it will often be necessary for a specific proposal to be outlined prior to discussion of the idea. Initial student suspicion and wariness is to be expected – this factor is considered in more detail later.

As self assessment may be quite a novel idea it is important to give students an opportunity to discuss it fully and allow them to influence the way in which it is used. Such involvement can lead to more effective implement-ation, but staff need to avoid being drawn into practices which they do not believe to be educationally sound. The modification of proposals in the light of student concerns and ideas is likely to lead to a greater degree of ownership of the practice by students than would be the case if the approach to self assessment were unilaterally imposed. This is desirable for all categories of self assessment, but vital when there is an emancipatory interest.

Two possible areas of conflict in initial discussions are evident in my experience:

- It is quite common for students to wish to use time spent or effort expended as a criterion for judging their work, and this is generally not acceptable to staff.
- Conversely, staff assessing students' work often use criteria which they have not revealed and which they may not even have acknowledged to themselves that they are using. This practice leads to a mystification of assessment and inhibits students developing appropriate criteria of their own.

The solution to both problems lies in explicit communication. The difficulty of using effort as a criterion must be confronted at the start – effort does not reflect outcomes – and staff must be prepared to acknowledge their own criteria for assessing work even if it is difficult for them to articulate what these are. It is desirable, as a general rule, for both staff and students to be open about their criteria and their judgements. Only in this way can these be available for critical scrutiny, and only thus can students learn to appreciate the full range of considerations which are relevant to the kind of work in which they are engaged. The introduction of self assessment would ideally be accompanied by a review of all the ways in which staff communicate what counts as good work in the subject and the nature of the feedback provided by staff to students on other course-related tasks.

It is tempting to take an existing self assessment strategy off-the-shelf and use it directly in one's own course. The use of other people's strategies has limitations, however. While examination of different approaches used elsewhere can be very useful in prompting consideration of what may or may not be appropriate, it is rare that any of these will sufficiently fit the existing local context to be used without modification. In the same way that allowing students to suggest modifications and using their ideas to improve the strategy leads to better ownership and commitment to the approach, so the modification of existing strategies by teachers prior to introducing them leads to an approach more suited for the immediate teaching and learning context.

Finally, at the start, options other than self assessment may need to be considered. As discussed in Chapter 3, self assessment is one of a much wider range of options to prompt student reflection on learning, foster learning-how-to-learn skills and support deep approaches to learning. It fits well with these other approaches and can be used in conjunction with them; however, it is manifestly not the solution to all problems of learning.

## Getting committed

Some teachers see themselves as chiefly responsible for the inculcation of the knowledge and practices of the discipline or profession rather than the pursuit of other educational goals. The result is that in teaching they focus almost exclusively on the formal content of the subject. This in turn can lead to inadequate consideration of the attitudes and needs of students, and neglect of the second-order skills (eg, learning-how-to-learn) which are required for both learning and for professional practice. Other teachers, as we have seen in Chapter 3, see themselves as conduits for the knowledge which students need to acquire. Neither of these conceptions of teaching are likely to lead students to adopt deep approaches to learning or to successful engage with self assessment.

In addition, some staff see themselves as having power and are loathe to 'give it up'; they may find some forms of self assessment too challenging to encompass within their courses. Any shift of emphasis in assessment, even self assessment which is not used for grading, changes patterns of influence in a course and can lead to students asking questions about the appropriateness and fairness of existing assessment procedures. While this is generally a positive development which helps to demystify the assessment process, it can mean that staff have to justify their practices in unfamiliar ways.

As with all innovations, it is important that staff embark on schemes to develop student self assessment procedures only when they themselves understand and become committed to the values which underpin this whole area. These values are contained in the premises discussed in Chapter 2 and the views of learning in Chapter 3. They include principally the encouragement of student autonomy in learning and student responsibility for critical evaluation of their own work. When there is a compatibility of values there is a greater likelihood that the necessary adaptations required in getting self assessment to work effectively will be undertaken in a way which is consistent with the basic premises. Risks will have to be taken, risks of putting some decisions in the hands of students, but it is only when the basic premises are accepted that it will be possible to justify some of these risks (cf. Cowan, 1988).

On the other hand there are many examples of staff who may not be fully committed to these ideas, or relatively neutral about the values involved, who nevertheless find it feasible to engage in self assessment activities with their students. They might do this as a means of exploring their potential and testing out their own response to the new values and ideas. Some may initially be attracted to self assessment to solve resource problems only then to find themselves discovering that the educational benefits are persuasive also.

In sum, the ways staff conceptualise their role as teachers, and the attitudes they hold towards their position, might not in all cases match closely enough the conditions necessary for effective implementation of student self assessment. It is tempting to think that the introduction of self assessment into a course might address its existing problems. This is rarely the case. On the contrary, it is important to appreciate that the introduction of self assessment by itself cannot bring significant benefits if a course already stands in need of revision of teaching methods or teacher-centred assessment procedures.

## Responding to student concerns

It is not realistic to expect students to greet self assessment as a wonderful new development to which they will respond enthusiastically. Many will be justifiably wary. Many will have encountered teachers who propose a new way of teaching or who have talked about students taking responsibility, only to find themselves floundering in some new system whose rules they don't understand or which seems particularly time-consuming or of little benefit. It is even worse when students hear the rhetoric of a new approach, but experience the old approach again.

There is also a countervailing expectation when students start any new course. It is that the new course 'will be one that is interesting and involving and in which I will do well'. At the beginning, students are often willing to try new ideas. They will persist with them if they see the benefit and if their teachers maintain a suitable and consistent context in which they can operate. They are more likely to take a positive view if their teachers appear confident about what they are doing.

Some concern about student resistance to self assessment was revealed in the survey of staff using self assessment discussed in Chapter 11, but is this concern of great significance? In many cases there is resistance. If self assessment is introduced with little rationale in a course which has excessive demands on students, resistance is not surprising. Such resistance often says more about the culture of the course, the relationship between staff and students and the contradictions between what a teacher claims and what students experience than anything to do with self assessment. It is always worth taking such apparent resistance seriously as it indicates that the course is not working as the teacher would like.

In many circumstances it may be in students' best interests to resist and it may also be appropriate for them to do so. These are when self assessment appears to be introduced as a substitute for staff providing good quality feedback, when the overall load demands of a subject are too high or when there is no perceived benefit. Students' concerns need to be heard and clarified and responded to in a way which shows that they have been heeded. Changes may not need to be substantial, but they do need to be seen by students as related to the issues which they have raised.

It does not matter how intrinsically well-designed a self assessment activity might be, it is the specifics of how it is implemented which significantly influence how well it is received. This will influence how students perceive the approach and it is this which really counts.

If it is assumed that students have had their initial concerns satisfactorily addressed, the next step is for them to experience a process which they accept as valid. The elements of such a process are likely to involve:

- a clear rationale: what are the purposes of this particular activity?
- explicit procedures: students need to know what is expected of them
- reassurance: of a safe environment in which they can be honest about their own performance without the fear that they will expose information which can be used against them
- confidence: that other students will do likewise, and that cheating or collusion will be detected and discouraged.

There is a strong need for students to have a specific rationale for the self assessment activity. This must relate both to their long-term goals, but more importantly, the immediate payoff to students must be apparent. If there is no immediate benefit – for example, it doesn't assist them with the assessed course requirements – then there are questions to be raised about why the assessment requirements are as they are, or about why self assessment has been introduced in a part of the course which is not important enough to be otherwise assessed.

It is difficult for students to change their habits and attitudes towards monitoring their own learning if self assessment is introduced at the end of a course. However, it is also difficult for students entering from school to change the habits acquired there. They will have had many years of being socialised into expectations of authority-dependence and unilateral assessment by staff. It is probably at the beginning of any course that students ought to first encounter the concept of self assessment if it is to be taken seriously and applied effectively. Notwithstanding the problems of transition from school, the introduction should be made at the earliest possible stage, and the skills practised thereafter, most desirably in a sequence of subjects throughout the years of their course.

Similarly, within a particular subject, students should know what is expected of them at the beginning and should not have the idea of self assessment introduced once they have already developed an expectation of what is to occur. There are always competing demands in the timetable and it is quite difficult to make room for new content or for a new approach. However, many successful self assessment exercises have been built around an existing activity in a course (an examination, or a class exercise) through making variations in the process.

There needs to be plenty of time for discussion/clarification with students, but it can be necessary to set a deadline on the debate, otherwise student anxieties about assessment take over and the issue can become a running irritant throughout the term. My practice is to introduce the idea early in the semester and suggest a specific procedure during the first four weeks, before self assessment considerations start to conflict with other assessment pressures. That is, students are engaged in discussing the idea when they are least preoccupied with other tasks.

A particular issue which arises in the introduction of any new assessment procedure is that quite small variations in the approach adopted can produce very different responses from students. These should be anticipated and adaptations, often quite small, need to be made. For example, instructions need to be explicit and unambiguous and specific details need to be given about what students should do. Asking students to list the level of performance required in particular aspects of an assignment and asking them to make a judgement about each one is normally more effective than simply requiring them to give unjustified ratings on, say, a five-point scale.

One might hope that in a setting where there were no formal assessment constraints students would acknowledge the value of monitoring their own learning and willingly undertake it. However, it is sometimes necessary to offer some sort of incentive. There are three options: making these incentives intrinsic to the task, making them extrinsic, or combining elements of the two. Incentives could include:

- appealing to pure intellectual curiosity
- persuading students of the interest and value of the exercise
- awarding marks for self assessment
- building it in as a course requirement
- allocation of class time or substitution for other assignments, rather than expecting students to take it on as an extra task
- using it for contracting for a grade.

In an ideal context it may be sufficient to appeal to students' best interests. But in many course cultures it is necessary for staff to demonstrate their belief in the value of self assessment in a tangible fashion, by providing at least some extrinsic incentive.

## Dealing with the institution

The introduction of self assessment practices can have the effect of raising quite profound questions about:

- the role of courses: are they to inculcate knowledge, develop students' intellectual skills, or what?
- the educational purposes of professional courses: are they simply pre-service training or do they have broader educational goals?
- the ways in which courses are organised: if students are expected to take responsibility for their learning, why is this discouraged in practice?
- the validity of the assessment procedures associated with courses: why is the development of self assessment skills not an integral part of all assessment practices?

Considerations of questions such as these sometimes lead to changes in parts of the curriculum or, at least, pressure to review courses. It can also lead to resistance on the part of colleagues as these questions can rarely be confined to a single subject within a course. There is nothing more likely to make colleagues unsympathetic to one's position than comments by students which imply that colleagues should change their practices because of what you are doing. It is not a matter of rational discourse about the merits of change. It is often experienced as one person unilaterally placing items on a departmental agenda through student pressure.

The simplest way of circumventing this problem is to discuss with colleagues plans to introduce self assessment right from the start and gain their acceptance, if not their approval. This is clearly the best strategy in many departments. However, in others any public announcement about the adoption of self assessment is likely to provoke challenges to one's right to do it. 'It wasn't included when the course was approved', or 'It doesn't form part of the existing assessment guidelines', are favourite arguments. I have been in at least two situations, many years ago, where I did not judge it politic to formally inform my colleagues that I was using self assessment. I believed that they would have tried to stop me because I was challenging the dominant teaching and assessment ethos of the department. I also believed that while I might have persuaded them of my point of view, the amount of time and energy I would have had to expend was not worth it. On both occasions I revealed my practices to them once I could demonstrate that they were working well.

There are surprisingly few examples of problems of acceptance by external agencies. Indeed, unless there is a substantial shift of formal assessment weighting towards student-generated grades, the use of innovative methods designed to improve the quality of learning are naturally regarded quite sympathetically. My own experience has been that external accrediting bodies have been favourably inclined towards to the introduction of self assessment. However, problems have arisen within institutions when the visits of external accrediting committees have been used as excuses to impose conservative teaching and learning regimes. When self assessment has been introduced as part of assessment strategies (as distinct from teaching and learning strategies) there are examples of them being subject to quite hostile scrutiny prior to the involvement of external bodies. Self assessment seems to provoke in some staff an irrational fear, contrary to any evidence, that the institution will be seen as condoning the lowering of standards and introducing courses that are insufficiently serious.

Such perceptions are a trap for the unwary innovator and can be disconcerting. There is no substitute for careful preparation of the ground and the collection of supporting evidence from within the institution and elsewhere that the proposed practices are not only acceptable, but have a positive impact on learning. This is perhaps as it should be. 'Tinkering' with assessment is fraught with dangers and should be done only in full awareness of the possible consequences. It is unfortunate that moves towards adding to assessment burdens in ways which encourage bad study habits of overload and memorisation are not subject to equally rigorous scrutiny.

## Evaluating self assessment practices

It is particularly important to evaluate self assessment practices as the effects of such procedures are especially sensitive to the ways in which they have been implemented. It is necessary to ensure that they are suitably adapted to meet local circumstances. Evaluation needs to be conducted to ensure that self assessment meets the needs of students and teachers and contributes to learning in ways which have been anticipated. It is also often necessary to satisfy a wider audience. It is always needed to aid the development of the practice.

The most important feature of any evaluation is that it is systematic. A systematic approach is required to avoid an overemphasis on impressionistic and informal information which might, for example, come from a few vocal students or a cutting remark from a colleague. It is also required to ensure that it is not only information which supports one's point of view which is collected. It is easy to inadvertently word a questionnaire, for example, so that students are not given the opportunity to express what they feel. Items which solicit both positive and negative views are needed.

Examples of evaluation can be found in earlier chapters as well as in the literature. Chapter 6 gives examples of questionnaire items which have been used to determine student acceptability and to monitor changes in procedures over time. Chapter 7 provides a simple, open-ended question-naire which can be used when student numbers are sufficiently small for the collation of qualitative answers to be managed quickly. The literature provides other examples of evaluation items, for example, in Edwards and Sutton (1991), Stefani (1994) and Williams (1992).

There are three main aspects of evaluation relevant here. These are associated with different purposes:

*Assisting in effective establishment (developmental testing)*. Evaluation of this kind is needed before it can be said that self assessment has been properly introduced. It involves collecting data to check if implement-ation has occurred in the ways desired. Modifications to the process used are made immediately the need for them is identified. The evaluation activities are often informal and involve close liaison with students, and any other parties involved, so that they understand the practice in the way it is intended and that they can do what is expected of them.

*Improving educational processes in the medium term (formative evalu-ation)*. This is connected with information which will be of assistance to the staff and students directly involved, but it is more comprehensive than that gathered through developmental testing. Questionnaires and inter-view schedules may be devised to collect data in ways that will allow comparisons from one round of implementation to another. This can demonstrate progressive improvements in the self assessment process as it is refined from year to year in the light of feedback.

*Enabling overall benefits to be judged (summative evaluation)*. Other parties are also interested in the outcomes of the use of self assessment, but their focus is often quite different to that of the initiators. Data on overall effects are of less interest to the immediate parties concerned as they will have already formed their own views. It is such summative data, along with longitudinal and experiential data from formative evaluations, which allows inferences about self assessment as an educational practice to be made.

The three aspects of evaluation relate to different intents, but they can easily merge. Data generated for one purpose are often used for another and this can lead to confusion and misinterpretation. For example, in the first two purposes above, rich and detailed information which may be critical of a particular practice is required to identify areas for change and development. However, for summative purposes, more general and balanced judgements are needed which set the self assessment process being evaluated alongside other practices with similar intents.

The three aspects of evaluation also reflect three levels of acceptance of the practice being examined. At the first level of acceptance, staff and students directly involved must be assured that the specific self assessment activity works for them. At the second level of acceptance, students and staff are reassured through formative evaluation activities that other staff and students have found similar self assessment activities appropriate and worth pursuing. At the third level of acceptance, third parties such as colleagues elsewhere, administrators and researchers are able to draw secure conclusions about the effectiveness of the types of self assessment being examined.

The difference of focus of these purposes goes some way towards explaining why teachers persist with an innovation in the face of evidence that shows that it is not working. The data in which they are interested and which influence them are of quite a different kind to those which are compelling to colleagues and administrators.

The first aspect of evaluation normally preceeds the second and third as there is no point reaching a conclusion about self assessment even at a local level if it is not implemented well. If judgements were made about the effectiveness of lecturing on the basis of the first example of an inexperienced lecturer, then we would draw false conclusions about the effectiveness of lecturing. Similarly with self assessment. There have been so few examples of evaluation of mature self assessment processes over time that it is not yet possible to draw conclusions about their long-term effects. The fact that positive results have been obtained from newly tried strategies augers well for future development of self assessment.

Most examples of evaluation practice of self assessment have come in the first and second categories: evaluation to improve the process. Where there have been examples of the third category (judging overall benefits) these have usually been through a few additional questions slipped into a questionnaire design to seek improvements or through students' results in final assessments.

While it is important to be able to undertake specific evaluation studies which focus on self assessment, much course and subject evaluation will take place in a wider context. Self assessment will be but one of many considerations. Whether or not evaluation is specific to self assessment activities or more general, it is important that it focuses on those factors which are related to student learning, rather than those associated with features of teacher style or local administrative arrangements.

## Conclusions

This chapter has drawn attention to the importance of effective implementation. It has emphasised involving students and gaining their commitment through responding to their real concerns. It has also pointed to wider issues in dealing with institutional concerns and in effective evaluation of self assessment practices. The following two chapters consider details of the design of self assessment strategies and the particular issue of how other students can be used effectively in the self assessment of their peers.

# Chapter 15

# How can Self Assessment Strategies be Designed?

Self assessment activities clearly need to be designed in response to particular needs, particular circumstances and particular subject matter. There are many different practices influenced by different motives, and they emphasise different key ideas and strategies. In some practices, for example, subject-matter concepts are central; in others, transferable skills are dominant. And, as we have seen in Chapters 5 and 11, they are driven by different interests.

An effective strategy is one which gains student commitment, links well with the subject matter, fits the context and forms part of a broader strategy for encouraging students to take greater responsibility for learning. There are some pointers which are helpful in considering how to design a self assessment strategy and, especially, how to avoid some of the pitfalls. This chapter is mostly based on my own experience of working with a wide variety of courses. It is unlikely that all of the features discussed in this chapter will appear in any given example, but if too many are absent, the self assessment process designed may not meet any of its goals.

## Considering the assessment and learning context

Self assessment has to be compatible with the nature of the course of which it is a part, otherwise it can easily be seen as an isolated exercise or mere add-on that is not significant for the course of study. The overall assessment and learning context needs to be carefully considered. The aspects of the context which tend to be important are:

- Other assessment tasks and work demands. For example, will involvement in a self assessment exercise assist students in completing formally assessed tasks later? Will it fit well within the total workload of students relative to other subjects? Will it consolidate student learning to date? Will

189

it enable students to better understand topics which follow?

- The educational goals of the subject. For example, is it related to central ideas and concepts? Will it assist students in appropriating key knowledge in the subject? Will it enable students to communicate their understandings more effectively?
- Students' experience of undertaking self assessment. For example, do students need to be convinced of the worth of self assessment? Will they need practice in specifying criteria? How specific will guidelines for self assessment need to be?
- The competitive/cooperative climate in the course. In some circumstances students will resist self assessment unless the activity formally counts as part of the grading system. This is usually related to the overall climate of competition or cooperation which it is difficult for individual teachers to influence directly.

I am inclined to only use self marking (ie, the giving of numerical marks or grades) in limited circumstances as the artefacts of marking can detract from student engagement with criteria and standards for work in a given area. Conditions in which self marking may be educationally justified are:

- when students are very new to the domain and cannot recognise what counts as good; models and worked examples may be required
- when it is a preliminary stage to self assessment proper
- when it is used in association with distancing devices to help students look afresh at their work (eg, through provision of a detailed sequences of steps, the use of peer feedback or through getting them to first mark the work of a peer)
- when the rating scale used does not have any connotations of what is socially desirable (eg, it does not relate to specific classes of honours, or involves a percentage with an assumed pass mark)
- when the sub-components of the task, not global marking, are emphasised (eg, specific checklists or detailed marking schedules are used)
- when all scales and points on scales are explicit (ie, not marking as a percentage or out of 10 without the categories for each mark specified).

### The particular demands of the subject

The demands of the subject and the educational outcomes of the course have to be considered. While some aspects of self assessment are likely to have the character of generic skills, many are situation-specific or specific to a particular domain of knowledge. Just because someone is effective in self assessment in mechanical engineering does not imply that they would be equally effective in, say, surgery. It is not a simple matter of different knowledge requirements, but the structure of domains of knowledge and different epistemologies of problem-solving. What constitutes an appropriate solution differs from one field to the next. Not only this, but within a given area there are the different kinds of knowledge interest which were explored in Chapter 5.

It is prudent to assume that self assessment is usually domain-specific rather than a transferable skill, ie, it will be necessary for students to develop self assessment with respect to a particular body of knowledge and its associated epistemology rather than in a way which assumes that the body of knowledge is not a significant factor. There may well be some academic skills which are more broadly transferable, eg, some aspects of verbal communication, but I believe that it is generally wiser to assume that there is less transferability than one might hope for. When looking for relevant examples of self assessment strategies, it is useful to consider what domain of knowledge and what kinds of knowledge interests one is dealing with and look for examples in those areas.

## Choosing appropriate tasks and processes for self assessment

The design of a self assessment activity involves bringing together an appropriate self assessment strategy and a suitable task that is pertinent to a particular stage of students' development in a given course. The choice of what to assess and the process of doing so is as crucial in self assessment as it is in any assessment context. It may be even more important as there are severe practical limits on the number of self assessment exercises students can undertake in any course. The adaptation of a task to make it one which is a particularly good use of students' time repays the initial effort required.

Successful selection of a particular task and process is likely to depend on the extent to which one:

- asks learners to make judgements on matters on which it is reasonable for them to do so. There is often a threshold of knowledge below which a learner's understanding is so low that meaningful assessments cannot be made. If assessments are expected in these situations it is not surprising if students do not take them seriously as they betray a lack of respect for them – 'rubbing in' a lack of knowledge!
- uses cues for success which are embedded in the content as much as possible. The more the task is one which involves the use of intrinsic subject matter cues, the more the exercise becomes a meaningful one.

For example, an exercise in communication could be designed so that learners get verbal and non-verbal responses from an audience before completing the task rather than completing the task without feedback, or the choice of a scientific problem-solving exercise which can be checked by simple order-of-magnitude type calculations.

- chooses situations in which there are external sources of evidence and benchmarks (standards) which can be drawn upon, or multiple sources of evidence or multiple judgements are available. For example, in asking for a critique of an argument, a variety of critical reviews from different perspectives may be made accessible or, in making a laboratory measurement, students may be expected to use tolerances which are readily available to them.
- avoids situations in which criteria for success are matters of opinion or taste (unless the goal is the exploration of aesthetic judgements). If a second *staff* member would likely give a differing opinion from the first, then great care must be exercised in how self assessment might be used.
- avoids incentives for mis-assessment. That is, it avoids situations in which students can 'beat the system' by not approaching self assessment in an authentic way, ie, by 'going through the motions' or collusion without engagement in the task.
- chooses the specific rather than the global, ie, situations in which students can imagine undertaking a specific task. For example, Peirce *et al.* (1993) found that it was better to get language students to explain a movie plot in French rather than have them compare their language proficiency with a Francophone peer.
- limits the number of criteria which must be considered simultaneously at first. If multiple criteria are to be applied, guidelines on sequencing or consolidating judgements may need to be given. For example, when assessing a report, suggest that emphasis be initially given to looking at the general sequence of the argument, rather than detailed forms of expression.
- develops detailed guidelines on how the process is to be undertaken, preferably after discussion with students. What is apparently clear in the lecture hall often becomes unclear when a week later students try to recall what was discussed. It is important to spend time considering what ambiguities might exist in the proposed task. Self assessment is difficult enough for students when their task is clear. One way of thinking about this is to consider how a naive student would misread the instructions. Strategies should normally be in writing so they can be more easily discussed and students can refer back to them. The success of good self assessment (like good assessment) is in the details of the task – anyone

can design a grand plan which doesn't work, but crafting what ends up as a simple exercise involves a great deal of skill.

**Key choices**

Once the area to be assessed has been determined, a number of decisions are required to focus on the major features of a particular design:

- In what forms should students express their assessments? Should rating scales be used or should assessments be entirely qualitative? There is a wide range of opinion on this matter. However, I have been moving increasingly away from the use of rating scales towards self assessments which lead to a qualitative outcome and involve students in making detailed value judgements about their work. My view now is that it is important to avoid the use of simple rating scales, especially those in which the specific meaning of each point is not explicit. It means little for a student to rate themselves as seven out of ten. What is important are the factors which lead the student to conclude that six and eight are inappropriate ratings. These discriminatory factors are the ones which are influential in learning, not the summary grade to which they might lead. If grades or points are to be used there is benefit in only selecting the mark after a process of discussion or clarification with peers.
- How can self assessment abilities be developed over time? It is unrealistic to expect excellent assessments at first. If students do demonstrate initial excellence in self assessment this may be a good reason for not spending more time on developing their skills in that particular area.
- How can it be ensured that self assessment activities are of direct benefit to students? Self assessment should always lead to some kind of action or outcome of value to students (ie, one that they believe is of value to them).

Finally, it is worth keeping in mind that iteration and modification to the exercise will always be needed. It is very difficult to create a good self-assessment exercise which works well the first time it is used. Many of the examples given in earlier chapters (eg, in Chapters 6, 7, 9 and 10) were the result of many years of incremental modification.

## Engaging learners in considering criteria and standards

The central aspect of any self assessment process is the extent to which it engages learners effectively with the criteria and standards which it is appropriate to apply to any given work. On the one hand students are not experts and cannot be expected to have as sophisticated appreciation of criteria as their teachers; on the other, they will never develop such an appreciation without direct engagement with such criteria.

## Criteria for judging performance

One of the most difficult aspects of self assessment for students, and necessarily for staff, is thinking in terms of criteria. Very often teachers have a notion of what are the standards they should apply to a particular kind of work, for example an essay, but they have difficulties in articulating them. They know what is good when they see it, but they find it hard to describe it to others (Pirsig, 1974). This is an issue which goes to the heart of teaching in higher education: if teachers are unable to clearly specify their standards for good work, how can students learn to produce it? Dealing with tacit knowledge takes us beyond the scope of this book, but it is important for staff to exert themselves to be as clear as possible about what criteria are, and what would constitute satisfactory achievement.

## Clarifying the concept of assessment criteria

In all cases it is necessary for the concept of criteria for assessment to be presented in operational terms with which all participants are familiar. This may take the form of asking: 'How would you distinguish good from poor work in this subject?', or 'What would be the factors which characterise a good assignment in this course?' It is not a good idea to ask students to guess what criteria their teachers would use as this may trivialise and personalise the issue and discourage students from thinking for themselves.

## The elements of satisfactory criteria

Criteria should include information about:

- the area to be assessed,
- the aims to be pursued, and
- the standards to be reached.

Moreover, these should all be spelled out at such a level of detail as will make it possible for the person making the judgement to know the extent to which the criteria have been met. This represents an ideal case however, and in practice rather less than this may be adequate under circumstances where it can be demonstrated that the appropriate standards in the given subject can be applied without their being stated explicitly.

### Strategies for generating criteria

Although the objective is for students to reach their own decisions about criteria for assessing themselves, and hopefully about how they arrive at such criteria, it is important to understand the facilitative role the teacher plays in this process. Two techniques which can be used for this purpose are structured written schedules for developing individual criteria and structured group activities for reaching consensus on common criteria.

*Structured written schedules* have been found most useful when used as a basis for self assessment by individual students (as distinct from a class group). They consist of a list of written instructions to guide each student through a sequence of steps involving:

- identifying the criteria which they consider appropriate to apply to their work,
- clarifying these criteria, and
- assessing the priority or emphasis which they wish to give to each.

These steps consist of questions which are as easy to complete as possible. A starting point might be:

1. List the factors you would take into account in assessing your assignment.
2. List the factors you would take into account when assessing another person's assignment.
3. Look through each list carefully and decide if you could recognise each item in the work of someone else. Rewrite any item in your list that you could not recognise in someone's work.
4. Reread your list. Could each item be readily understood by someone else without explanation? Rewrite any ambiguous statements.
5. Decide what priority you would place on each item. Number them in order of importance.
   (Adapted from Boud and Tyree, 1980)

Once satisfactory criteria have been generated in this way, students can then use them as the yardsticks by which they judge their own performance. In some cases this will consist simply of awarding themselves a mark with respect to each criterion, and then making a statement justifying that mark. Alternatively, they may simply make a statement indicating the extent to which they have satisfied each criterion (eg, in Chapter 9).

*Structured group activities* can be used when it is desired to generate common criteria for a class, as is frequently the case when students enrolled in a particular subject are expected to be assessed using identical criteria. The use of identical criteria is the usual way teachers make assessments.

If students are to be involved in generating these criteria for purposes of self or peer assessment, it becomes necessary to find ways in which they can, as a group, identify, discuss and agree upon a common set of them. One method which has been found particularly useful is based upon the nominal group technique (Delbecq *et al.*, 1975). The word 'nominal' is used as the group functions as a group in name only and the interactions between members are restricted by certain rules. The following is one way of using that technique for generating self and peer assessment criteria:

1. Students are briefed in advance of the meeting that they will be expected to produce a number of criteria, say three, which will be considered by the class as a whole. To assist them at this stage they may be given a handout which gives them some guidance on how criteria for assessment might be phrased and what will happen in the meeting.
2. The meeting is conducted by either the teacher or a colleague who is experienced in the use of nominal group methods. If the teacher leads the session it is particularly important that he or she be non-judgemental about the criteria which are generated during the process and resist indicating either verbally or non-verbally their own thoughts about the criteria which are being discussed. The reason for this is that students may be inhibited from presenting their own responses when they hear teachers expressing their own opinions or values. If the teacher feels that it is not possible to maintain this role, then this is ground for bringing in someone else who can be a neutral facilitator.
3. The leader of the session invites each person in turn to read out *one* of the criteria from their prepared list. This is written on a large sheet of paper where it can be seen by everyone. The process continues with as many cycles around the group as are necessary for all criteria to be listed. Chalkboards or whiteboards, unless very large, or overhead projectors, cannot be used as it is not possible to display all the criteria which are normally generated. Once the criteria have been recorded there is a period for clarification and for combining statements covering the same ground. Participants may be asked to suggest headings under which the criteria may be grouped. At this stage a straw vote may be taken on whether the criteria are acceptable. Students may agree to use the complete list, or to rate and choose the high priority items.

## Considering what is known about assessment design and student differences

While this book focuses on self assessment and presents research on self assessment practices, there is experience from related areas of assessment to be considered also. While some of it, eg. on the reliability of marking, is relatively well known, there is also work from the psychology of self presentation and the area of gender differences which raises important questions about the design of self assessments.

## Reliability of markers

While Chapter 13 discussed how to improve reliability of marking, parallel advice can improve the effectiveness of self assessments even when grades are not to be formally recorded. Recommendations would include:

- establishing explicit criteria for satisfactory and unsatisfactory performance. Whatever else is generated, a decision about whether the work meets minimum standards is often useful;
- using scales in which all the categories are unambiguously defined, for example, by avoiding five-point scales in which the end points only are defined or where vague descriptions such as good/very good or average/about average are used;
- using scales which are no more detailed than required, for example, by avoiding scales with more than a readily comprehensible number of categories;
- training self assessors through practising the application of accepted criteria to typical examples of work followed by discussion between peers to reach consensus on the interpretation of the criteria.

## Self presentation

A fundamental problem for all assessment is that students are not only dealing with the ostensible assessment task, but they are managing an impression of themselves. This occurs even when marking is done anonymously. This adds an extra dimension to self assessment over that which is apparent. When students have an audience for their assessment they are projecting a view of themselves which may cloud the information which the other person notices and forms their judgement on. Sometimes, for example, maintaining the impression of being an unambitious student who is not trying hard can overwhelm the demonstration of competence (cf. Snyder, 1987).

## Research on gender differences

While the outcomes of research on male/female differences are far from unambiguous, work to date (see Chapters 12 and 17) suggests that the following matters should also be considered in designing self assessment

**197**

strategies. These recommendations should be treated with great care as it is easy to fall into the kind of gender-stereotyping this research seeks to avoid:

- Ensure that the effects of the particular exercise on the self esteem of students is considered (women may be more adversely affected than men when 'deficiencies' are exposed).
- Avoid social norms as criteria for judgement (eg, by directing attention away from considering what an 'average' student would consider a good response).
- Avoid students making direct comparisons with each other (use objective criteria not those which have interpersonal implications).
- Avoid public presentations of self assessment unless other specific steps to create a suitable climate to protect self esteem have been made (eg, establishing a high-trust environment).
- Avoid activities which involve tasks or examples which have masculine or feminine connotations (eg, a task where men present technical and women the social arguments in favour of a proposal).
- Avoid competition in self assessments.
- Consider using female–female or male–male pairings and pairings of students similarly matched in ability for giving one-to-one feedback.
- Consider whether self assessments might be affected by more modest self presentational styles of female students in social settings.

## Conclusion

While this chapter has provided many suggestions to influence the design of self assessment strategies, it would be impossible to address all the considerations discussed here in a given instance. It is necessary to be pragmatic when introducing self assessment for the first time and start with a reasonably straightforward exercise which students can readily appreciate. More sophisticated tasks drawing on additional features discussed here might be introduced at later stages.

The most important design consideration of all is viewing the process from the point of view of typical students who might encounter it. The intrinsic merits of the process are irrelevant if students do not interpret the activity in the ways anticipated. It is the perceptions students have of the task, not the teacher's perceptions of it, which will govern how students will act. One way of dealing with this is to take the proposed self assessment plan and subject it to the imagined criticism of different students. If they were being completely open and frank, what would they say is unrealistic, what would be realistic for them to do and not do? If they undertook the exercise as envisaged, what would their outcomes look like? Do these perceptions lead to a task which has the desired outcomes and is a worthwhile element of the course?

# Chapter 16

# How can Peers be Used in Self Assessment?

One of the greatest misconceptions about self assessment is that it can be undertaken in isolation from others. While it would be possible to envisage self assessment processes of this kind, most examples in higher education require the involvement of other parties. The defining feature of self assessment is that the individual learner ultimately makes a judgement about what has been learned, not that others have no input to it. While there are many strategies which involve staff inputs, most interest and activity has been shown in the role of peers, that is, other students who are studying alongside the learner. How can such people be used most effectively? What guidelines might be adopted for the use of peers in self assessment?

Learning is enhanced through maximising the opportunities for students to discuss their work with others. Organising self assessment with an element of peer discussion or feedback can be very desirable. Smith and Hatton's (1993) research suggests that students engage in a greater level and depth of reflection when they discuss their work with a peer as distinct from discussion with a specifically trained staff member or in a specially designed written assignment. If this is generally true, it would lead one to build peer discussion and feedback into most learning and hence most self assessment exercises. Such discussion can involve students in disclosing their tentative views and uncertainties without having to justify themselves to an authority figure and formulating responses to a wide range of questions. It is self regulating, and it is inexpensive of staff time.

## Making judgements, giving feedback

One of the most valuable contributions anyone can make to another person's learning is constructive comment. Whether as a student or as a teacher each one of us has the capacity to provide useful information which will help others learn more effectively. The contribution of other students can be a very useful input into the self assessment process. They have had an opportunity to observe their peers throughout the learning process and often they have a more detailed knowledge of the work of others than have their teachers. My own use of peer assessment in conjunction with self assessment, and others' experience suggests (Falchikov, 1995), that formal peer assessment which leads to peer determined grades is generally to be avoided. It can be disruptive of cooperation between students and lead to jealousies and resentment. Reactions have been most positive when students have given specific feedback of a descriptive nature for the benefit of their peers and no grading has taken place. In these circumstances, peer assessment serves to inform self assessment.

Everyone has the capacity for giving useful feedback, however, some people are more effective than others. The skills of giving and receiving feedback can be developed if attention is given to the attributes of worthwhile feedback and how to provide it in ways which enhance learning. There are many characteristics of worthwhile feedback but the most important is the way in which it is given. The tone, the style and the content should be consistent and provide the constant message: 'I appreciate you and what you have done and whatever else I say should be taken in this context'. Some advice on giving helpful feedback is listed below.

The desirable characteristics of peer feedback are no different from those of any other type of feedback from others, including that from teachers. In general such feedback is specific, descriptive, predominantly non-judgemental in tone and form, directed towards the goals of the person receiving it and well timed. It also refers to the particular work under consideration. This 'work' may be of any type: an essay, a class contribution, a design, some behaviour, a project in any form: written, oral, graphic, etc. In the list below, the term 'work' or 'contribution' is used to describe the matter on which feedback is given. Feedback should not refer to attributes of the person not manifested in that work. Helpful feedback makes a conscious distinction between the person – who is always valued – and particular acts or specific work – which may be subject to critical comment. This distinction emphasises that the person is not identical to what he or she does, and their work or actions are not the same as the person, though this should not be taken as justification for a person abrogating responsibility for his or her behaviour. No matter how distasteful a person's acts might be, feedback will only be effectively communicated if their common humanity is respected. It is also normally necessary for students to be given, or for them to establish, clear guidelines on what is being assessed and the form of the assessment activity.

One of the practical constraints on using peer feedback is the amount of time required for students to gain sufficient appreciation of each others' work to enable valid comments to be made. It is particularly important for them to have time to examine and think about the work on which they are giving feedback, otherwise their comments can be superficial. This implies that, except in very small classes (perhaps of less than six students), it is not possible for a student to get feedback from all others even if this were thought desirable.

Realistically, it is unlikely that one person can give sufficiently detailed and useful feedback to more than a few others. The extent to which this is possible also depends on the complexity of the work and the degree to which it is publicly available for discussion and comparison. It can be easier to engage in peer feedback in a design class when drawings and sketches are displayed than it is in a subject which normally requires the production of essays. Even so, students are not used to commenting on the work of others. They therefore need more time than staff to do this, both in order to appreciate the criteria which they are using and to formulate their responses.

Once students have gained some distance from their work and perhaps received feedback from others, they are then in a position to make their own judgements using the criteria which they have earlier identified. It is quite common for additional criteria to become apparent at this stage, so it is necessary for the procedures which are adopted to be sufficiently flexible for these to be accommodated. One form of self assessment involves individuals making a judgement in a small group setting and then seeking feedback from peers prior to arriving at a final assessment (as in the staff development example in Chapter 10). However, a supportive and mature group is needed for this to be effective.

I have been involved in many discussions about positive and negative feedback and the use of praise in feedback. There appears to be close to a consensus on this topic. We all know what it is like to be on the receiving end of bad feedback: we feel 'got at', 'attacked', 'put down', 'damned' and generally invalidated as a person. Some of the basic characteristics of bad feedback are that it is directed globally at the person; it is unhelpful, that is, it does not suggest what otherwise might be done; it is ill-judged, it comes from the needs of the critic rather than the needs of the person receiving it; and it can provide a weight of destructive comment from which it is difficult for a person to surface: it is dehumanising.

Useful feedback, on the other hand, affirms the worth of the person and gives support whilst offering reactions to the object of attention. Thus the person providing the feedback shows that he or she values the person who is receiving it and the provider is sensitive to that person's needs and goals.

Offering feedback to someone else about their work indicates both that the giver cares enough about that person to spend time and that their work is worthy of attention.

This does not mean that only praise should be given, in fact phoney or contrived praise, or praise directed at the person rather than what they have done, can be quite counterproductive – it can feel patronising or controlling. Critical matters should be raised in an overall supportive context in which the parties can trust one another. Great care should be taken in formulating authentic responses which pay attention to both positive and negative aspects of work and presenting these in as helpful a way as we can while keeping in mind the inevitable vulnerability of the learner. We should neither praise falsely nor withhold comments on features which are executed well.

Kohn (1993) has undertaken a detailed review of the literature on rewards and the use of praise and made it available in a readable and provocative form. He argues from empirical research, against popular belief among teachers, that praise is not helpful to learning and has undesirable longer-term consequences. He points out that 'the most notable aspect of a positive judgement is not that it is positive but that it is a judgement' (p. 102). The problem with praise is not as some people seem to think, that it is overdone, but it is with the nature of the praise. Praise comes from the perspective of those who give it and comes on their terms. It implicitly places the person who gives it in a position of authority over the recipient as it assumes that their judgements are crucial.

The solution Kohn proposes to the problem of praise is to keep in mind two general principles that might be thought of as the standards against which all praise should be measured. The first principle is *self determination*. With every comment we make – and specifically, every compliment we give – we need to ask whether we are helping that individual to feel a sense of control over his or her life. Are we encouraging them to make their own judgements about what constitutes a good performance (or a desirable action)? Are we contributing to, or at least preserving, their ability to choose what kind of person to be? Or are we attempting to manipulate their behaviour by getting them to think about whether they have met our criteria? The other principle is *intrinsic motivation*. Are our comments creating the conditions for the person we are praising to become more deeply involved in what they are doing? Or are they turning the task into something they do to win our approval? He points out that to determine the likely effect of praise with respect to these two guidelines, we need to examine, first, our own motives (Kohn, 1993, pp.106–7).

## Offering feedback

If you wish to give helpful feedback, you should:

- *Be realistic.* Direct your comments towards matters on which the person can act. Don't make suggestions which are entirely outside the scope of what the person can do. Constructive comments can be helpful so long as they respect the other person's way of doing things.
- *Be specific.* Generalisations are particularly unhelpful. Base your comments on concrete observable behaviour or materials. Always check your general impressions or inferences against the particular and use the particular in your response. Focusing on behaviour implies that it is something related to a specific situation that might be changed. The person should be given sufficient information to pinpoint the areas to which you are referring and have a clear idea of what is being said about those specific areas. Provide examples.
- *Be sensitive to the goals of the person.* Just because the other person's contributions have not met *your* goals doesn't necessarily imply that something is wrong. The person produced the work for a specific purpose and you should be aware of that purpose and give your views accordingly. This is not to say that you can't make comments from your own perspective but that you should be clear when you offer views in terms of your own goals and you should say that is what you are doing. Link your comments to their intentions; listen carefully to what they have to say. If there is a common task goal be careful to ensure that you have a shared interpretation of what that means.
- *Be timely.* Time your comments appropriately. It is no use offering feedback after the person receiving it has put the work aside and moved on to other things. Respond promptly when your feedback is requested: to be effective feedback must be well-timed.
- *Be descriptive.* Describe your views. Don't be evaluative or say what you think the person should feel. Don't be emotionally manipulative: you are offering your considered views which should have the characteristics described here; it is up to the other person to accept or reject them as he or she sees fit.
- *Be consciously non-judgemental.* Offer your personal view, do not act as an authority even if you may be one elsewhere. Give your personal reactions and feelings rather than value-laden statements. One way of doing this is to use comments of the type, 'I feel . . . when you . . .'
- *Don't compare.* Treat each person's work as their own, not part of some supposed competition with others. Be cautious about giving feedback in

a context in which the comments which you give one person will be compared with those of another. Such comparisons undermine intrinsic motivation.

- *Be diligent.* Check your response. Is it an accurate reflection of what you want to express? Have you perceived the contribution accurately? There is nothing more annoying than to receive criticism from someone who clearly hasn't bothered to pay attention to what you have done.
- *Be direct.* Say what you mean. Don't wrap it up in circumlocution, fancy words or abstract language.
- *Be positive.* Say what you appreciate. Don't just focus on what you react negatively towards. Try to find something which is genuinely felt, rather than being positive because you feel it is required.
- *Be aware.* Note your own emotional state before you give feedback. If you are anxious or defensive you may well distort otherwise helpful comments. Feedback is never a time for you to relieve yourself at the expense of the other person. Move to a focus on the person to whom you are relating and their needs, not yourself, before responding in any way. Don't overload them just because you have a lot to give.

## Receiving feedback

There is no point in asking others to give you feedback unless you are prepared to be open to it and to consider comments which differ from your own perceptions. As receiver:

- *Be explicit.* Make it clear what kind of feedback you are seeking. If necessary indicate what kinds you do not want to receive. The feedback from others is entirely for your benefit and if you do not indicate what you want you are unlikely to get it.
- *Be attentive.* Concentrate fully on what is being said. Focus on what the person wants you to know, not on what you would like to hear. You may want to use a tape recorder to capture verbal feedback to avoid being distracted by taking notes.
- *Be aware.* Notice your own reactions, both intellectual and emotional. Particularly notice any reactions of rejection or censorship on your part. If the viewpoint from which the other is speaking is at variance with your own do not dismiss it: it can be important to realise the misapprehensions of others. Some people find it useful to partially dissociate or distance themselves in this situation and act as if they were witnessing feedback being given to someone else.

- *Be silent.* Refrain from making a response. Don't even begin to frame a response in your own mind until you have listened carefully to what has been said and have considered the implications. Don't use the excuse of correcting factual errors to avoid hearing and resonating with the substance of what has been said. Don't be distracted by the need to explain: if you continue to feel that you need to give an explanation do it later after the feedback session, once you are sure you have attended to all that has been said.

There is no difference in principle between feedback given in written form and that in person. However, with written feedback there is normally no opportunity to resolve misunderstandings and it is necessary to be very explicit in specifying what types of feedback are desired and in formulating responses. In the written form more attention needs to be given to tone and style as there is no opportunity to adjust your response in the light of the immediate reactions of the other person.

## Conclusion

Peers are important in self assessment as they can provide to learners useful perspectives on their work. They can do this in ways which are more informal and less threatening in many circumstances than can teachers. However, they are frequently unused to doing so. They may therefore need support in the process through the provision of guidelines and opportunities to practise giving and receiving feedback.

PART V

# CONCLUSION

## Chapter 17

# What Issues in Self Assessment are Still to be Explored?

In this book we have examined a very wide range of self assessment practices used in a variety of disciplines and pursuing a diversity of educational goals. In an important sense, these are all merely illustrations of the potential of self assessment: a potential which has still to be fully realised. The basic message of the book has been that self assessment must be seen as much as a learning activity as an assessment practice. It can be justified primarily by resort to arguments about its role in improving learning although it has a secondary role in assessment where, under suitable circumstances, it can be used as part of the formal assessment system. Assessment, in all its guises, contributes to learning and influences what students spend their time on. So any use of self assessment must consider its relationship to other activities in the course of which it is a part.

It is now possible to set out some of the features of good practice in the use of self assessment in contrast to practice which is less effective. Table 17.1 might usefully serve as a checklist to examine a particular self assessment practice to identify where it might be modified so as to enhance its contribution to learning. As yet, there are very few current self assessment activities which consistently reflect the good practice column of the table; the points represent a direction to pursue.

**Table 17.1**  Features of good and poor practice in self assessment

| Good practice in self assessment | Poor practice in self assessment: |
|---|---|
| the *motive* for its introduction is related to enhancing learning | it is related to meeting institutional or other external requirements |
| it is introduced with a clear *rationale* and there is an opportunity to discuss it with students | it is treated as a given part of course *requirements* |
| student *perceptions* of the process are considered prior to the idea being introduced | it is assumed that processes which appear to work elsewhere can be introduced without modification |
| students are involved in *establishing criteria* | students are using criteria determined solely by others |
| students have a *direct role* in influencing the process | the process is imposed on them |
| *guidelines* are produced for each stage of the process | assessments are made impressionistically |
| students learn about a *particular subject* through self assessment which engages them with it | self assessment is only used for apparently 'generic' learning processes such as communication skills |
| students are involved in expressing understanding and judgements in *qualitative* ways | assessments are made on rating scales where each point is not explicitly defined |
| specific judgements with *justifications* are involved | global judgements without recourse to justificatory data are acceptable |
| learners are able to *use information* from the context and from other parties to inform their judgements | the activities do not draw on the kinds of data which are available in authentic settings |
| it makes an identifiable contribution to formal *decision-making* | no use is formally made of the outcomes |
| it is one of a number of complementary strategies to promote *self-directed and interdependent learning* | it is tacked on to an existing subject in isolation from other strategies |
| its practices *permeate* the total course | it is marginalised as part of subjects which have low status |
| staff are willing to *share control* of assessment and do so | staff retain control of *all* aspects (sometimes despite appearances otherwise) |

| | |
|---|---|
| qualitative *peer feedback* is used as part of the process | it is subordinated to quantitative peer assessment |
| it is part of a *profiling* process in which students have an active role | records about students are produced with no input from them |
| activities are introduced in step with the students' capabilities in *learning-how-to-learn* | it is a one-off event without preparation |
| the implications of research on gender *differences* and differences of presentational style *are considered* | the strategy chosen is assumed to work equally for all |
| the process is likely to lead to *development of self assessment* skills | the exercise chosen relates only to the specific needs of the topic being assessed |
| *evaluation* data are collected to assist in improvement and for determining its contribution to student learning | evaluation is not considered or is not used |

## Outstanding issues

Learner self assessment in higher education is an area which, as we have seen, is currently undergoing considerable development. New approaches are being introduced, experience in its application is being gained and reports on it are appearing regularly in the literature. There are many aspects still to explore. Here in the final chapter I consider three aspects among the many. First, some disturbing work on professional judgement is revealed. Questions are raised about the confidence which can be placed in the assessment judgements made by any party, be they staff, student or even someone with supposed professional expertise. This leads to a discussion of the limits of assessment. The importance of using a variety of perspectives on assessment is emphasised. Second, the role of self-esteem and self-confidence is discussed in the light of gender differences. Different responses by students to different self assessment tasks have been mentioned earlier. Here some research which connects student self esteem and self image with self assessment is mentioned and the possible implications for self assessment practice explored.

Third, questions are posed about future developments in self asses-sment. What issues might become significant and what areas of enquiry might illuminate new approaches to self assessment? While there is a growing body of research and professional practice which can inform present discussions, there are still some major areas to be examined.

The book ends with a self assessment. I return to the concerns raised at the beginning of the book and reflect on the criteria for success which were indicated there.

## Matters of judgement

Discussions of self assessment, like any discussions of assessment, make the assumption that it is possible for students or staff to make appropriate judgements about the performance and products of learning. It is assumed that there is always someone able to make a valid judgement of the matters under consideration. Disturbingly, the growing body of research on professional judgement casts doubt on the confidence with which we can hold this view. It points to the fact that there are problems in making judgements no matter who does it and sometimes these problems are quite profound (Nisbett and Ross, 1980). Some of them have been recognised in assessment practice generally, others have been ignored, perhaps hoping that they might disappear.

Plous (1993) has reviewed the literature on the psychology of judgement and decision-making and has drawn attention to the following points which are pertinent to assessment judgements:

- Perception is selective. That is, we do not see all the evidence there is to see: 'expectations and motivations brought to a situation influence perceptions of actual experiences, events and feelings' (p. 21).
- Commitment influences judgement. '. . . if you want someone to form more positive attitudes towards an object, get him (sic) to commit himself to own that object; if you want someone to soften his moral attitude towards some misdeed, tempt him so that he performs the deed, to harden attitude tempt him but not enough for him to do it . . . the pressure to feel consistent will often lead people to bring their beliefs in line with their behaviour' (pp. 29–30).
- Memory and hindsight biases judgement. People often distort or forget what their initial beliefs were. It is important to keep accurate records as even the most sophisticated decision-maker is susceptible to biases in memory and there is no better way to avoid these biases than maintaining careful contemporaneous notes and records. Memory is, by its very nature, reconstructive and highly dependent upon contextual factors (Hunter, 1964) (p. 37).
- Judgement depends on context. There are the contrast effect (assessment depends on what is being contrasted with what), the primacy effect

(factors considered first are seen as more important than later ones), the recency effect (the last impression carries the most weight), and halo effects (knowledge of an initial positive characteristic leads to other positive assessments) (pp. 38–47).

- Familiarity can offset context. When people are familiar with an issue, variations in context and order typically produce marginal changes; when people know little about an issue, they are more easily influenced.
- Questions profoundly influence answers. It is worth paying close attention to the structure and context of questions as the wording of a question significantly influences the answers people give (p. 62).

All these factors will influence assessments. However, Bruner (1990, p.17), in summarising much other literature, disturbs further our confidence in assessment. He suggests that

> . . . as in the careful studies reported by Lee Ross and Richard Nisbett, it is plain that people can describe correctly neither the basis of their choices nor the biases that skew the distribution of those choices. And if even more proof of this generalisation were needed, it could be found in the work of Amos Tversky and Daniel Kahnemann [cf. Kahnemann *et al.*, 1982].

Brehmer (1986) begins to undermine confidence in judgements on a much wider front when he reviews research which indicates that experts with years of experience are often no better than novices in making diagnoses. Knowledge from experience is not necessarily valid except when truth is manifest. 'The guarantee of validity is *not* in experience itself' (p. 706).

Learning is not a simple matter of adding new knowledge to an existing framework which is able to accommodate it. Some forms of knowledge act as a direct challenge to existing ways of seeing the world and they require the construction of new conceptual frameworks or learning schema before they can be fully assimilated. Many judgements are dependent on having a schema in place. When this is yet to be developed, assessors are more dependent on the judgements of others than later in their learning. The twofold notion of assessment presented earlier in the book (identifying criteria and making judgements) needs to be extended to take account of these complexities.

The important point is that all judgements are subject to these reservations. As we have seen in Chapter 12, research on marking differences does not indicate a sharp distinction between staff ability to assess and that of students. The spectrum is likely to overlap considerably and we need to consider the biases of each party. Staff are likely to be better at judging with respect to some criteria under some circumstances, students others. What the research on judgements calls into question is the appropriateness of any individual as the sole assessor. Assessors, be they staff or students, need the perspectives of others if they are not to be misled by the distractions of the context and their own predilections.

## Self esteem, self assessment and student differences

While this book has emphasised throughout the importance of focusing on explicit criteria and particular features of the *work* being assessed, there are obviously connections between how students view themselves and the assessments they make about particular achievements. The role of feelings and emotions in learning was discussed in Chapter 3. These, when manifest in what is called variously self confidence, self concept, self image and self esteem, have a profound influence on the assessments individual learners make of their own achievements. While, as we have seen earlier, there are steps which can be taken to focus learner's attention on observable evidence – away from preoccupation with self – there is still plenty of scope in most situations for learners to make inappropriate self assessments for reasons to do more with images they have of themselves than with present circumstances. These matters need to be explored in a variety of ways. Ideas from self-regulated learning and social cognitive perspectives (Bandura, 1986; Corno, 1986; Schunk, 1990) may contribute some insights, but it is likely that a broader range of conceptions will be needed to probe the subtle interactions between learners' past experience, current context and affective states.

The relationship between self image and self assessment has been explored most in the literature on gender differences. Studies clearly show that the social contexts in which self assessments occur have differential influences on participants. Differences in interpretation of the self assessment task have an impact on the outcomes. They also show that self assessment does not take place independently of others. While these studies focus on male/female differences, it is likely that similar effects would occur when other differences (eg, age, ethnicity) were present.

There is a vast body of research on male/female differences in self attribution and self esteem. This suggests that in a wide range of situations girls and women show low confidence relative to boys and men (Maccoby and Jacklin, 1974), that predictions about task performance may be consistently lower in women than men (Crandall, 1969) and that females may be more modest in their expectations of their performance than are males (Erkut, 1983; Kimball and Gray, 1982; Mura, 1987). However, the picture is quite complex and there are many specific exceptions to these findings. For example, while refuting the idea that women state lower expectancies as a show of modesty, Lenney (1977) concluded that girls and women show a lack of confidence only in certain situations such as when the task is considered as masculine, when the task is performed in a competitive situation, and when in the presence of highly competent others. Lenney and Gold (1982) found that women and men did not differ in their estimates of how many problems they had answered correctly, but women evaluated their performance more poorly than men in comparison to a 'highly competent' group of undergraduates. Similarly, Lenney, et al. (1983) found that women evaluated their own performance in comparison to a highly competent other more poorly than did men; however, no gender difference emerged when the comparison person was of average or low ability. A workplace study by Heilman and Kram (1978) suggests that a person's gender can act as a cue for how competent he or she is judged to be. Both male and female adult subjects judged men to be more competent than women, and women gave lower expectancies for personal success than men only when they were paired with a man, not when they were paired with a woman.

Daubman et al. (1992) take the view that self-presentational style is a factor which must be taken into account in self assessment, as well as self esteem. Their view is that the reporting or sharing of one's beliefs about one's abilities and performances takes place within an interpersonal interaction. Therefore self reports of ability and performance are potentially subject to the same self-presentational concerns that have been found to influence other behaviours. Thus the findings of lower self evaluations in women may be due not only to an internalised lack of confidence, but also to a characteristically more modest self-presentational style, which is triggered by certain social contexts. In social situations in which achievements are discussed, women might be concerned not only with others' evaluations of them, but also others' evaluations of themselves and with the implications that social comparisons about such evaluations and achievements might have for the immediate relationship. If this is the case, then a manipulation that explicitly makes the other potentially vulnerable to negative social comparison ought to result in even greater gender differences in estimates of one's own performance.

The work of Clark and Zehr (1993) suggests that there is a need to be cautious in accepting Lenney et al.'s (1983) view that women in an ambiguous achievement setting self-apply gender stereotypes. Their research gives support to Collis (1985) that women in such settings have different (and lower) views of themselves compared with women generally

– the 'we can, but I can't' paradox, and reinforces previous findings of gender differences in self confidence (Andrews, 1987; Erkut, 1983; Zuckerman, 1985).

Interpretation of this wider literature in the light of discussions of good practice in self assessment indicates once again the need for criteria to be specific, for there to be unambiguous guidelines about self assessment processes, an avoidance of direct comparisons between students and eschewal of a competitive context for self assessment. It also points to the need to be careful about considering more thoroughly the social context in which self assessment is conducted and implied comparisons which may be assumed by students. In addition it would also be prudent to avoid the public disclosure of self assessments unless there is a highly supportive context.

Much of the discussion of self assessment in this book has assumed that self assessment is basically a cognitive activity, in particular, a kind of cognitive skill. What is therefore mainly needed for the development of such a skill is feedback and practice. For many day-to-day applications this is quite sufficient. Unfortunately though, as we see here, it is not as simple as that. Because self assessment is so connected with how students view themselves as learners and because students need a strong commitment to engage in such self-monitoring activities, discussions of self assessment must inevitably also concern themselves with wider psychological and contextual matters.

## The future of self assessment

Self assessment is now clearly an idea whose time has come. The range and extent of self assessment practices at different levels, in different subjects and in different institutions indicates that it is becoming worryingly popular. Will we, in a few years time, be discussing it as an idea whose time has been and gone?

The best sign that work on self assessment will not disappear is that it is not associated with a very specific set of practices. As we have seen, the range of activities which take place under the heading of self assessment goes from the highly technical and subject-based to the expressive and transformative. The one thing these activities share is the emphasis they place on learners making decisions about their own learning. This may occur in a highly teacher-directed context, a student-directed one or one where there is interdependence. It is difficult to argue that students should not be actively engaged in monitoring their own learning. The debate centres on the ways in which this should occur and, increasingly, the frameworks we should use to think about it. This is a healthy focus because the form of self assessment must be governed by intention and context.

The trap which we need to avoid is self assessment becoming a set of techniques or common activities which are established without critical questioning. As soon as self assessment strategies are simply added to the curriculum without them being re-thought afresh in every new context with each group of students, self assessment will simply become a commodity, an instrument of a process which is not creative or emancipatory, but a mechanism of bureaucracy destined to become yet another requirement for students to cope with in an overcrowded curriculum.

In my view, self assessment needs to be seen alongside a set of practices which are respectful of students and which treat them as unique beings who are struggling with learning in a system which at times denies their intent, undermines their confidence, ignores their culture and concerns, and treats them as objects to be processed in terms of the priorities of the institution. Self assessment also needs to be seen as part of a cooperative enterprise in which students and teachers work with each other towards ends which both induct learners into new ways of thinking and action as well as provide the means for them to transform their practices as needed by changing circumstance.

The direction in which I anticipate work on self assessment moving therefore, is towards increasing its links with other practices to become an integral part of courses and not an add-on. One direction is that anticipated in Chapter 3. Self assessment can be viewed not as a distinct element of teaching and learning, but in relation to reflection, critical reflection and metacognitive practices. It is part of that set of activities which encourage students to take responsibility for their own learning, monitor their learning plans and activities, process their studying and assess their effectiveness. Self assessment then would become something which is embedded in courses, designed from the very start to assist students with their learning and integrated with the overall substructure of tasks, exercises, problem-solving activities and assessment assignments. Self assessment which can be clearly identified as a separate event would then disappear and, while it will be possible to discuss course design from a self assessment perceptive, it will not be possible to simply point to the self assessment activities.

The trend is therefore towards a shift of attention from looking at the distinct elements of courses to the total impact of the mix of activities. It is inconceivable, for example, to simultaneously introduce any one of the practices described in Chapters 6 to 11 into all the subjects a given student might be studying as part of a course. Repeating the same practice in parallel subjects would soon become tedious and time-consuming and be seen by students not as a useful learning strategy, but as yet another hurdle to be jumped. It is not just desirable for different subjects to use different approaches to self assessment, it will be essential if students are not to become overloaded by repetition.

The focus I believe will be on holistic course design rather than the assembling of individual parts, not withstanding the counter-trend towards modularisation. The impact of the whole milieu on learning will be paramount and assessment for purposes of certification will need to be constructed to take account of many of the negative consequences on learning which are apparent today. An emphasis on students demonstrating understanding of learning processes and schemas rather than particular product outcomes will be seen. Integrated systems of teaching/learning activities will be the subject of research and development and these will be influenced by work on reflection and reflective practice (Brookfield, 1995; Schön, 1991), negotiated learning and contract-driven approaches (eg, Anderson, *et al.*, forthcoming), self-regulated learning (eg, Corno, 1986), the development of professional expertise (Chi, *et al.*, 1988) and metacognition and self-monitoring (eg, Biggs, 1988; Flavell, 1979).

Any development of self assessment ideas will also be dependent on a more sophisticated and sensitive discourse of assessment and a shift in assessment talk away from an almost exclusive obsession with comparability and a misguided faith in universal 'standards'. Assessment discourse will need to be deconstructed to expose the ways in which its socially determined nature is disguised by a pretence that it is subject-matter standards which are being protected. This will not mean that absolute judgements of quality will be replaced by subjective and relativistic ones. Rather, the present subjective and relativistic approaches, for that is what they are, will evolve into ones which can be defended by resort to evidence about what students are actually able to accomplish and demonstrate.

The discourse of assessment will always be one involving power and control, and assessment will always betray actual rather than espoused values. It will therefore continue to be important and at the heart of any discussions of teaching and learning. The role of self assessment in exploring the discourse of assessment is to expose the fact that many of the decisions, assumed to reside exclusively in the hands of staff and other examiners, do not necessarily belong there and that a unilateral approach to student assessment can limit learning. Such an awareness may not shift assessment discourse in the wider society, but it will at least mean that discussions about assessment within the institution are made more explicit and therefore subject to greater critical scrutiny.

## In conclusion

It seems appropriate in ending this book on self assessment to return to the beginning to examine the extent to which the criteria set out there have been addressed. In the first chapter I listed my own criteria for judging the book. In ending, I reflect on them, consider some of the dilemmas with which I have been faced and offer some final comments.

### Inclusion of some autobiographical material to help make the ideas come alive

What place does autobiographical material have in a book on assessment? This was the question which I faced at the start. I have become committed over the years to the idea of writing oneself into publications to avoid the pretence which occurs when the person appears to be writing objectively. I believe that those involved in teaching and learning have to stand for something and that these values are rooted in their experience. I made a strong personal statement at the start where I thought it most appropriate, but later in the book I have played this down as I did not want the issues which drove me in my explorations to distract from the narrative which increasingly included many other collaborators and drew on documented research and innovations.

Yet to say that I was more personal at the beginning of the book implies an all too stark distinction between the personal and the academic. The choice of material has been mine. That choice has been informed by my personal experience of being assessed and of assessing myself, of seeing others being assessed and assessing themselves. My choice of material has also been informed by reading, writing and research in a number of fields related to these practices. The book is therefore inevitably idiosyncratic in its choice of material and in that sense too it is also a very personal book. It would have been possible to write as if the personal and autobiographical was absent. Most academic books do this. I chose to honour the uneasy tension between being open about the personal influences on my work and writing as if they do not exist. The book reflects where I am in relation to that tension. Neither a more 'objective' account, nor a more openly auto-biographical one would have been truly me.

### Clarity about what is and what is not covered

In starting the book I realised that many people take self-and-peer-assessment as if it were one connected idea. I wanted to challenge this and separate out self assessment, which I see as fundamental to all learning, from peer assessment, which is a useful adjunct. The book has concentrated almost exclusively on the first of these in order to right the balance which I saw as starting to tip in favour of the secondary concept (eg. Brown and Knight, 1994).

What has been an issue throughout is where the boundaries in thinking about self assessment are located. I have related it to learning, to assessment, to ideas about reflection, to experiential learning and I have explored a number of bodies of literature which are often unrelated. But where does it end? In a sense, in thinking about self assessment there are no boundaries. Narrowly viewed, it is merely an aspect of student assessment in higher education. More widely, it is an aspect of the very way we function as human and social beings. As I say, the choice of material is a personal one. I suspect that some readers will still be wondering why some content has been included, but I hope that as they extend their explorations these ideas will act as signposts to new horizons.

## Rooted in actual practice with examples given

There are very many examples of different kinds of self assessment practice throughout the book. The quandary which I faced, however, concerned what should be included of my own work in the field. In the end I decided to devote five chapters to examples of work I had been directly involved in. Some of them were originally reported over ten years ago, but were published in rather obscure places. I wanted to make this work accessible in so far as it was sufficiently well documented and evaluated to provide rich examples or interesting approaches. In spite of the age of some of these studies, they still have important lessons, particularly, I hope, for those new to self assessment.

Amongst the wide range of self assessment practices being used by other people, to some degree the choice of examples was a function of what was immediately available. I wanted to illustrate a range of uses rather than be comprehensive about the coverage of self assessment – the field is moving too fast for that to have a great deal of validity. It is interesting that among the examples, the use of the computer did not feature significantly. It is clear that the computer is being used increasingly widely for the management of assessment tasks. Its general use in innovative forms of self assessment, however, has yet to be widely explored.

## Underpinned by theory and research

Discussions of assessment have long been regarded as essentially pragmatic. Practices have developed largely without theoretical under-pinning. At the present time, there is still ambivalence among teachers in higher education about the use of theory. It is often regarded as the preserve of educationalists and psychologists and therefore remote from their practical concerns. Luckily this is changing with attempts that have been made in recent years to relate theory and practice closely (cf. the work of Ramsden, 1988a). In this book, theory has been introduced where I felt it had previously been lacking. The most important aspect of this is the grounding of self assessment in ideas about learning, and particularly about learning from experience. The latter, I know from colleagues who read earlier versions of the first few chapters, is a controversial decision. As one of them said, 'Why is there so much about experiential learning in a book about self assessment?' The simple answer is that my work on self assessment and learning from experience has been proceeding in parallel for many years. Rather than being discrete areas, I see them as different sides of the same coin. My interest in self assessment emerged from work on experiential learning and it has now taken me back into it. The two are complementary and each offers insights in discussions of the other.

So my choice of theory to underpin the ideas in this book is guided by my overarching sense of what makes for good education. But I have gone beyond these ideas in presenting relevant research. As has previously been mentioned, there are a number of areas of literature relevant to the present discussion which are quite discrete. There is a dilemma in presenting material from disparate research areas, in ensuring the coherence of the whole. I hope this coherence is provided first by the strong sense permeating the book of what self assessment is and is not, and second by the aura of questioning of all too often unquestioned practice which I have endeavoured to foster throughout. I don't know how well I have succeeded in this, but if this volume helps to bring to self assessment a greater critical awareness of the issues involved in its practice, then I shall be well pleased.

## Reasonably comprehensive in coverage of higher education

It is impossible to claim comprehensive coverage as there will always be someone's favourite study which has been neglected or authors ignored who might have had something interesting to say. My dilemma throughout was deciding what was in and what was out. Even up to the final deadline I was finding interesting self assessment studies. I am satisfied that there is enough here to demonstrate the extent of present practice. What I am less confident about is whether I have identified all the trends in theory and practice which will carry us forward over the next few years. In view of the paucity of theoretical work, and indeed truly grounded practical work in this area, this book has been able to take a small step in making such work more firmly based. It will be interesting to see what further conceptual work in this area will look like. When it emerges, I shall no doubt be wondering why I did not think to include it here.

## Of practical use to others in implementation

A major tension here was between grounding the book in research on the one hand and being practical on the other. There were severe limitations on the former, however, because research, as we have seen, is patchy and does not focus on many of the most important issues. On the other hand, practice, as always, is messy, and it is often difficult to know what to make of the amazing diversity of examples. The biggest problem I had in this regard, though, was in getting the balance right between neutral exposition and giving advice. Naturally, after working in this area for many years, I have a number of deeply held views about what works and what does not work and what are useful lines of development. Not only would being too direct about these risk alienating the reader and creating an excessively opinionated text, it would also contradict principles of self reflection and responsibility in learning which I have espoused for many years! Yet to leave out my working assumptions about good practice would have been to deprive the book of much of its utility. My compromise has been to temper the advice by providing ideas for reflection rather than dogmatic statements of what must be done. However, I think the ardency of my desire for self assessment to reflect my conception of good practice has, at times, led me to proselytise.

## Linked to ideas in teaching and learning

To separate out self assessment from the vast range of other teaching and learning ideas and practices is artificial. So although relating self assessment to other ideas is a feature of the book, there is a sense in which they never were separate. I hope that some conceptual clarity on these relationships has, however, been achieved.

Another problem which I faced, and which I still do not believe is satisfactorily addressed, is that of linking self assessment, reflection and critical reflection. To this might be added, at the risk of becoming too technical, metacognition. These are all closely related ideas but they arise from different traditions, have different emphases and draw on different views of the world. They have overlapping concerns but it is not a simple matter to combine the ideas they represent. To have done so would have led me into complex theoretical, indeed philosophical, discussions which would have detracted from the pragmatic aims of the book. All I can hope for is that until some new ways of encompassing them is proposed, some cross-fertilisation will occur. The boundaries between self assessment and reflection are by no means clear. At present it may be helpful to think of them as separate. However, as we saw earlier, emancipatory self assessment practices will take us beyond traditional teaching and learning into new realms of thinking and acting where our present conceptual distinctions disappear. Indeed, in writing these final paragraphs I wonder whether it is more useful to think of myself as writing a self assessment or engaging in reflection.

A common experience in reviewing self assessment criteria once a task has been completed, is that invariably one realises that to start again would involve changing the criteria. Some old ones may be discarded and new ones take their place. In my case here, I don't think I would want to discard any of those listed above, but I would want to add some additional questions:

## To what extent does the work transform the conceptions of those who engage with it?

This book was written with the aim of moving forward debates about self assessment through discarding some old conceptions – self assessment is about marking – and establishing new ones – self assessment is about learning. There are other ideas which are also being promoted here, but the key one is the shift from an assessment to a learning perspective. The main reason why I would want to introduce learner self assessment into a course I was conducting is to improve the quality of learning. Through focusing on what counts as criteria for good work and through being actively engaged in making decisions about whether their work meets these requirements, students take responsibility for their learning and make the course their own. I like to think that I have made a convincing case for this. However, argument, by itself, does not transform thinking. It is not only in arguing a case, but in the mélange of examples, the discussions of research literature as well as my own reflections, the occasional handout and discussion of issues in practice, that the book has the potential to influence change. All of this provides material to inform readers' critical reflection on practice. Only time will tell whether it does so.

## To what extent will the book be used to support contrary agendas?

This is the most difficult criterion of all and the most worrying. In the end, a writer has absolutely no control over how a text will be used. However, pointers can be set down which say, in effect, 'don't go there'. I am conscious that conclusions will be drawn from my material which are in opposition to

221

those which I have drawn myself. I know too that some people will follow some of the examples without an awareness of or a concern for the warnings. All I can do, and have done, is to urge the reader to take into account the key factors. I must acknowledge that readers will make their own interpretations no matter what is written. In the end, the writer has to let go. This is exactly the same process as teachers have to go through in implementing self assessment. They can present the idea and the process, but in the end, the students will make of it what they wish. No matter what is done by way of self assessment, learners are ultimately responsible for their own learning.

# References

Anderson, G, Boud, D and Sampson, J (1994) 'Expectations of quality in the use of learning contracts', *Capability: The International Journal of Capability in Higher Education*, 1, 1, 22–31.

Anderson, G, Boud, D and Sampson, J (forthcoming) *Learning Contracts: A Practical Guide*, London: Kogan Page.

Andrews, P H (1987) 'Gender differences in persuasive communication and attribution of success and failure', *Human Communication Research*, 13, 372–85.

Argyris, C and Schön, D A (1974) *Theory in Practice: Increasing Professional Effectiveness*, San Francisco, C A: Jossey-Bass.

Armstrong, M T (1978) 'Assessing students' participation in class discussion', *Assessment in Higher Education*, 3, 3, 186–202.

Armstrong, M T and Boud, D (1983) 'Assessing class participation: an exploration of the issues', *Studies in Higher Education*, 8, 1, 33–44.

Arnold, L, Willoughby, T L and Calkins, E V (1985) 'Self-evaluation in undergraduate medical education: a longitudinal perspective', *Journal of Medical Education*, 60, 21–8.

Assiter, A and Shaw, E (1993) *Using Records of Achievement in Higher Education*, London: Kogan Page.

Atkins, M, Beattie, J and Dockrell, W B (1993) *Assessment Issues in Higher Education*, Sheffield: Employment Department, Further and Higher Education Branch.

Bailey, G D (1979) 'Student self-assessment: helping students help themselves', *Kappa Delta Pi Record*, 15, 3, 86–8, 96.

Baird, J R and White, R T (1982) 'Promoting self-control of learning', *Instructional Science*, 11, 227–47.

Ball, C (1990) *More Means Different: Widening Access to Higher Education*, London: Royal Society of Arts, Industry Matters.

Ballard, B and Clanchy, J (1988) 'Literacy in the university: an "anthropological" approach', in Taylor, G, Ballard, B, Beasley, V, Bock, H, Clanchy, J and Nightingale, P (eds) *Literacy by Degrees*, Buckingham: Society for Research into Higher Education and Open University Press.

Bandura, A (1986) *Social Foundations of Thought and Action: A Social Cognitive Theory*, Englewood Cliffs, NJ: Prentice-Hall.

Barnett, R (1990) *The Idea of Higher Education*, Buckingham: Society for Research into Higher Education and Open University Press.

Barnett, R (1994) *The Limits of Competence: Knowledge, Higher Education and Society*, Buckingham: Society for Research into Higher Education and Open University Press.

Barrows, H S and Tamblyn, R M (1976) 'Self-assessment units', *Journal of Medical Education*, 51, 334–6.

Barrows, H S and Tamblyn, R M (1980) *Problem-Based Learning: An Approach to Medical Education*, New York: Springer.

Bawden, R and McKinnon, C (1980) 'The portfolio', *HERDSA News*, 2, 2, 4–5.

Beaty, L and McGill, I (1992) *Action Learning: A Practitioners Guide*, London: Kogan Page.

Becker, H, Geer, B and Hughes, E C (1968) *Making the Grade: The Academic Side of College Life*, New York: John Wiley.

Beeler, K D (1976) 'A student self-evaluation tool', *Humanistic Educator*, 14, 3, 104.

Benett, Y (1993) 'The validity and reliability of assessments and self-assessments of work-based learning', *Assessment and Evaluation in Higher Education*, 18, 2, 83–94.

Berger, P and Luckmann, T (1967) *The Social Construction of Reality*, Harmonsworth: Penguin.

Biggs, J B (1987) *Student Approaches to Learning and Studying*, Melbourne: Australian Council for Educational Research.

Biggs, J B (1988) 'The role of metacognition in enhancing learning', *Australian Journal of Education*, 32, 127–38.

Biggs, J B and Moore, J P (1993) *The Process of Learning*, (3rd edn), Sydney: Prentice-Hall of Australia.

Bishop, J B (1971) 'Another look at counsellor, client, and supervisor ratings of counsellor effectiveness', *Counselor Education and Supervision*, 10, 319–23.

Black, P J (1969) 'University examinations' *Physics Education*, 3, 2, 93–9.

Blatchford, P (1992) 'Academic self assessment at 7 and 11 years: its accuracy and association with ethnic group and sex', *British Journal of Educational Psychology*, 62, 35–44.

Blumhof, J and Broom, C (1991) 'Student self-evaluation sheets: skills development', Unpublished handout, University of Hertfordshire, Division of Environmental Sciences.

Borman, C A and Ramirez, C (1975) 'Evaluating counseling practicum students', *Counselor Education and Supervision*, 15, 48–54.

Boud, D (1981) 'Independence and interdependence in distance education', in Ellington, H and Percival, F (eds) *Aspects of Educational Technology 15. Distance Learning and Evaluation*, London: Kogan Page, 55–60.

Boud, D (1988a) 'Moving towards autonomy', in Boud, D (ed.) *Developing Student Autonomy in Learning*, (2nd edn), London: Kogan Page, 17–39.

Boud, D (ed.) (1988b) 'Assessment and Evaluation in Problem-Based Learning', special issue of *Assessment and Evaluation in Higher Education*, 13, 2.

Boud, D (1989) 'The role of self assessment in student grading', *Assessment and Evaluation in Higher Education*, 14, 1, 20–30.

Boud, D (1990) 'Assessment and the promotion of academic values', *Studies in Higher Education*, 15, 1, 101–111.

Boud, D (1991) *Implementating Student Self Assessment*, (2nd edn), Sydney: Higher Education Research and Development Society of Australasia.

Boud, D (1992) 'The use of self-assessment schedules in negotiated learning', *Studies in Higher Education*, 17, 2, 185–200.

Boud, D (1995) 'Assessment and learning: contradictory or complementary?', in Knight, P (ed.), *Assessment for Learning in Higher Education*, London: Kogan Page 35–48.

Boud, D and Falchikov, N (1989) 'Quantitative studies of student self-assessment in higher education: a critical analysis of findings', *Higher Education*, 18, 5, 529–49.

Boud, D and Feletti, G (eds) (1991) *The Challenge of Problem-Based Learning*, London: Kogan Page.

Boud, D and Holmes, W H (1981) 'Self and peer marking in an undergraduate engineering course', *IEEE Transactions on Education*, E-24, 4, 267–74.

Boud, D and Knights, S (1994) 'Designing courses to promote reflective practice', *Research and Development in Higher Education*, 16, 229–34.

Boud, D and Lublin, J (1983) 'Student self assessment: educational benefits within existing resources', in Squires, G (ed.) *Innovation through Recession*, Guildford, Surrey: Society for Research into Higher Education, 93–9.

Boud, D and Prosser, M T (1980) 'Sharing responsibility: staff-student cooperation in learning', *British Journal of Educational Technology*, 11, 1, 24–35.

Boud, D and Prosser, M T (1984) 'Sharing responsibility for learning in a science course: staff-student cooperation', in Knowles, M S and Associates, *Andragogy in Action*, San Francisco, CA: Jossey-Bass, 175–88.

Boud, D and Tyree, A L (1980) 'Self and peer assessment in professional education: a preliminary study in law', *Journal of the Society of Public Teachers of Law*, 15, 1, 65–74.

Boud, D and Walker, D (1990) 'Making the most of experience', *Studies in Continuing Education*, 12, 2, 61–80.

Boud, D *et al.* (1972) *Experiential Techniques in Higher Education*, Guildford: University of Surrey, Human Potential Research Project, Centre for Adult Education.

Boud, D, Churches, A E and Smith, E M (1986) 'Student self assessment in an engineering design course: an evaluation', *International Journal of Applied Engineering Education*, 2, 2, 83–90.

Boud, D, Cohen, R and Walker, D (1993) 'Understanding learning from experience', in Boud, D, Cohen, R and Walker, D (eds) *Using Experience for Learning*, Buckingham: SRHE and Open University Press, 1–17.

Boud, D, Keogh, R and Walker, D (1985) 'Promoting reflection in learning: a model', in Boud, D, Keogh, R and Walker, D (eds) *Reflection: Turning Experience into Learning*, London: Kogan Page, 18–40.

Boyd, H and Cowan, J (1985) 'A case for self-assessment based on recent studies of student learning', *Assessment and Evaluation in Higher Education*, 10, 3, 225–35.

Boydell, T and Pedler, M (eds) (1981) *Management Self-Development: Concepts and Practices*, Aldershot: Gower.

Brehmer, B (1986) 'In one word: not from experience', *Acta Psychologica*, 1980, 45, 223–41, reprinted in Arkes, H R and Hammond, K R (eds), *Judgement and Decision Making: An Interdisciplinary Reader*, Cambridge: Cambridge University Press, 705–19.

Brew, A (1988) *Research as Learning*, unpublished PhD thesis. University of Bath.

Brew, A (1993) 'The partnership degree: idea to reality', *Research and Development in Higher Education*, 14, 264–71.

Broadfoot, P (1979) 'Communication in the classroom: a study of the role of assessment in motivation', *Educational Review*, 31, 1, 3–10.

Brookfield, S (1995) *Becoming a Critically Reflective Teacher*, San Francisco, CA: Jossey-Bass.

Brown, S and Knight, P (1994) *Assessing Learners in Higher Education*, London: Kogan Page.

Bruner, J S (1990) *Acts of Meaning*, Cambridge, MA: Harvard University Press.

Burgess, H (1992) *Problem-Led Learning for Social Work Education: The Enquiry and Action Learning Approach*, London: Whiting and Birch.

Burgess, H and Jackson, S (1990) 'Enquiry and action learning: a new approach to social work education', *Social Work Education*, 9, 3, 3–19.

Burke, R J (1969) 'Some preliminary data on the use of self-evaluations and peer-ratings in assigning university course grades', *Journal of Educational Research*, 62, 10, 444–8.

Butler, S (1982) 'Assessing the journal: an exercise in self evaluation', *English Quarterly*, 14, 4, 75–83.

Candy, P (1988) 'On the attainment of subject-matter autonomy', in Boud, D (ed.) *Developing Student Autonomy in Learning*, (2nd edn), London: Kogan Page, 59–76.

Candy, P, Crebert, G and O'Leary, J (1994) *Developing Lifelong Learners through Undergraduate Education*, NBEET Commissioned Report No. 28. Canberra: Australian Government Publishing Service.

Candy, P, Harri-Augstein, S and Thomas, L (1985) 'Reflection and the self-organized learner: a model of learning conversations' in Boud, D, Keogh, R and Walker, D (eds) *Reflection: Turning Experience into Learning*, London: Kogan Page, 100–116.

Chester College (1993a). 'Outdoor activities training initiative', unpublished course materials, Chester College, Cheyney Road, Chester.

Chester College (1993b). 'The PGCE student handbook: appraisal of practical teaching', unpublished course materials, Chester College, Cheyney Road, Chester.

Chi, M T H, Glaser, R and Farr, M J (eds) (1988) *The Nature of Expertise*, Hillsdale, NJ: Lawrence Erlbaum Associates.

Chiu, L H (1975) 'Influence of student teaching on perceived teaching competence', *Perceptual and Motor Skills*, 40, 872–4.

Churches, A E (1982) 'Simple design-and-build projects as an aid to teaching engineering design', in Langdon, R *et al.* (eds) *Proceedings, Design Research Society Conference Vol. 5: Design Education*, 20–23 July, 36–41.

Churches, A E, Boud, D and Smith, E M (1986) 'An evaluation of a design-and-build project in mechanical engineering', *International Journal of Mechanical Engineering Education*, 14, 1, 45–55.

Clark, J and Zehr, D (1993) 'Other women can: discrepant performance predictions for self and same-sex other', *Journal of College Student Development*, 34, 31–5.

Cochran, S B and Spears, M C (1980) 'Student self-assessment and instructors' ratings: a comparison', *Journal of the American Dietetic Association*, 76, 253–7.

Collis, B (1985) 'Psychosocial implications of sex differences in attitudes toward computers: results of a survey', *International Journal of Women's Studies*, 8, 207–13.

Corno, L (1986) 'The metacognitive control components of self-regulated learning', *Contemporary Educational Psychology*, 11, 333–46.

Courts, P L and McInerney, K H (1993) *Assessment in Higher Education: Politics, Pedagogy, and Portfolios*, Westport, CT: Praeger.

Cowan, J (1975) 'The ability to appraise one's own work', *Higher Education Bulletin*, 3, 127–8.

Cowan, J (1988) 'Struggling with student self-assessment', in Boud, D (ed.) *Developing Student Autonomy in Learning*, (2nd edn), London: Kogan Page, 192–210.

Crandall, V C (1969) 'Sex differences in expectancy of intellectual and academic reinforcement', in Smith, C P (ed.) *Achievement-Related Motives in Children*, New York: Russell Sage Foundation, 11–45.

Crocker, A C and Cheesman, R G (1988) 'The ability of young children to rank themselves for academic ability', *Educational Studies*, 14, 1, 105–10.

Dahlgren, L-O (1984) 'Outcomes of learning', in Marton, F, Hounsell, D and Entwistle, N (eds) *The Experience of Learning*, Edinburgh: Scottish Academic Press, 19–35.

Daines, J M (1978) 'Self evaluation of academic performance in a continuously assessed course of study', *Research Intelligence*, 4, 1, 24–6.

Daubman, K A, Heatherington, L and Ahn, A (1992) 'Gender and self-presentation of academic achievement', *Sex Roles*, 27, 3/4, 187–204.

Davies, A (1994) 'Evaluating a deep approach to assessment', Paper presented at the Second International Symposium on Improving Student Learning, Oxford: Oxford Brookes University.

Davis, J K and Rand, D C (1980) 'Self-grading versus instructor grading', *Journal of Educational Research*, 73, 4, 207–11.

Delbecq, A, Van der Ven, A M and Gustafson, D H (1975) *Group Processes for Program Planning: A Guide to Nominal Group and Delphi Processes*, Glenview, IL: Scott Foreman.

Denehy, G E and Fuller, J L (1974) 'Student peer evaluation: an adjunct to preclinical laboratory evaluation', *Dental Education*, 38, 200–203.

Denscombe, M and Robins, L (1980) 'Self-assessment and essay writing', *Teaching Sociology*, 8, 1, 63–78.

Dewey, J (1933) *How We Think: A Restatement of the Relation of Reflective Thinking to the Educative Process*, Boston, MA: Heath and Co.

Doleys, E J and Renzaglia, G A (1963) 'Accuracy of student prediction of college grades', *Personnel and Guidance Journal*, 41, 6, 528–30.

Ebel, R L (1974) 'Marks and marking systems', *IEEE Transactions on Education*, E-17, 76–92.

Edwards, R M (1989) 'An experiment in student self-assessment' *British Journal of Educational Technology*, 20, 1, 5–10.

Edwards, R M and Sutton, A (1991) 'A practical approach to student-centred learning', *British Journal of Educational Technology*, 23, 1, 4–20.

Eisner, E W (1993) 'Reshaping assessment in education: some criteria in search of practice', *Journal of Curriculum Studies*, 25, 3, 219–33.

Elliott, J (1978) 'Classroom accountability and the self-monitoring teacher', in Harlen, W (ed.) *Evaluation and the Teacher's Role*, Basingstoke: Macmillan Education, 47–90.

Elton, L and Laurillard, D M (1979) 'Trends in research on student learning', *Studies in Higher Education*, 4, 87–102.

Entwistle, N J and Entwistle, A C (1991) 'Contrasting forms of understanding for degree examinations: the student experience and its implications', *Higher Education*, 22, 205–27.

Entwistle, N J and Marton, F (1994) 'Knowledge objects: understandings constituted through intensive academic study', *British Journal of Educational Psychology*, 64, 161–78.

Entwistle, N J and Ramsden, P (1983) *Understanding Student Learning*, Beckenham: Croom Helm.

Erkut, S (1983) 'Exploring sex differences in expectancy, attribution, and academic achievement', *Sex Roles*, 9, 217–31.

Everett, M S (1983) 'Influence of trait anxiety on self-grading', *Educational Directions*, 8, 1, 4–9.

Falchikov, N (1986) 'Product comparisons and process benefits of collaborative peer group and self assessments', *Assessment and Evaluation in Higher Education*, 11, 2, 146–66.

Falchikov, N (1995) 'Improving feedback to and from students', in Knight, P (ed.) *Assessment for Learning in Higher Education*, London: Kogan Page 157–166.

Falchikov, N and Boud, D (1989) 'Student self-assessment in higher education: a meta-analysis', *Review of Educational Research*, 59, 4, 395–430.

Fazey, D M A (1993) 'Self-assessment as a generic skill for enterprising students: the learning process', *Assessment and Evaluation in Higher Education*, 18, 3, 235–50.

Feletti, G L (1980) 'Evaluation of a comprehensive programme for the assessment of medical students', *Higher Education*, 9, 169–78.

Filene, P O (1969) 'Self-grading: an experiment in learning', *Journal of Higher Education*, 40, 451–8.

Fincher, R-M E and Lewis, L A (1994) 'Learning, experience, and self-assessment of competence of third-year medical students in performing bedside procedures', *Academic Medicine*, 69, 4, 291–5.

Fincher, R-M E, Lewis, L A and Kuske, T T (1993) 'Relationships of interns' performances to their self-assessments of their preparedness for internship and to their academic performances in medical school', *Academic Medicine*, 68, 2, S47–S50.

Flavell, J H (1979) Metacognition and cognitive monitoring: a new area of cognitive-developmental inquiry, *American Psychologist*, 34, 10, 906–11.

Forehand, L S, Vann, W F, and Shugars, D A (1982) 'Student self-evaluation in preclinical restorative dentistry', *Journal of Dental Education*, 46, 4, 221–6.

Franklin, A (1994) 'Letter to the editor', *RSA Journal*, CXLII, 5447, March, 66.

Fuqua, D R, Johnson, A W, Newman, J L, Anderson, M W and Gade, E M (1984) 'Variability across sources of performance ratings', *Journal of Counselling Psychology*, 31, 2, 249–52.

Gaier, E L (1961) 'Student self estimates of final course grades', *Journal of Genetic Psychology*, 98, 63–7.

Gale, J (1984) 'Self-assessment and self-remediation strategies', in Henderson, E S and Nathenson, M B (eds). *Independent Learning in Higher Education*, Englewood Cliffs, NJ: Educational Technology Publications, 99–140.

Gibbs, G (1981) *Teaching Students to Learn*, Buckingham: The Open University Press.

Gibbs, G (1995) 'Changing lectures' conceptions of teaching and learning through action research', in Brew, A (ed.) *Directions in Staff Development*, Buckingham: SRHE and Open University Press, 21–35.

Gonczi, A (1994) 'Competency based assessment in the professions in Australia', *Assessment in Education*, 1, 1, 27–44.

Gordon, M J (1992) 'Self-assessment programs and their implications for health professions training', *Academic Medicine*, 67, 10, 672–9.

Gould, N and Taylor, I (eds) (in preparation), *Reflective Learning for Social Work*, Aldershot: Ashgate Publishing.

Gray, T G F (1987) 'An exercise in improving the potential of exams for learning', *European Journal of Engineering Education*, 12, 4, 311–23.

Greenfield, D G (1978) 'Evaluation of music therapy practicum competencies: comparisons of self- and instructor ratings of videotapes', *Journal of Music Therapy*, 15, 1, 15–20.

Grimmett, P P and Erickson, G L (eds) (1988) *Reflection in Teacher Education*, New York: Teachers College Press.

Guptara, P (1994) 'Letter to the editor', *RSA Journal*, CXLII, 5450, June, 13–14.

Habermas, J (1987) *Knowledge and Human Interests*, Transl. Shapiro, J, London: Polity Press, first published in German 1968 by Suhrkamp Verlag.

Hager, P, Gonczi, A and Athanasou, J (1994) 'General issues about assessment of competence', *Assessment and Evaluation in Higher Education*, 19, 1, 3–16.

Hammond, M and Collins, R (1991) *Self-Directed Learning: Critical Practice*, London: Kogan Page.

Hartog, D and Rhodes, E C (1935) *An Examination of Examinations*, Basingstoke: Macmillan.

Hassencahl, F (1979) 'Contract grading in the classroom', *Improving College and University Teaching*, 27, 1, 30–33.

Haswell, R H (1993) 'Students self-evaluations and developmental change', in MacGregor, J (ed.) *Student Self-evaluation: Fostering Reflective Learning*, New Directions for Teaching and Learning No 56, San Francisco, CA: Jossey-Bass, 83–100.

Hayes, E and Colin, S A J (eds) (1994) *Confronting Sexism and Racism*, New Directions for Adult and Continuing Education No. 61. San Francisco, CA: Jossey-Bass.

Hayes, S L and Hayes, R A (1973) 'Towards objective assessment of class participation', *Journal of the Society of Public Teachers of Law*, 12, 323–32.

Hedges, P D (1993) 'The assessment of individuals in a group-based simulated public inquiry', Paper presented at the Higher Education for Capability Conference, Using Assessment to Develop Student Capability, University College, London.

Heilman, M E and Kram, K E (1978) 'Self-derogatory behaviour in women fixed or flexible: the effects of co-workers' sex', *Organisational Behaviour and Human Performance*, 22, 497–507.

Henbest, R J and Fehrsen, G S (1985) 'Preliminary study at the Medical University of Southern Africa on student self-assessment as a means of evaluation', *Journal of Medical Education*, 60, 66–8.

Heron, J (1974) *The Concept of the Peer Learning Community*, Guildford: Human Potential Research Project, University of Surrey.

Heron, J (1981) 'Self and peer assessment', in Boydell, T and Pedler, M (eds) *Management Self-Development: Concepts and Practices*, Aldershot: Gower, 111–28.

Heron, J (1988) 'Assessment revisited', in Boud, D (ed.) *Developing Student Autonomy in Learning*, (2nd edn), London: Kogan Page, 77–90.

Heywood, J (1989) *Assessment in Higher Education*, (2nd edn), London: John Wiley.

Higgs, J (ed.) (1988) *Experience-Based Learning*, Sydney: Australian Consortium on Experiential Education.

Hoffman, R A and Geller, M I (1981) 'A comparison of self-evaluations and classroom teacher evaluations for aides in a pre-student teaching field experience program', *Teacher Educator*, 17, 2, 16–21.

Holzbach, R L (1978) 'Rater bias in performance ratings: superior, self-, and peer ratings', *Journal of Applied Psychology*, 63, 5, 579–88.

Hunter, I M L (1964) *Memory*, Harmonsworth: Penguin Books.

Huntley, J F (1976) 'Academic evaluation and grading: an analysis and some proposals', *Harvard Educational Review*, 46, 4, 612–31.

Huscroft, M (1993) 'Finding ways for staff and students to participate in assessment', Paper presented at the Higher Education for Capability conference, Using Assessment to Develop Student Capability, University College, London.

Institute of Physics (1988) *Physics in Higher Education*, London: Institute of Physics.

Israelite, L (1983) 'Adult student self-evaluation', *Performance and Instruction Journal*, 22, 5, 15–16.

Jackson, M W (1988) 'Patterns of self assessment in a political analysis course'. Unpublished manuscript, Department of Government, University of Sydney.

Jasper, M (1994) 'The use of a portfolio in assessing professional education', Paper presented at the Second International Symposium on Improving Student Learning. Oxford: Oxford Brookes University.

Jessup, G (1991) *Outcomes: NVQs and the Emerging Model of Education and Training*, London, Falmer Press.

Justice, D O and Marienau, C (1988) 'Self-assessment: essential skills for adult learners', in Hutchings, P and Wutzdorff, A (eds) *Knowing and Doing: Learning Through Experience*, New Directions for Teaching and Learning. No. 35. San Francisco, CA: Jossey-Bass, 49–62.

Kagal'niak, A I and Iashchishin, K E (1992) 'The development of self-assessment of future teachers' professionally significant qualities', *Russian Education and Society*, 34, 8, 43–56

Kahnemann, D, Slovic, P and Tversky, A (1982) *Judgement Under Uncertainty: Heuristics and Biases*, New York: Cambridge University Press.

Keefer, K E (1971) 'Characteristics of students who make accurate and inaccurate self-predictions of college achievement', *Journal of Educational Research*, 64, 9, 401–4.

Kegel-Flom, P (1975) 'Predicting supervisor, peer, and self-ratings of intern performance', *Journal of Medical Education*, 50, 812–5.

Kennell, J H, Tempio, C R and Wile, M Z (1973) 'Self-evaluation by first year medical students in a clinical science programme', *British Journal of Medical Education*, 7, 4, 230–8.

Kimball, M M and Gray, V A (1982) 'Feedback and performance expectancies in an academic setting', *Sex Roles*, 8, 999–1007.

Knight, P (1993) *An Assessment Toolkit*, Lancaster: Unit for Innovation in Higher Education, University of Lancaster.

Knowles, M S and Associates. (1986) *Using Learning Contracts*, San Francisco, CA: Jossey-Bass.

Knowles, M S (1975) *Self-directed Learning: A Guide for Learners and Teachers*, New York: Association Press.

Kohn, A (1993) *Punished by Rewards*, Boston, MA: Houghton Mifflin.

Kolb. D (1984) *Experiential Learning: Experience as the Source of Learning and Development*, Englewood Cliffs, NJ: Prentice-Hall.

Kramp, M K and Humphreys, W L (1993) 'Narrative, self-assessment and the reflective learner', *College Teaching*, 41, 3, 83–8.

Lambeth, S and Volden, C (1989) 'Portfolios: they work for RNs', *Journal of Nursing Education*, 28, 1, 42–4.

Lan, W Y, Bradley, L and Parr, G (1993) 'The effects of a self-monitoring process on college students' learning in an introductory statistics course', *Journal of Experimental Education*, 62, 1, 6–40.

Larson, M B (1978) 'Multiple copies of exams encourage self-grading', *Engineering Education*, 68, 5, 435–7.

Lave, J (1988) *Cognition in Practice: Mind, Mathematics and Culture in Everyday Life*, New York: Cambridge University Press.

Lenney, E (1977) 'Women's self-confidence in achievement settings', *Psychological Bulletin*, 84, 1–13.

Lenney, E and Gold, J (1982) 'Sex differences in self-confidence: the effects of task completion and of comparison to competent others', *Personality and Social Psychology Bulletin*, 8, 74–80.

Lenney, E, Gold, J and Browning, C (1983) 'Sex differences in self-confidence: the influence of comparison to others ability level', *Sex Roles*, 9, 925–42.

Linn, R L, Baker, E L and Dunbar, S B (1991) 'Complex, performance-based assessment: expectations and validation criteria', *Educational Researcher*, 20, 8, 15–21.

Loacker, G and Jensen, P (1988) 'The power of performance in developing problem-solving and self-assessment abilities', *Assessment and Evaluation in Higher Education*, 13, 128–50.

Luke, C and Gore, J (eds) (1992) *Feminisms and Critical Pedagogy*, London: Routledge.

Lyotard, J-F (1984) *The Postmodern Condition: A Report on Knowledge*, translation from the French by Bennington, G and Massumi, B, Manchester: Manchester University Press, first published 1979, Les Editions de Minuit.

Lyte, V J and Thompson, I G (1990) 'The diary as a formative teaching and learning aid incorporating means of evaluation and renegotiation of clinical learning objectives', *Nursing Education Today*, 10, 228–32.

Maccoby, E E and Jacklin, C N (1974) *The Psychology of Sex Differences*, Stanford, CA: Stanford California Press.

McDonald, R J and Sansom, D (1978) 'Use of assignment attachments in assessment', *Assessment in Higher Education*, 5, 1, 45–55.

McGeever, P J (1978) 'Student self-grading in the introductory American politics course', *Teaching Political Science*, 5, 3, 319–30.

MacGregor, J (1993) 'Learning self-evaluation: challenges for students', in MacGregor, J (ed.). *Student Self-Evaluation: Fostering Reflective Learning*, New Directions for Teaching and Learning No. 56. San Francisco, CA: Jossey-Bass, 35–46.

McVey, P J (1976) 'Standard error in the mark for an examination paper in electronic engineering', *Proceedings of the Institution of Electrical Engineers*, 123, 8, 843–4.

Magin, D J and Churches, A E (1988) 'What do students learn from self and peer assessment?', in *Designing for Learning in Industry and Education*, Canberra: Australian Society for Educational Technology, 224–33.

Mandell, A and Michelson, E (1990) *Portfolio Development and Experiential Learning: Purposes and Strategies*, Chicago: Council for Adult and Experiential Learning.

Marienau, C (1994) 'Self-assessment and performance in the workplace', in *Proceedings of the 35th Annual Adult Education Research Conference*, Knoxville, TN: College of Education, University of Tennessee, Knoxville, 241–6.

Marshall, J and Reason, P (1993) 'Adult learning in collaborative action research: reflections on the supervision process', *Studies in Continuing Education*, 15, 2, 117–32.

Marton, F, Hounsell, D and Entwistle, N (eds) (1984) *The Experience of Learning*, Edinburgh: Scottish Academic Press.

Maslow, A H (1966) *The Psychology of Science*, New York: Harper and Row.

Mason, C L (1992) 'Concept mapping: a tool to develop reflective science instruction', *Science Education*, 76, 1, 51–63.

Mayer, E A (1992) *Educating for Excellence: Business/Higher Education Round Table 1992 Education Surveys*, Commisioned Report No. 2, Camberwell, Victoria: Business/Higher Education Round Table.

Messick, S (1989) 'Validity', in Linn, R L (ed.) *Educational Measurement*, (3rd edn), New York: Macmillan, 13–104.

Millar, C, Morphet, T and Saddington, T (1986) 'Curriculum negotiation in professional adult education', *Journal of Curriculum Studies*, 18, 4, 429–43.

Miller, C M L and Parlett, M (1974) *Up to the Mark: A Study of the Examination Game*, Guildford: Society for Research into Higher Education.

Moore, W S and Hunter, S (1993) 'Beyond "mildly interesting facts": student self-evaluations and outcomes assessment', In MacGregor, J (ed.) *Student Self-Evaluation: Fostering Reflective Learning*, New Directions for Teaching and Learning No. 56, San Francisco, CA: Jossey-Bass, 65–82.

Moreland, R, Miller, J and Laucka, F (1981) 'Academic achievement and self-evaluation of academic performance', *Journal of Educational Psychology*, 73, 3, 335–44.

Morton, J B and Macbeth, W A A G (1977) 'Correlations between staff, peer, and self assessments of fourth year students in surgery', *Medical Education*, 11, 3, 167–70.

Mueller, R H (1970) 'Is self-grading the answer?', *Journal of Higher Education*, 41, 3, 221–4.

Mura, R (1987) 'Sex-related differences in expectations of success in undergraduate mathematics', *Journal of Research in Mathematics Education*, 18, 15–24.

Murstein, B I (1965) 'The relationship of grade expectations and grades believed to be deserved to actual grades received', *Journal of Experimental Education*, 33, 4, 357–62.

Nisbett, R E and Ross, L (1980) *Human Inference: Strategies and Shortcomings of Social Judgement*, Englewood Cliffs, N J: Prentice-Hall.

Novak, J D and Gowin, D B (1984) *Learning How to Learn*, New York: Cambridge University Press.

O'Kane, J M (1971) 'Having students do the grading', *Improving College and University Teaching*, 19, 331–2.

O'Neill, G P (1985) 'Self, teacher and faculty assessments of student teaching performance: a second scenario', *Alberta Journal of Educational Research*, 31, 2, 88–98.

Orpen, C (1982) 'Student versus lecturer assessment of learning: a research note', *Higher Education*, 11, 567–72.

Oskarsson, M (1980) *Approaches to Self-Assessment in Foreign Language Learning*, Pergamon: Oxford.

Otter, S (1992) *Learning Outcomes in Higher Education: A Development Project Report*, London: UDACE

Palmer, A, Burns, S and Bulman, C (eds) (1994) *Reflective Practice in Nursing: The Growth of the Professional Practitioner*, Oxford: Blackwell Scientific.

Parks, A G and Zurhellen, H S (1978) 'Student attitudes towards the grade contract', *Improving College and University Teaching*, 26, 4, 239–42.

Pastol, G (1993) 'Turning a test into a learning situation', *Methomix*, occasional publication of the Teaching Methods Unit, University of Cape Town, Rondebosch, South Africa, 15, 1, 3–4.

Payne, R, Eaton, D and Short, C (1993) 'Using portfolios to record progress and assess achievement', in Assister, A and Shaw, E (eds) *Using Records of Achievement in Higher Education*, London: Kogan Page, 87–91.

Pease, D (1975) 'Comparing faculty and school supervisor ratings for education students', *College Student Journal*, 9, 1, 91–4.

Pedler, M J (ed.) (1991) *Action Learning in Practice*, (2nd edn), Aldershot: Gower.

Peirce, B N, Swain, M and Hart, D (1993) 'Self-assessment, French immersion, and locus of control', *Applied Linguistics*, 14, 1, 25–42.

Perkins, E R and Anderson, D C (1981) *Self-Assessment in the National Health Service*, Nafferton: Studies in Education Ltd.

Peterson, J M (1979) 'Me and my critics: students' responses to architectural jury criticism', *Studies in Art Education*, 20, 2, 64–7.

Pettman, J J (1991) 'Towards a (personal) politics of location', *Studies in Continuing Education*, 13, 2, 153–66.

Pirsig, R (1974) *Zen and the Art of Motorcycle Maintenance: An Inquiry into Values*, London: Bodley Head.

Pitishkin-Potanich, V (1983) 'On evaluating students knowledge', *Higher Education in Europe*, 8, 2, 18–22.

Plous, S (1993) *The Psychology of Judgment and Decision Making*, New York: McGraw-Hill.

Polczynski, J J, and Shirland, L E (1977) 'Expectancy theory and contract grading as an effective motivational force for college students', *Journal of Educational Research*, 70, 238–41.

Poppen, W A and Thompson, C L (1971) 'The effect of grade contracts on student performance', *Journal of Educational Research*, 64, 9. 420–24.

Ramsden, P (1987) 'Improving teaching and learning in higher education: the case for a relational perspective', *Studies in Higher Education*, 12, 275–286.

Ramsden, P (1988a) *Improving Learning: New Perspectives*, London: Kogan Page.

Ramsden, P (1988b) 'Studying learning: improving teaching', in Ramsden, P (ed.) *Improving Learning: A New Perspective*, London: Kogan Page, 13–31.

Reason, P and Marshall, J (1987) 'Research as personal process', in Boud, D and Griffin, V (eds). *Appreciating Adults Learning: From the Learner"s Perspective*, London: Kogan Page, 112–26.

Reason, P and Rowan, J (eds) (1981) *Human Inquiry: A Sourcebook of New Paradigm Research*, Chichester: John Wiley.

Ries, A L, Kreit, L H and Podshadley, D W (1971) 'A comparison of dental student self-evaluations with predicted and actual teacher evaluations', *Journal of Dental Education*, 35, 493–5.

Robinson, J, Saberton, S and Griffin, V (eds) (1985) *Learning Partnerships:*

*Interdependent Learning in Adult Education*, Toronto: Department of Adult Education, Ontario Institute for Studies in Education.

Rogers, C R (1983) *Freedom to Learn for the 80s*, Columbus, Ohio: Charles E Merrill.

Rorty, R (1989) *Contingency, Irony and Solidarity*, Cambridge: Cambridge University Press.

Rotem, A and Abbatt, F R (1982) 'Self-assessment for teachers of health workers: how to be a better teacher', *WHO Publication 68*, Geneva: World Health Organization.

Rowntree, D (1987) *Assessing Students: How Do We Know Them?*, London: Kogan Page.

Ryle, G (1949) *The Concept of Mind*, London: Hutchinson.

Saberton, S (1985) 'Learning partnerships', *HERDSA News*, 7, 1, 3–5.

Schön, D A (1983) *The Reflective Practitioner: How Professionals Think in Action*, London: Temple Smith.

Schön, D A (1987) *Educating the Reflective Practitioner: Towards a New Design for Teaching and Learning in the Professions*, San Francisco, CA: Jossey-Bass.

Schön, D A (ed.) (1991) *The Reflective Turn*, New York: Teachers College Press.

Schunk, D H (1990) 'Goal setting and self-efficacy during self-regulated learning', *Educational Psychologist*, 25, 1, 71–86.

Schutz, A (1972) *The Phenomenology of the Social World*, Translated by Walsh, G and Lehnert, F. London: Heinemann.

Sclabassi, S E and Woelfel, S K (1984) 'Development of self-assessment skills in medical students', *Medical Education*, 84, 226–31.

Sheppard, C and Gilbert, J (1991) 'Course design, teaching method and student epistemology', *Higher Education*, 22, 229–49.

Shirts, M A (1968) 'The college grade contract', *The Educational Forum*, 32, 4, 456–8.

Smith, D L and Hatton, N (1993) 'Reflection in teacher education: a study in progress', *Education Research and Perspectives*, 20, 1, 13–23.

Smith, R M and Associates, (1990) *Learning-to-Learn Across the Lifespan*, San Francisco, CA: Jossey-Bass.

Snyder, M (1987) *Public Appearances/Private Realities: The Psychology of Self-Monitoring*, New York: W H Freeman and Co.

Solomon, M (1994) Personal communication.

Somervell, H (1993) 'Issues in assessment, enterprise and higher education: the case for self-, peer and collaborative assessment', *Assessment and Evaluation in Higher Education*, 18, 3, 221–49.

Spencer, J (1993) 'Assessment of interpersonal skills', paper presented at the

Higher Education for Capability Conference, Using Assessment to Develop Student Capability, University College, London.

Stanton, H E (1978) 'Self-grading as an assessment method', *Improving College and University Teaching*, 26, 4, 236–8.

Stefani, L A J (1994) 'Self, peer and group assessment procedures', in Sneddon, I and Kremer, J (eds) *An Enterprising Curriculum: Teaching Innovations in Higher Education*, Belfast: HMSO, 25–46.

Stephenson, J and Laycock, M (eds) (1993) *Using Learning Contracts in Higher Education*, London: Kogan Page.

Stover, R V (1976) 'The impact of self-grading on performance and evaluation in a constitutional law course', *Teaching Political Science*, 3, 3, 303–10.

Stuart, M R, Goldstein, H S and Snope, F C (1980) 'Self-evaluation by residents in family medicine', *Journal of Family Practice*, 10, 4, 639–42.

Sumner, F C (1932) Marks as estimated by students, *Education*, 32, 429.

Taylor, H (1971) 'Student reaction to the grade contract', *Journal of Educational Research*, 64, 7, 311–14.

Taylor, K (1995) 'Sitting beside herself: self assessment and women's adult development', in Taylor, K and Marienau, C (eds) *Learning Environments for Women's Adult Development: Bridges Toward Change. New Directions for Adult and Continuing Education, No. 65*, San Francisco, CA; Jossey-Bass.

Taylor, K and Marienau, C (1993) 'Self-assessment: a source for individual and organisational learning', *Contemporary Education*, 64, 3, 166–9.

Thomas, K (1990) *Gender and Subject in Higher Education*, Buckingham: SRHE and Open University Press.

Thomas, L F and Harri-Augstein, E S (1977) 'Learning to learn: the personal construction and exchange of meaning', in Howe, M J A (ed.) *Adult Learning: Psychological Research and Applications*, London: John Wiley, 85–104.

Towler, L and Broadfoot, P (1992) 'Self-assessment in the primary school', *Educational Review*, 44, 2, 137–51.

Trigwell, K, Prosser, M and Taylor, P (1994) 'Qualitative differences in approaches to teaching first year university science', *Higher Education*, 27, 1, 75–84.

Van Riper, B W (1982) 'Facilitating systematic self-assessment: a role for teachers in contemporary appraisal', *Education*, 103, 1.

Vygotsky, L S (1978) *Mind in Society: The Development of Higher Psychological Processes*, Cambridge, MA: Harvard University Press.

Walker, D (1985) 'Writing and Reflection', in Boud, D, Keogh, R and Walker, D (eds) *Reflection: Turning Experience into Learning*, London: Kogan Page, 52–68.

Waluconis, C J (1993) 'Self-evaluation: settings and uses', in MacGregor, J (ed.), *Student Self-Evaluation: Fostering Reflective Learning*, New Directions for Teaching and Learning No. 56. San Francisco, CA: Jossey-Bass, 15–34.

Warner, D A and Akamine, T (1972) 'Student reactions to college grade contracts', *The Educational Forum*, 36, 389–91.

Weil, S and McGill, I (eds) (1989) *Making Sense of Experiential Learning: Diversity in Theory and Practice*, Buckingham: Society for Research into Higher Education and Open University Press.

Wheeler, A E and Knoop, H R (1981) 'Self, teacher and faculty assessments of student teaching performance', *Journal of Educational Research*, 75, 3, 171–81.

White, E M (1985) *Teaching and Assessing Writing*, San Francisco, CA: Jossey-Bass.

Wilcox, K (1988) 'Student self-evaluation in a first year Australian politics course', unpublished manuscript, Department of Government, University of Sydney.

Williams, E (1992) 'Student attitudes towards approaches to learning and assessment', *Assessment and Evaluation in Higher Education*, 17, 1, 45–58.

Wolf, A (1995) *Competence-Based Assessment*, Buckingham: Open University Press.

Woods, D R (1990) 'Developing students problem-solving skills', *Journal of College Science Teaching*, 19, 3, 176–9.

Woods, D R (1994) *Problem-Based Learning: How to Gain the Most from PBL*, Waterton, Ontario: Donald. R Woods. Distributed by the McMaster University Bookstore, Hamilton, Ontario.

Woolliscroft, J O, TenHaken, J Smith, J and Calhoun, J G (1993) 'Medical students' clinical self-assessments: comparisons with external measures of performance and the students' self-assessments of overall performance and effort', *Academic Medicine*, 68, 4, 285–94.

Ziegler, A L (1992) 'Developing a system of evaluation in clinical legal education', *Journal of Legal Education*, 42, 4, 575–90.

Zimmerman, B J (1986) 'Becoming a self-regulated learner: which are the key subprocesses?', *Contemporary Educational Psychology*, 11, 307–13.

Zuckerman, D M (1985) 'Confidence and aspirations: self-esteem and self-concepts as predictors of students' life goals', *Journal of Personality*, 53, 543–60.

# Index